WITHDRAWN

Green
Escapes

Green Escapes

The Guide to Secret Urban Gardens

Key to Garden Types

 Botanic
Gardens created to display a scientific and diverse collection of plants, often displayed in botanical groupings.

 Community
Gardens created and cultivated by and for local community members. Such gardens often include productive gardens as well as community areas and wildlife gardens.

 Conservatory
Gardens where the plants are grown inside and within some form of protective structure affording protection from the external environment. Includes atriums.

 Courtyard
Gardens made within a partially or fully enclosed space. Includes courts, walled enclosures and peristyle courtyards. Excludes roof gardens.

 Edible
Gardens cultivating primarily edible plants. Includes orchards, vegetable gardens, herb gardens, allotments, cottage gardens and kitchen gardens.

 Green Space
Secluded spaces designed for free public access and use, usually with expanses of lawn or hard surfacing with beds and borders of mixed plantings and often shaded by trees. Includes squares, plazas, garden walks, vertical gardens, water gardens and parks.

 Historic
Gardens, parks and green spaces that have a significant historical context and/or layout. Includes castle grounds, forts and archaeological sites.

 Museum and Sculpture
Gardens created or existing as part of a museum or gallery, and sculpture gardens.

 Plantsman
Gardens in which the rich and diverse plant collection and/or planting design is the most noteworthy element.

 Pleasure Garden
A public garden (often originally created as a private garden) of sophisticated design that within its layout contains a range of different structural elements, planting and ornamental features.

 Pocket Park
A small park (usually less than 0.5 hectare in size) often created on an empty building plot or on small, irregular pieces of land between buildings.

 Religious and Memorial
Gardens and green spaces that have a dominant religious connection. Includes churchyards, cemeteries, cloisters, monuments, temples and memorial gardens.

 Rooftop
Green spaces or gardens created above street level and/or atop a building.

Wildlife
Gardens created primarily as nature reserves or havens for native flora and fauna.

Introduction
Toby Musgrave

There is no doubt that cities the world over are dynamic, exciting and alluring. More than 50 per cent of the world's population lives in urban areas, and many inspiring cities are high on tourists' 'bucket lists'. However, whether as a resident, worker or a visitor, spending time in the city can become overwhelming, and when it does we long to escape the urban jungle and to find solace in nature and green space. Indeed, study after academic study has shown that using green space reduces stress and improves both psychological and physical health.

Of course, the world's famous cities are graced with large, equally famous public parks that are enjoyed by myriads of people every day, and are treasured as an integral part of each city's urban character and identity: Hyde Park in London, the Jardin des Tuileries in Paris, Zabeel Park in Dubai, Jingshan Park in Beijing, the Royal Botanic Garden in Sydney, Alameda Central in Mexico City and Central Park in New York City, to name just a few. These generous and familiar green spaces, with their lawns, lakes, flower beds and trees, bring not only positive social benefits but also create significant ecological advantages, for they contribute to carbon sequester, sound damping, air filtration, stormwater attenuation and the regulation of ambient temperature, and encourage wildlife, thus increasing urban biodiversity.

Equally significant but perhaps more charming are 'green escapes': the compact hidden gems and secret oases that are often unknown even to many locals, though they may be just around the corner from home, the office or a bustling tourist attraction. Such intimate spaces are full of character, usually quieter and much less busy than their famous counterparts. Whether for residents leading ever more frenetic lives in our ever-growing, ever more crowded and congested metropolises, employees with precious minutes to spend on a lunch break, or tourists resting aching feet and reflecting on the exciting and stimulating experience of exploring unfamiliar streets and sites, these green escapes are the perfect refuge. Small, intimate and peaceful, they are places where one feels at ease, and can relish the quietude and allow the mind to refresh. *Green Escapes* therefore offers an antidote to urban life, revealing these more obscure and gardenesque, verdant and tranquil hideaways, with the aim of encouraging the discerning garden-lover, traveller or resident to seek them out and to enjoy and be stimulated by them.

Carefully selected, these rewarding green escapes are much more than just refuges to soothe the soul, stimulate the senses and revivify the psyche, however. Because their size, design and features are human-scale, they are easy to relate to and can be inspirational, both to inspire the spirit and as a source of ideas for gardeners. They are engaging and revealing because of their human-interest stories – many are made and maintained by devoted teams of volunteers – and the tales and anecdotes associated with them. And many are also made more enjoyable simply because part of the experience is the quest that one must undertake to seek them out.

Every green escape in this book is singular. One of the great delights of this collection is its diversity, whether of shape and layout, style and form, planting and ornament, age, history, cultural identity or type. Thus it includes pleasure gardens hidden physically behind walls (Yipu Yuan, the Garden of Cultivation in Suzhou; p.44), deep in an old part of town (the Dutch Period Museum in Colombo; p.79), within the architecture of domestic complexes (Naranjestan-e Qavam in Shiraz; p.87) and within larger green spaces (Himeji Garden, in Adelaide's embracing Park Lands; p.13). There are intimate courtyards accessed via a narrow passage (TechWorld Plaza in Washington DC; p.323) and there are former industrial lands, now transformed (The Rail Park in Philadelphia; p.315); there are productive gardens on rooftops (FOOD ROOF Farm in St Louis, Missouri; p.321), monuments (South Park Street Cemetery in Kolkata; p.73), and community wildlife gardens (Natuurtuin Slatuinen in Amsterdam; p.159). There are also 'best-kept secrets', which is to say those hidden not from view but from the general urban consciousness (Wendy's Secret Garden in Sydney, Greenace Park in New York City and Praça dos Cristais in Brasilia; pp.19, 332 and 355).

In terms of location, most of these green escapes are in city centres, downtown, in the Central Business District, in the historic heart or in other areas of the city that visitors are likely to be exploring. However, some delightful gardens worthy of a small excursion beyond the downtown area are also included in this book, such as the gardens of Vaucluse House in Sydney, Alcatraz Island in San Francisco and the Museo de Arte Español Enrique Larreta in Buenos Aires (pp. 23, 299 and 363).

Above all these physical criteria, however, is the metaphysical requirement that all the green escapes featured here are places of repose: urban havens that provide succour and into which anyone may retreat in search of comfort, relief and ease. All are places that – irrespective of design, style or global location – are a pleasure to be in and from where one emerges revitalized, uplifted, inspired and ready to face the city once more. Wherever you are in the world, do have fun discovering and enjoying these special places.

Note for Reader

The gardens are organized geographically into six chapters for each of the continents – Oceania, Asia, Europe, Africa, North and Central America, and South America. Within each continent or chapter, the countries are also organized geographically, generally from north to south, west to east, with the individual gardens then sequenced alphabetically by city. Cities featuring five or more gardens have their own city maps and these cities fall at the end of each country or regional section. The maps in this book are intended as a guide to the general location and to indicate the spread of secret city gardens in each place. Readers should refer to printed or digital maps for accurate way-finding. Digital maps may also be used to generate lat/long coordinates to be used with a GPS. Each garden is presented with its name, its street address to allow navigation directly, as well as the garden type (see key on previous page and the coloured tabs on each page) and a brief description. A Visitor Information section at the back of the book (see p.364) provides more detailed information about visiting the gardens, including websites, additional access details and opening times, as well as providing further information about guided tours or cafes on site.

Oceania

1 **Himeji Garden**
Adelaide, p.13
2 **Old Parliament House
Rose Gardens**
Canberra, p.14
3 **The System Garden**
Melbourne, p.15
4 **Docklands Community
Garden** Melbourne, p.16
5 **Harold Boas Gardens**
Perth, p.17
6 – 10 See **Sydney Map,** p.18

Himeji Garden
Adelaide

📍1
283 South Terrace,
SA 5000
(enter via South
Terrace, between
Pulteney St & Hutt St)
Open: see p.364
Free

Within Wita Wirra park, a part of the southern Adelaide Park Lands (the grassy belt that rings the city centre), is an enclosed, traditionally styled Japanese garden. It was a gift from the Japanese city of Himeji to symbolize the two becoming Sister Cities in 1982. With its Japanese lanterns popping up between neatly clipped bushes, boulder-sized stepping stones crossing the waterlily-covered pool, gravel viewing garden and tea house, the design is a hybrid of two distinct styles: 'lake and mountain' and 'dry'. It contains all the hallmarks of Japanese gardens, evoking the beauty of nature in a relatively small space (it may be walked around in fifteen minutes). But do not hurry, for this is a contemplative oasis, and with its complementary mix of sunny and shady spots it is lovely to visit whatever the season. The garden opened in 1985, and later in that decade the design (by Adelaide City Council) was improved by the Japanese landscape designer Yoshitaka Kumada in order to adhere more closely to traditional principles.

**Old Parliament House
Rose Gardens**
Canberra

● 2
18 King George Terrace,
Parkes, ACT 2600
Daily: 07.00–20.00
(summer); 07.00–
17.00 (winter)
Free

To pass through the tall, neatly clipped hedges enclosing the large U-shaped gardens hidden on either side of Old Parliament House is to be transported to a different continent and a different time. With their grass tennis courts, bowling green and cricket pitch, formal rose gardens set in lawn, seating pavilions, wisteria-clad pergolas and rose arbours, the gardens are quintessentially colonial English and Arts and Crafts in style. In the eastern House of Representatives Garden, the Ladies Rose Garden features hybrid teas and floribundas, and the Macarthur Rose Garden China, tea and noisette types. Look out for the Women's Suffrage Commemorative Fountain, too, a lovely jetting water feature. In the western Senate Garden, the Rex Hazlewood Rose Garden features historic Asian and European roses, and the Broinowski Rose Garden has shrub types. Indeed, it was Robert Broinowski, secretary of the Joint House Department and Usher of the Black Rod, who laid out the gardens, in 1931. Once the privileged realm of parliamentarians, the gardens were opened to the public in 2004.

The System Garden
Melbourne

📍 3
The University of
Melbourne, Parkville
Campus, VIC 3010
(between Professors
Walk & Royal Parade)
Open Mon–Fri:
09.00–17.00
Free

This fascinating garden on the University of Melbourne campus, some 3 kilometres north of the Town Hall, was established by Professor Frederick McCoy in 1856 as an educational resource for botany students, three years after the founding of the university itself. Following a period of neglect in the twentieth century, it was restored, and today the plants are arranged according to the Cronquist classification system, which groups related plants. With examples from all major land plant groups, including mosses, ferns, cycads, conifers and angiosperms (flowering plants), the garden offers an opportunity to observe the similarities and differences in form and flower structure among members of the same plant family. But it is also an attractive, shady and quiet garden in which to relax and enjoy an al fresco lunch. The original garden was circular and probably laid out by the English garden designer Edward La Trobe Bateman in consultation with McCoy; though now only a quarter of its original size, it retains some original features, including the central tower of the conservatory and an Osage orange tree.

Docklands Community Garden
Melbourne

📍 4
Geographe St,
Docklands, VIC 3008
(between Bourke St
& Collins St)
Open: 24/7
Free

Just west of the downtown gridiron, the 200-hectare Docklands became part of the City of Melbourne in July 2007. As part of this new urban development, the Docklands Community Garden was created between Bourke and Collins streets. Its main feature is a slightly sunken oval lawn fringed with eucalyptus and set with shaded seats. Far more fun and interesting, however, is the community vegetable garden that occupies the southernmost corner of the plot. With raised beds and planters made from timber and other materials salvaged from the development project, this is really a backyard for Docklands residents, but all are welcome to enjoy it, and there is plenty of seating, including the circular communal bench. The garden operates on an honesty principle of 'take something, put something back': in return for harvesting, residents either plant herb or vegetable seedlings, or make a donation – whether financial or in kind, of gardening materials. Come at the weekend and you may end up in deep horticultural conversation with a green-fingered resident.

Harold Boas Gardens
Perth

● 5
Corner of Wellington
St & Havelock St,
WA 6005
Open: 24/7
Free

To be found on the corner of Wellington and Havelock streets in West Perth, set amid modern office and apartment buildings, this mature, well-maintained garden provides a green and tranquil respite for city workers and visitors alike. The layout and style are informal and natural, and it is all the more relaxing for that. The garden, with its gently sculpted topography, was originally planted in 1900 and today features varied groups of shrubs, sinuous borders of perennials, luxuriant shade-giving trees, tree ferns and palms, expansive sculpted and manicured lawns, several lakes, a gentle stream and the focal point, a waterfall. Here and there among the shrubberies and in secret nooks, wooden benches are carefully positioned. There is also a small children's play area, and the garden is a popular spot for wedding photographs. Bring a picnic, spend some time reading, or lie on the sun-dappled lawn and take a nap. Formerly known as Delhi Square, the garden was renamed in 1976 after Harold Boas (1883–1980), a prominent local town planner, architect and Jewish community leader.

●N

0   600 1200 1800
yd.

Wendy's Secret Garden
Sydney

● 6
Lavender Bay,
NSW 2060 (at the
junction of Walker St
& Lavender St)
Open: 24/7
Free

Hidden away, this enchanting garden is squeezed between the coast of Lavender Bay and Clark Park, beyond which runs Lavender Street. Clark Park is simply lawn shaded by palms, but if you venture down the slope you can enjoy the verdant delight of Wendy's Secret Garden, created by local resident Wendy Whiteley who has transformed an area of wasteland into this tropical paradise. Cascading down the hillside, this invigorating garden feels artless, but that belies the skilful layout and planting. Whiteley has let nature work its magic, and the result is a riot of native ferns, foliage and flowers, towering palms and fig trees. The winding paths and flights of steps have an exotic ambience. Enclosed by the greenery are patches of lawn dotted with statues and sculptures, offering the perfect place to sit, enjoy a picnic and take in the spectacular view over Sydney Harbour. Yet among all this life and joy is sadness, for Whiteley created this jewel as grief therapy following the deaths of her husband, the artist Brett Whiteley, in 1992 and her only daughter, Arkie, in 2001.

**Lex and Ruby
Graham Gardens**
Sydney

📍 7
Cremorne Point
Reserve, Milson Rd,
Cremorne Point,
NSW 2090
Open: 24/7
Free

A particular delight of Sydney is to experience its stunning harbour setting from the water. Take the ferry from Circular Quay to Mosman on the north shore and disembark at the Cremorne Point Reserve, a mix of bushland and cultivated land, to find this most romantic of gardens on the eastern side. The story began in 1959, when, during his morning swim, Lex Graham recovered an elephant's ear corm from the harbour. He planted it for Ruby, his girlfriend (and later wife), between the roots of a nearby coral tree, where it thrived, inspiring the couple to clear the rubbish- and weed-covered slope, make winding paths and beds, and fill them with whatever they could get their hands on: Agapanthus spp., Callistemon, Clivia, Crinum, Cyathea, Hibiscus, Philodendron, and so on. With no masterplan beyond their own passion, the garden evolved organically over the decades. The result is a beautiful and tranquil testament to a couple's love. While here, do climb down to the Robertson Point lighthouse and/or take a dip in the harbourside Maccallum Pool, a great sunbathing spot with superb views.

**Balfour Street
Pocket Park**
Sydney

● 8
Balfour St,
Chippendale,
NSW 2008
(at the junction
of Chippendale
& Broadway)
Open: 24/7
Free

This small, award-winning neighbourhood park, designed by Jane Irwin Landscape Architecture, is a community meeting place, a pedestrian gateway to Central Park (formerly the Carlton United Brewery) and a connection between the inner city suburbs of Chippendale and Broadway. It is also a refreshing place simply to pause on a bench and enjoy the birdsong. It opened in 2010 and is to be found a short distance southwest of Central Station, at the corner of Balfour and O'Connor streets. In order to celebrate the heritage of its site and be a sympathetic modern insert, the design style is geometric and formal and the dominant decorative medium is brick, which is used in a series of colours and patterns. The north–south drainage swale with its interesting lighting and associated chequerboard pattern at its southern end shows particularly delightful and inventive uses of this detailing. There are a number of shade-giving trees and a small lawn; the perimeter planters are filled with a ground cover of ivy, and the small geometric beds with native taxa.

**Paddington
Reservoir Gardens
Sydney**

● 9
251–255 Oxford St,
Paddington, NSW 2021
Daily: 07.00–19.00
Free

Sydney's Oxford Street offers some wonderful examples of Victorian architecture, and something unusual, reminiscent of an archaeological site worthy of Rome. Indeed, the Reservoir Gardens have been (somewhat disingenuously!) called the Southern Baths of Caracalla. Sitting on iron pillars raised to street level is a large planter that shades the pool beneath and creates an interesting reflection. Descend the steps to below street level and you enter what was once a reservoir supplying this then rapidly expanding part of the city. The reservoir stopped supplying water in 1899, and, after reincarnations as a car park and a petrol station, some enlightened souls decided to salvage this significant piece of industrial architecture. Now a heritage-listed monument, the gardens opened in 2009 following a project that conserved much of the original structure, added modern elements and repurposed the space. Stroll the boardwalk, enjoy the foliage, including tree ferns and ornamental gingers, and rest on the lawn or benches. Return at sunset to discover the space transformed yet again by lighting.

Vaucluse House
Sydney

📍10
69A Wentworth Rd,
Vaucluse, NSW 2030
Open: 24/7 (see p.364
   for house)
Free (admission fee
   for house)

This is a rare survivor of a nineteenth-century harbourside estate, complete with splendid outbuildings and grounds. It is about twenty minutes east of downtown Sydney by bus 325, which stops outside the gate. More fun and more lovely, though, is to take the ferry from Circular Quay to Watson's Bay and walk the 2 kilometres along the shore via Parsley Bay. The Gothic Revival house is set in 10 hectares of gardens, paddock, bush and beach. Its productive kitchen garden is a riot of heritage fruit and vegetables, specifically those available in the colony in the mid-nineteenth century. The pleasure garden retains its Victorian design, with lawns and sand paths passing beneath mature trees among shrubberies and borders of perennials and seasonal colour. The house was built from 1827 by the explorer and writer William Charles Wentworth around the core of a cottage erected in 1805 by the Irish convict-knight Sir Henry Browne Hayes. Wentworth and his wife, Sarah, continued to develop the house and the estate until his death in 1872, installing the veranda and stone fountain in about 1861.

1   **Highwic** Auckland, p.25
2   **Eden Garden** Auckland, p.26
3   **Riccarton House and Bush** Christchurch, p.28
4   **Te Wepu Native Garden** Christchurch, p.29
5   **Olveston Historic Home** Dunedin, p.30
6   **Katherine Mansfield Birthplace** Wellington, p.31

Highwic
Auckland

● 1
40 Gillies Ave,
Newmarket, 1023
(enter from
Mortimer Pass)
Daily: 10.30–16.30
  (closed Christmas
  Day & Good Friday)
Admission fee

To visit Highwic, which is hidden by mature trees and high hedges, is to step back in time, into the daily life of a wealthy colonial family. The estate was built by English immigrants Alfred and Eliza Buckland in the early 1860s, and remained in the family until it was purchased for preservation as a historic monument in 1978. One of the finest Carpenter Gothic houses in the country is complemented by 1.2 hectares of garden that retains much of its Victorian layout – and is allegedly haunted by a big, black spectral dog. Dominated by a large lawn (there are both lawn tennis and croquet courts), the informal garden has curving pathways (including the meandering Lovers' Walk), a fern house and beds edged with clipped hedges and filled with old-fashioned annuals and perennials. The volcanic outcrop rockery in the northwestern corner is particularly prettily planted, and there are some splendid original specimens, notably camellias, Norfolk Island pines by the croquet lawn and front entrance, and pines, now underplanted with clivias. Look out for native species, too, including tī kōuka, ferns, nīkau palm and a large tōtara.

Eden Garden
Auckland

📍2
24 Omana Ave,
Epsom, 1023
Daily: 09.00–16.00
  (closed Christmas
  Day)
Admission fee

Nestled in an abandoned quarry at the foot of the eastern slope of the extinct Mount Eden volcano, this award-winning 2.2-hectare informal garden is a plantsman's paradise. Paths wind among pools and waterfalls and between the floral fireworks of foliage and flowers, a rich mix of native and exotic imported taxa. The garden was established in 1964 by horticulturalist Jack Clark, and today, strolling from the level central area to the rocky, steep and uneven perimeter of the old quarry, you can fully appreciate and enjoy the canopy of mature specimen trees and shrubs that complement the carefully structured underplanting of shade-loving taxa. This is also an all-year-round garden. Spring highlights include flowering bulbs, camellias, ornamental cherries and rhododendrons; summer is a mass of perennials and lilies (also look for the Vireya rhododendrons); autumn is all about seasonal leaf colour, with superb Japanese maples; and in winter it is the foliage of the evergreens and sculptural forms of the deciduous trees. While you are here, do ascend to the summit of Mount Eden.

**Riccarton House
and Bush**
Christchurch

● 3
16 Kahu Rd,
Riccarton, 8041
Open: 24/7 (see p.364
for house times)
Free (admission fee
for house)

A mere 3.5 kilometres west of Christchurch city centre is this floriferous garden, a beautiful mix of history and nature. Near the house, neatly clipped hedges enclose beds of roses, which also smother the pergola; other beds are full of perennials. Explore the grounds at your leisure, take a guided tour of Riccarton House (1856) and examine Deans Cottage. Built in 1843 for the pioneering Scottish émigré brothers William and John Deans, the latter is the oldest building on the Canterbury Plains. The estate is bordered by the River Avon, which the brothers renamed after the Avon Water, which bounded their grandfather's property in Lanarkshire. Beyond the sweeping lawns and mature trees is the Riccarton Bush (or Pūtaringamotu). Conserved at the behest of the Deans family in 1914, this is the region's sole remnant of kahikatea floodplain forest and is thus nationally significant. Marvel at the magnificent 600-year-old evergreen kahikatea trees (*Dacrycarpus dacrydioides*), as well as specimens of hīnau (*Elaeocarpus dentatus*), mataī (*Prumnopitys taxifolia*) and tōtara (*Podocarpus totara*).

Te Wepu Native Garden
Christchurch

● 4
154 Papanui Rd,
Merivale, 8014
By reservation only
   (see p.364)
Admission fee

A little north of the city centre and the expansive North Hagley Park (which is home to the unmissable Botanic Gardens) is an everyday suburban road. But it contains a delightful surprise: an award-winning 0.2-hectare garden framed by a huge lime tree (planted in 1882) and featuring primarily native taxa. There are ferns galore in the fernery, and hebes, lancewoods and New Zealand flax, to name but a few. However, this is not just a plant collection but also a plantswoman's artful arrangement, which melds native with non-native exotics. Other highlights include the two Japanese-inspired gardens with eye-catching *objets trouvés*, and St Albans Creek, which runs through the property and is home to ducks and eels. The current owner's great-grandfather H.R. Webb built a mansion in the area in 1881 and named it Te Wepu, Maori for 'web'. The garden is part of this former estate, and both garden and house were rebuilt after the devastating earthquake of 2011. The house is also a B&B, so why not stay in the room that opens on to a self-contained garden and courtyard?

Olveston Historic Home
Dunedin

● 5
42 Royal Terrace, 9016
Daily: 09.00–17.00 (closed Christmas Day)
Free (admission fee for house)

Set on a gentle slope a little north of the Octagon, in the city centre, this is an English country house in the city. To complement it, a formal garden was made (now restored), comprising a series of terraces, lawns set with square beds, herbaceous borders and hedge-edged beds of seasonal colour (in spring the show of bulbs is lovely). Some of the plants, notably the fine rhododendrons and native specimens, are original. Be sure to visit the functioning kitchen garden, and don't miss the large heated conservatory, now restored to its Edwardian glory and filled with a collection of hothouse treasures. The plans for the thirty-five-room mansion in Jacobean style came from the desk of the famous British architect Sir Ernest George, and the house was built in 1904–6 as the home of the Theomin family. This 'time capsule' property was gifted to the city of Dunedin by Dorothy Theomin in 1966, and today the interior (accessible only on a guided tour) displays the antiques and artworks gathered from all over the world by her father, an avid collector.

Katherine Mansfield Birthplace
Wellington

📍 6
25 Tinakori Rd,
Thorndon, 6011
Open: see p.364
Free (admission fee
for house)

'The mind I love must have wild places, a tangled orchard where dark damsons drop in the heavy grass, an overgrown little wood, the chance of a snake or two, a pool that nobody's fathomed the depth of, and paths threaded with flowers planted by the mind.' So wrote Katherine Mansfield (1888–1923), New Zealand's most internationally famous author. The garden is only a ten-minute walk from Wellington's Parliament buildings and old St Paul's Cathedral, and it is a delight. The present garden dates from 1988, shortly after the house was restored. In its layout and planting it attempts to be authentic to late nineteenth- and early twentieth-century colonial garden design, with an Arts and Crafts feel. Behind a cream picket gate the small front garden features a rectangular lawn, a straight path, a bench, and borders of 'period correct' plants. In the back garden (which is smaller than it once was), the plantings around the lawn place more emphasis on natives, and notable trees include medlar, lilac, Japanese flowering cherries and the native kōwhai (*Sophora microphylla*) and karaka (*Corynocarpus laevigatus*).

Asia

Gong Wang Fu (Prince Gong's Mansion)
Beijing

● 1
17 Qianhai West St,
ShiChaHai, Xicheng
District
Open: see p.364
Admission fee

Central Beijing boasts many green spaces; most are large, but it is possible to find smaller ones here and there. One of the most beautiful is that of the city's most exquisite and best-preserved imperial mansion. Set a little north of the Shichahai lakes and dating from 1777, the buildings and gardens were made for Heshen, infamous as the most corrupt official in Chinese history. A favourite of the Qianlong Emperor (r.1735–96), he was subsequently forced to commit suicide by the Jiaqing Emperor. The confiscated mansion passed to Prince Qing in 1799 and subsequently Emperor Xianfeng transferred it to Prince Gong. The 2.8-hectare Fantastical Gardens (Cuijin Yuan) are to the north of the mansion. Surrounded by artificial mountain peaks, the ponds, caves and pavilions are distributed picturesquely, while twenty contrived scenic spots ensure a rich, subtle and varied experience. Highlights include the rockery hills and Qiaoxiang Path, the Bat Pond and, facing the main gate, the Peak of Solitary Joy, crowned with a 5-metre-tall monolith (a sculptural Taihu stone) excavated from the bed of Lake Tai, near Suzhou.

Wenshu Temple
Chengdu

● 2
66 Wenshuyuan St,
CaoShiJie, Qingyang
District
Daily: 08.00–18.00
Free

Dating from the Tang Dynasty (AD 618–907), this is the most impressive and best-preserved Buddhist temple in Chengdu. The present grounds were built in 1697, during the Qing Dynasty, and the buildings with their relics and artworks, and the joss-stick-scented courtyards, are fascinating to explore. Once your inner culture vulture is sated, there is the shaded, verdant garden to roam. Paths edged with low hedges meander among features and plantings that are not discernibly ordered, yet unite harmoniously. In a pool stands a boat-shaped stone planter with a lion's face, in which grows a pavilion-shaped topiary; there are also venerable *penjing* (bonsai). There is a small seating pavilion and groves of bamboo, palms and ferns, informal ponds with islands and a formal rectangular pool in which stands a naturalistic rockery and a moon gate. After soaking up this somewhat eclectic admixture, adjourn to the Tea House for a cup of tea and enjoy people-watching – it is a popular spot with locals, who come to play chess, read or knit, or just hang out. There is also an excellent vegetarian restaurant.

**Hu Xueyan Gu Ju
(Hu Xueyan's Former
Residence)**
Hangzhou

● 3
18 Yuanbao St,
Shangcheng District
Daily: 08.00–17.30
Admission fee

Hu Xueyan (1823–85) was the most influential businessman and banker of the late Qing Dynasty in China, and spared no expense in the construction of his house and garden. The garden displays the beauties of nature, albeit artistically exaggerated and miniaturized. One of the highlights is the artfully arranged rockwork composed of sculptural, almost tortured-looking yet wholly natural rocks, and within it is the largest artificial karst grotto-cave in China. Water is the central theme, and deliciously reflects its surroundings, creating a second, mirrored garden. Another delight is the ingenious and maze-like way in which the architectural forms integrate with those of the garden and the planting. This quality constantly stimulates both the eye and the mind and imbues the experience with a purposeful tranquillity. The complex was completed in 1875 and opened to the public in 2001 following a major restoration. The luxurious residence (5,815 square metres in total) is an interesting blend of traditional Chinese and Western architectural styles and features, and contains an exquisite collection of arts and crafts.

Dominion Garden
Hong Kong

● 4
31–43 Queen's Rd East,
Wan Chai
Open: 24/7
Free

Squeezed into an empty plot on the western fringe of Wan Chai district, close to Central district, this pocket park was created as part of the Old Wan Chai Revitalisation Initiatives and opened in November 2012. The area was one of the earliest settlements in Hong Kong, and this is the perfect place for a break on the Wan Chai Heritage Trail. The surfacing of abstract drifts of white concrete and black paviours is vaguely reminiscent of Roberto Burle Marx's Copacabana beach promenade in Rio de Janeiro. Punctuating it are raised concrete planters full of foliage shrubs and shading trees. Begin your stop by reading the interpretive copper panels, before sitting on the curvaceous concrete bench that winds its way around the perimeter of the park and simultaneously retains raised beds. At the back of the square space is a high stone wall, from which a sculptural fig tree grows, and a flight of steep steps ascends to Sun Street. After dark the park is subtly lit with lights on poles and LEDs underneath the concrete bench.

Pak Tsz Lane Park
Hong Kong

📍 5
Square behind
Aberdeen St,
Hollywood Rd,
Gage St & Peel St,
Central
Open: 24/7
Free

In the Central and Western district of Hong Kong Island, Pak Tsz Lane Park was opened in 2012 as part of the centenary celebrations of the Xinhai Revolution, which resulted in the establishment of the Republic of China in 1911. Surrounded by tenement buildings and adjacent to the rear of 52 Gage Street, where the revolutionaries met, this is a truly hidden pocket park. It is deliberately so, because the narrow lanes that lead to it afforded the revolutionaries various quick escape routes. In spite of this, the revolutionary leader Yeung Ku-wan was assassinated at his home on Gage Street by Qing agents in 1901. With a colour scheme of black, white and green, the park – the work of the architectural practice Ronald Lu & Partners – is attractively illuminated at night and includes raised beds with integral benches, an interactive exhibition on the Revolution, and a historically themed play area. The main feature is a covered seating area with a bronze sculpture of a Western-dressed man cutting the *queue* (pigtail) of a Chinese man wearing traditional Manchu clothes – a symbol of liberation from Qing rule.

Wenmiao Tea Garden – Confucian Temple Lingxing Gate
Kunming

● 6
96 Renmin Middle Rd, Wuhua District
Daily: 08.30–17.00
Admission fee

Sometimes one needs to escape the grind of the urban experience and give the soul, mind and body a change of scene – and that is always aided by a good cup of tea. Wenmiao Tea Garden is central, a ten-minute walk southeast of the great Cuihu (Green Lake) Park on Renmin Zhong Lu (Renmin Middle Road) and to the east of Wen Miao Xi Xiang (Wenmiao West Alley). The site was formerly a Confucian temple (it is sometimes still referred to as the Confucian Temple Lingxing Gate), and the smallish grounds include a good variety of trees, shrubs in pots and flowers together with the obligatory pool, pavilions, rockwork and bridge. Pass through the ornamental, painted gateway and find one of the two tea houses. This may not be the quietest place to revivify the spirit – it is popular with locals, who come to drink green tea, talk and play mahjong and cards – but it has authentic colour, flavour and atmosphere in abundance. Sit in one of the pavilions, under the trees or among the bamboo and enjoy a cultural people-watching experience. The tea is pretty good, too.

Lou Lim Ieoc Garden
Macau

● 7
10 Estrada de Adolfo
Loureiro
Daily: 06.00–21.00
Free

Surrounded by skyscrapers and high-rise apartment blocks, this nineteenth-century garden modelled on the famous classical scholar gardens of Suzhou is a surprise awaiting discovery. And it looks extra-special when illuminated at night. Pass by the cheerful pots of flowers, through a moon gate and into a miniaturized, stylized natural landscape. Narrow paths wind through bamboo groves, past flowering shrubs and weeping willows, and between artificial rockwork mountains (do explore the hidden spaces within). The central feature is the large pond planted with waterlily and lotus (*Nelumbo nucifera*). The juxtaposed Spring Grass Pavilion in colonial style is a touch incongruous, but it was good enough for the Chinese revolutionary Sun Yat-sen, who stayed here in 1912. A nine-turn bridge (to confuse evil spirits) weaves across the northern end of the pond to another pavilion, and beyond is the imposing colonial-style mansion. Both house and garden were begun in 1870 by Lou Kau, a wealthy Chinese merchant, and completed by his son, after whom the garden is named.

Yuyuan (Garden of Happiness)
Shanghai

● 8
218 Anren St,
Huangpu District
Daily: 08.30–16.45
Admission fee

In the northeast of the Old City, close to the Bund or Waitan waterfront, this delightful garden was completed in 1577. It was made by Pan Yunduan, a Ming Dynasty official, for his parents to enjoy in their old age. The garden was subsequently neglected, modified extensively in the 1760s, damaged severely during the Opium Wars of the mid-nineteenth century and, finally, restored in 1956–61. Compact and exquisite within its 2 hectares, this is a classical Chinese garden of six sections or scenic areas, each with its own character. The winding paths, framed views, pavilions, rockeries, terraces and ornamental ponds contrive to create a total of forty-eight carefully composed scenic spots. Perhaps most dramatic is the Great Rockery, the largest and oldest in the region south of the Yangtze. Encountered upon entering the garden, it rises to a height of 14 metres. To the south of the original garden, but now integrated within it, the Inner Garden was created in 1709 as a separate entity. It offers a different vista at every step, and some of the most attractive scenery in Yuyuan.

**Bei Ban Yuan
(North Half Garden)**
Suzhou

📍 9
Scholars Hotel,
60 Baita East Rd,
Pingjiang District
Daily: 08.00–21.00
Free

There are two Half Gardens in Suzhou: one on Renmin Road in the south, and the North Half Garden or Bei Ban Yuan, just south of the famous Lion Forest Garden. Built during the reign of the Qianlong Emperor (r.1735–96), it is now the private garden of the Scholars Hotel, and although open to non-guests it attracts few visitors. The garden is compact and elegant. The residential buildings that would have been to the north of the pool have sadly disappeared, and today the garden is to the east of the buildings, with the pool at its centre, surrounded by winding covered walkways and waterside pavilions. The two-and-a-half-storey tower with protruding eaves at each level in the northeast part of the garden is unique within Suzhou's classical gardens. Also famous is the 150-year-old sweet osmanthus *(Osmanthus fragrans)*, whose blossoms smell delicious in autumn. While enjoying a cup of tea, contemplate the garden's name, which reflects the philosophy behind the design. The garden's name and design is a dialectic that contentment is the key to happiness.

Yipu Yuan (Garden of Cultivation)
Suzhou

📍10
5 Wenya Lane,
Jinchang District
Daily: 07.30–17.00
Admission fee

This small garden is hidden down a narrow lane near the historic area of Shantang Jie in the northwest of the old city. It is hard to find: take a rickshaw, since a taxi cannot get down the lane, or risk becoming quickly lost in the tiny side streets. But the adventure is well worth the effort. With its central pool reflecting the waterside buildings, features and plantings, it may not be as well maintained as its more famous cousins, but it has a truly authentic feel: join the locals drinking tea in the pavilion overlooking the pond. Built by Yuan Zugeng in 1541 and remodelled by successive owners, the garden is a particularly fine example of late Ming Dynasty (1368–1644) design. Laid out in a clear north–south arrangement of pavilions, a large pond, a rock mountain and trees, with small courtyards in the southwest defining secondary views, the garden is characterized by the elegance and simplicity of its components. Its name translates as Garden of Cultivation and also worth a special mention is the passageway down which cascades a riot of climbing roses.

**Shuzhuang Huayuan
(Shuzhuang Garden)**
Xiamen

● 11
Tianwei Rd,
Siming District
Daily: 07.30–17.30
Admission fee

Perched between cliff and ocean, this striking garden was built in 1913 on the south coast of Gulangyu Island by the Taiwanese businessman Lin Erjia to remind him of his childhood home. The pools, bridges, rockeries and manicured plantings echo the great scholar gardens, but this is demonstrably modern. Taking full advantage of its dramatic setting and running down the slope to the sea, it is a combination of dynamism, peace and apparently infinite space. The last is created ingeniously by a combination of hiding and revealing elements (including the sea) and vistas, engendering a curiosity that encourages the visitor to move through the garden, and by taking full advantage of the borrowed views. The garden itself can be divided into two parts: the Garden of Hiding the Sea (Canghaiyuan) and the Garden of Making-up Hills (Bushanyuan). In each are five carefully composed views to be enjoyed from the various pavilions. Particularly impressive is the rockwork maze. One of the pavilions is home to a renowned piano museum – it's not unusual to be treated to an impromptu recital.

**Lin Ben Yuan Yuandi
(The Lin Family
Mansion and Garden)**
New Taipei City

📍12
9 Ximen St, Banqiao
Open: see p.365
Admission fee

Successive generations of the Lin family (of Chinese descent) developed their agricultural businesses from 1778 to become both Taiwan's largest landowner and its wealthiest family. This house, a testament to their success, was built in 1851. The family returned to China in the wake of the Japanese invasion of 1895, and both house and garden fell into disrepair. Restored in the 1980s, it is now the country's most complete surviving example of traditional southern Chinese garden architecture, and is composed of four distinctive elements: artificial rockwork mountains, pools, planting and architecture. The complexity, variety and unity of the design are carefully engineered to create a series of ever-changing, man-made yet naturalistic scenes and experiences in a limited footprint. Chinese gardens were intended for entertaining and also to stimulate the mind. Walk the maze-like pathways, find a quiet corner with a view that appeals to you and reflect on the designer's intention that, through the creation of views, the garden would bring happiness and enlightenment.

Huwon (Rear Garden), Changdeokgung Palace
Seoul

📍 13
99 Yulgok-ro, Waryong-dong, Jongno-gu
Open: see p.364
Admission fee

Changdeokgung (Prospering Virtue) Palace is one of the Five Great Palaces built by the Joseon Dynasty (1392–1910) kings, listed by UNESCO, and a must-see when visiting Seoul. Behind is a secret garden, albeit a large one, of 32 hectares. Huwon, also known as Biwon (Secret Garden), was constructed in the early fifteenth century for the use of the royal family. The naturalistic layout is more akin to a rambling Chinese scholar garden than a Japanese stroll garden, but it is not a copy of either, rather one of the best representations of Korean garden art. As you meander among the 26,000-plus trees, some more than 300 years old, you come across focal elements such as a large lotus pond, landscaped lawns and man-made hills, a stream and pavilions – the outstanding Buyongjeong Pavilion reopened in 2012 after major restoration. The garden is sculptural in winter, with bare trees and frozen pools, and verdant and floriferous in summer, but perhaps at its best seen with its exceptional show of leaf colour in autumn. To visit you must pre-book a guided tour (available in English) via the website.

Japan

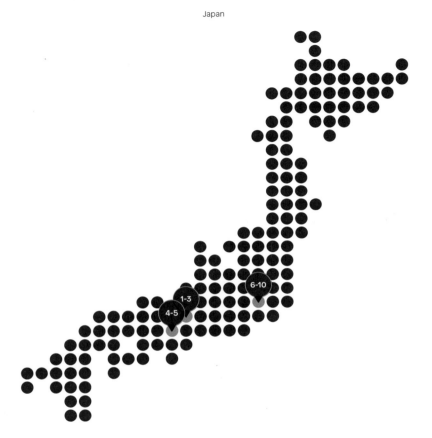

**Shigemori Mirei Kyutaku
(Mirei Shigemori Residence)**
Kyoto

9 1
34 Yoshidakamiojicho,
Sakyo-ku
By appointment only
(see p.365)
Admission fee

Kyoto is a city of gardens, but many are historic and royal or religious. This delightful example, visitable by arrangement only, is the private, domestic garden made by Shigemori Mirei (1896–1975), one of Japan's most respected twentieth-century garden designers and scholars. Viewed from a covered veranda or an internal room – which is sparsely decorated, with *shoji* screens that can be positioned to define specific vistas – the garden contains many of Shigemori's signature touches, including sinuous stone paving, and may be considered a case study of his ideas and principles. Set within curving drifts of moss and raked gravel, four rock configurations symbolize the Isles of the Blessed, and the 'blue rock' of chlorite schist from Shikoku island represents a ship. The garden's two tea pavilions (dating from 1953 and 1969) are a combination of traditional and modern design, as is the small *tsubo niwa* or courtyard garden. The residence itself is a traditional Edo Period town house dating from 1789, and was acquired by Shigemori in 1943 from the Shinto Suzuka order.

**Namikawa-ke
(Namikawa Residence)**
Kyoto

● 2
388 Horiike-cho,
Higashiyama-ku
Open: see p.365
Admission fee

Hidden away in the narrow streets south of the impressive Heian-jingu shrine (which itself has lovely gardens) is a picturesque villa, once the residence of the artist Namikawa Yasuyuki (1845–1927). This small, intricate viewing garden has echoes of a tea garden; to stand within the house and look out over it engenders a feeling of calm contentment. At the foot of the granite steps leading down from the enclosed veranda is a *tsukubai* water basin. From here, stepping stones set in moss lead into the garden, which is ornamented and lit with Japanese lanterns set in the beds of carefully positioned and clipped evergreen shrubs, over which rise trees. The main feature is an informal pond, which extends intriguingly under the main building and is inhabited by koi. Today the house is a museum to this master of *cloisonné*, the ancient craft of decorating metalwork objects, who became famous internationally in the 1880s.

**Shirakawa-in
(Shirakawa-in Garden)**
Kyoto

● 3
16 Okazaki Hoshojicho,
Sakyo-ku
Daily: until 21.00
Free

Close to both the famous Heian-jingu and the great gardens of Nanzen-ji and Konchi-in temples, Shirakawa-in is a *ryokan*, or traditional Japanese inn. Regarded by many aficionados as the best of its kind in Japan, it offers inexpensive accommodation, but it is also possible to visit the garden without being a guest. Behind the wooden building hides a small but atmospheric strolling garden with carefully positioned rocks, gravel paths and a small lake surrounded by manicured shrubs and artfully shaped yet seemingly natural-looking black pines (*Pinus thunbergii*). There is also a tea house in the southeastern corner. The view from the large open windows of the restaurant is superb, but for a panorama, ascend to the balcony on the second floor. In style the garden is in keeping with the traditions of the Edo Period (1603–1868), but it was made by the renowned garden designer Ogawa Jihei (1860–1933), who also worked on Murin-an garden, ten minutes' walk to the south. However, the garden's history began in the early Heian Period (794–1185), when courtly villas and gardens were built in this area.

**Osaka Station City
Roof Gardens**
Osaka

📍4
**North Gate Building,
Osaka Station City,
3-1-1 Umeda, Kita-ku
Yawaragi-no-niwa
 Garden**
 Daily: 07.00–23.30
Kaze-no-hiroba Plaza
 Daily: 07.00–24.00
Tenku-no-noen Farm
 Daily: 07.00–21.00
Free

The labyrinthine Osaka Station is the biggest and busiest in western Japan, and navigating it can be overwhelming. Thankfully, three places within the complex allow the visitor to escape and decompress. The station itself is at the centre of Osaka Station City, bookended by the South and North Gate buildings, two tower blocks full of shops, restaurants and leisure outlets. On the upper storeys of the latter block are three gardens. The Yawaragi-no-niwa Garden (Peaceful Garden), on the tenth floor, is a modern take on the traditional viewing garden, with gravel, rocks, moss and pine trees. Sit on one of the square stone seats and enjoy the views of the garden and the city skyline beyond. One floor up, via a flight of steps, is the Kaze-no-hiroba Plaza (Garden of the Wind). This linear, paved garden plaza with trees in planters and lots of seating is breezy and noted for its scented and brightly coloured flowers. The water feature is a favourite with children. Finally, on the fourteenth floor is the Tenku-no-noen Farm (Heavenly Plantation), a small, productive garden and vineyard that is tended by local residents.

Namba Parks
Osaka

● 5
2-10-70 Nanbanaka,
Naniwa-ku
Daily: 10.00–24.00
Free

The words 'massive residential block and office tower complex' conjure up mental images of soul-destroyingly dull architecture bereft of greenery. However, built on the site of the city's former baseball stadium, Namba Parks is a refreshing and verdant antithesis. This stunning, sloping eight-level rooftop park connects to the street and encourages passers-by to enter and explore the lush terraces. This is a dynamic space with green elements subtly and skilfully integrated within and among the architecture and contours. The 'landscape events' to be discovered and enjoyed include groves of trees, rocky outcrops and cliffs, ponds, streams and waterfalls, lawns and superbly planted raised beds; there are even private vegetable plots. But at no time does the green space feel contrived or overbearing. Indeed, the artistically planned and perfectly maintained planting creates quiet pockets in which to sit, have a snack and enjoy the harmony of nature and architecture. Namba Parks was designed by the Jerde Partnership in 2003 and is twenty minutes' train ride due south of Osaka railway station.

N

```
0    700  1400 2100
                      yd.
```

**Asakura-choso-kan
(Asakura Museum
of Sculpture)**
Tokyo

● 6
7-18-10 Yanaka, Taito-ku
Open: see p.364
Admission fee

Just west of the sprawling Yanaka Cemetery and only five minutes'
walk from Nippori Station on the Yamanote rail line, this museum is
dedicated to the father of modern Japanese sculpture, Asakura
Fumio (1883–1964), who was renowned for his realistic representations of people and cats. In fact the house, studio and garden were
designed by the artist himself in 1928–35. The building has two wings:
a Japanese-style residential space and a Western-style studio space.
On top of the latter is an attractive modern roof garden with raised
beds and a bronze sculpture; it allows a view over the whole building, including the statues topping the roofs and the courtyard garden below. At ground level and enclosed by both wings of the house,
the latter rectangular garden is not to be entered. With its dominant
koi pool crossed by boulder-sized stepping stones, its gnarled,
propped trees and evergreen planting, it is a viewing garden in the
truest sense of this Japanese tradition. However – and as intended
– delightful views of the garden can be enjoyed from the various
rooms of the building.

**Denpo-in Teien
(Denpo-in Garden)
Tokyo**

● 7
2-3 Asakusa, Taito-ku
Open: see p.364
Admission fee

In the heart of the Asakusa district and immediately southwest of Senso-ji (Tokyo's oldest Buddhist temple, completed in AD 648) stands Denpo-in Temple. It is the residence of the Abbot of Senso-ji, and his private garden is closed for most of the year. But for about seven weeks from mid-March it is possible to visit this hidden delight. With its informal lake, waterfalls and bridges, carefully shaped, mounded lawns ornamented with neatly trimmed pines, naturalistic rock arrangements, expanses of emerald-green moss and rustic tea house, the 1-hectare garden is beautiful and manicured in the way only Japanese stroll gardens can be. The contrived, ever-changing scenes simultaneously appear to be a miniature natural landscape and a composed work of art. With luck the weeping cherry trees will be in blossom; there is a great view of the *goju-no-to* (five-storey pagoda), and the Abbot's special tea is also served, free of charge. Enter through the Tokubetsu Gallery building, where an exhibition of the temple's artworks is included in the ticket price.

**Sukiyabashi
(Sukiyabashi Park)**
Tokyo

● 8
5-1 Ginza, Chuo-ku
Open: 24/7
Free

This small triangular park is at the entrance to Ginza, the thriving, much-visited international centre for tourism and commerce within the special ward of Chuo in the heart of Tokyo. It is a welcome patch of green among the tall buildings of concrete and glass, hidden away close to the busy Harumi Dori road with the raised Tokyo Expressway almost directly above it. The paved surfaces – their geometric patterns picked out by different-coloured paviours – are enlivened with planters and raised beds, the black concrete edgings of which double as benches. Additional benches are positioned under the trees, whose number was supplemented in 2016 by twenty Friendship-Blossoms dogwood trees (*Cornus florida*) – a gift from the Bridging Foundation and the US Department of State to celebrate commercial ties between the United States and Japan. At the rear of the park the level is raised by a flight of shallow steps (and a ramp). Complementing the denser plantings is a multi-armed stainless-steel clock-cum-octopus sculpture, a real eye-catcher when illuminated at night.

**Nezu Bijutsukan
(Nezu Museum)
Tokyo**

📍 9
6-5-1 Minamiaoyama
Open: see p.365
Admission fee

The museum and garden – designed in 1906 in the *shinzan-yukoku* (deep mountains and mysterious valleys) style – were formerly the residence of the businessman and politician Nezu Kaichiro (1860–1940), who built the collection of pre-modern Japanese and East Asian art that is on display today. However, both were severely damaged in the Second World War, and had to be restored and rebuilt (the 2006 extension is by the architect Kengo Kuma). The lush, surprisingly hilly 1.7-hectare garden is truly an urban oasis, and delightful for the way in which the architecture and garden meld seamlessly – in large part because of the stone lanterns and other artefacts that Nezu purchased for the garden. Take the winding paved paths and lose yourself in the verdant naturalistic landscape with its two ponds connected by small streams and waterfalls, rich plantings, tree groves and rocks. There are places to sit and enjoy the scenes with the various rustic buildings carefully positioned here and there, as well as a tea house where a tea ceremony can be enjoyed.

**Happo-en
(Happo-en Garden)**
Tokyo

📍 10
1-1-1 Shiroganedai,
Minato-ku
Open: see p.364
Free

Walk a little east from the Tokyo Metropolitan Teien Art Museum and escape from the metropolis into this beautifully maintained haven. The name means 'garden beautiful from eight angles', and this is a 3.3-hectare strolling garden to be enjoyed at leisure. It is also popular for wedding photographs, so don't be surprised if you are asked to join the bride in her traditional kimono. At the centre is an informal, colourful koi-filled lake, over which the *suichin* (a waterside arbour) seems to float. The garden looks spectacular in spring, when the pale-pink *sakura* (cherry blossom) is out, and is also lovely when the azaleas bloom a little later; the autumn show of fiery leaves as the Japanese maples turn is simply stunning. Be sure to admire the bonsai trees displayed on wooden benches lining the paths: most are in their second century, and one is a remarkable 520 years old. The garden dates from the early seventeenth century, during the Edo Period, although what is seen today was remodelled in 1915 by the industrialist Kuhara Fusanosuke, who also added the two tea houses.

Baan Phor Liang Meun Terracotta Garden
Chiang Mai

📍1
Pra Pok Klao Rd Soi 2,
Tambon Phra Sing,
Amphoe Mueang
(near junction with
Phra Pok Klao 2 Ko.
Alley)
Daily: 08.00–17.00
Free

Chiang Mai, the largest and most culturally significant city in northern Thailand, is home to hundreds of elaborate Buddhist temples, some of which have gardens. Yet one of the most tranquil green spaces to be found in the old city is technically an outdoor showroom. Just to the north of the Chiang Mai Gate market on the south side of the old town, within the Old City moat, is a walled enclosure pierced by an imposing brick gateway. Inside is a world of quiet, green jungle lushness, a seemingly forgotten garden of mossy, uneven cobblestones across and through which tree roots insinuate themselves, snake-like. Indeed the space has a distinctly temple-like quality on account of the ancient-looking, moss-patinated terracotta figurines, busts and pots artlessly positioned and piled here and there. Sit in one of the chairs with a refreshing drink and enjoy the cool, the shade pierced by dancing sunbeams, the sound of trickling water and the chirping of birds. The pieces are for sale – ask in the large teak house opposite the entrance to the garden if tempted by anything.

**Van Mieu
(Temple of Literature)
Hanoi**

📍 2
58 Quoc Tu Giam, Van
Mieu, Dong Da
Open Tue–Sun: 08.30–
11.30 & 13.30–16.30
Admission fee

A rare example of well-preserved traditional Vietnamese architecture, the Temple of Literature was constructed in 1070 by the Emperor Ly Thanh Tong and dedicated to Confucius. It is also home to the Quoc Tu Giam (Imperial Academy, Vietnam's first university, 1076). The walled temple grounds have five courtyards. The first two are pleasant, shady green spaces (but do keep off the grass); the third contains a large, square waterlily pool, the Well of Heavenly Clarity; and the last two are paved and ornamented with bronze vessels. This combines to provide respite from Hanoi's noisy and frenetic street life. It is possible to rest on one of the eighty-two stone turtles that support the stelae on which are engraved the names of the 1,307 doctors who took the eighty-two examination courses between 1442 and 1779. Look out, too, for the ornate stone tables featuring miniature rocky landscapes complete with buildings and bonsai trees. Beyond the fifth courtyard the circularish Văn lake is pleasant to stroll around, and adjacent to the courtyard complex is the grassy, shady Vuon hoa Quoc Tu Giam (Quoc Tu Giam Park).

Fort San Antonio Abad
Manila

📍 3
BSP Complex, Roxas
Blvd, Malate
Open: 24/7
Free

This green escape in the Malate district can be a bit of a challenge to find. The fort is now within the confines of the Central Bank complex, tucked away behind the Metropolitan Museum, between Roxas Boulevard and Mabini Street and a little southwest of the Zoological and Botanical Garden. Pass beneath the imposing yet elegant carved stone archway and into a green oasis surrounded by thick walls, some surmounted with cannon. Neatly clipped grass is the dominant element, but there are also borders planted with palms and tropical foliage plants, creating a quiet and relaxing enclosed space to hide out in for a while. The fort dates from 1584, during the Spanish Colonial period, and was erected in what was then a separate hamlet of Malate to guard both Manila and the Manila–Cavite route. It subsequently fell into the hands of the British (1762) and the Americans (1898), and was used as a bunker by the Japanese during the Second World War. It suffered considerable damage in the years following the conflict before being restored in the 1970s.

**Butterfly Garden
at Changi Airport
Singapore**

📍 4
Terminal 3, Departure
Transit Lounge, Level
2 & 3
Open: 24/7
Free

Most international airports are at best a trying experience where the well-being of the traveller is sacrificed for retail opportunity. Changi is a very pleasant exception, for here – in addition to plenty of shops and restaurants – are leisure facilities to entertain the weary traveller. The floral displays are always picture-perfect: there are about 500,000 plants in the airport, which runs its own nursery. In Terminal 2, do look out for the Orchid Garden, with its koi pond, and the Enchanted Garden, which combines flowers and ferns with sculptures and sparkling lights. But best of all is the Butterfly Garden in Terminal 3. This two-level glass tube with views out over the gated planes is a world first, an airport garden designed specifically as a habitat for tropical butterflies. Resplendent with a 6-metre-high natural-rock waterfall and planted with tall palms, lush foliage and a profusion of flowering plants (including orchids), this make-believe jungle is – depending on the time of year – home to about 1,000 butterflies representing about forty species. It is illuminated at night.

Ann Siang Hill Park
Singapore

📍5
78 Club St
Open: 24/7
Free

Just north of the somewhat manicured Telok Ayer Park, on the outskirts of Chinatown, is an unusual linear park. The official address is listed here, but the best way to discover this hidden gem is to make for the Thian Hock Keng Temple at 158 Telok Ayer Street. Next to it is the entrance to Telok Ayer Green, a pocket park that is a delightful oasis. Walk through to the exit on Amoy Street, turn left, walk 30 metres and turn right into Side Lane. Once you pass the Old Well you are at the start of the Hill Park. Paths and flights of steps take you upwards, a world away from the chic bars and eateries that now inhabit the elegantly restored early twentieth-century shopfronts, in a tranquil, winding journey around a hill that was formerly a failed nutmeg plantation (look out for the surviving nutmeg tree). The ascent offers refreshing views of the old and new city juxtaposed, and at the summit is a romantic climber-clad bower where you can sit and enjoy a wider outlook before exiting on to Ann Siang Road.

**Pura Jagatnatha
(Jagatnatha Temple)
Denpasar**

● 6
Jalan Mayor Wisnu,
Dangin Puri, Bali
Daily: 09.00–17.00
Free (donation is
requested)

A walk down Denpasar's streets is a pretty manic experience at the best of times, but look around: small Hindu 'temple-lets' can be spied at intervals between the houses. Pura Jagatnatha is particularly important, being both downtown and the city's largest temple. That is not to say that it is overwhelming. Quite the contrary, for within the peaceful compound are fishponds and courtyard prayer spaces surfaced with cobbles and grassy strips. Here it is possible to sit and unwind in the shade of a venerable tree. Built in 1953 and dedicated to the supreme god, Sanghyang Widi Wasa, the temple is in active use and appropriate dress is expected – a sarong will do fine. Visiting when it is crowded with worshippers – for example at the monthly festivals of new and full moon, when leather shadow-puppet (*wayang kulit*) performances occur – only adds to the spiritual experience. Leave the temple at its western perimeter and cross Jalan Udayana to the large Puputan Badung park, which boasts grassy expanses and a large water feature commemorating the Dutch massacre of 1906.

**Taman Kodok Menteng
(Menteng Frog Park)
Jakarta**

📍7
Jalan Sidoarjo No 3,
RT.3/RW.5, Menteng,
Kota Jakarta Pusat
Open: 24/7
Free

Just south of the large Taman Menteng is this smaller but older pocket park, commonly called Frog Park because of its amphibian ornamentation. The park was renovated in 2012 and, surrounded by a patterned surface of yellow and red paviours, the central feature is the circular Dancing Fountain, with jets of water emerging both from the frogs around the circumference and up from beneath the paving. It's very cooling – and very popular with children. There is plenty of seating, including beneath the stone-and-metal pergola that surrounds the part of the fountain that faces the park entrance, making this a shady, quiet retreat from the city. The planting is mostly at the perimeter and includes banyan trees and palms, and at ground level a well-maintained mix of foliage and flowering tropical taxa including banana, *Canna* spp. and *Dieffenbachia*. For more tranquil water visit Lake Lembang Park (Taman Situ Lembang), ten minutes' walk east. With its different-coloured tropical waterlilies and fringe of tall trees, it is a very relaxing place to find a shady bench and soak up some of the local colour.

1 **Mehtab Bagh (Moonlit Garden)** Agra, p.69
2 **Mughal Gardens, Rashtrapati Bhavan (President's Residence)** Delhi, p.70
3 **Jantar Mantar** Jaipur, p.71
4 **Chokelao Bagh (Mehrangarh Fort Gardens)** Jodhpur, p.72
5 **South Park Street Cemetery** Kolkata, p.73
6 **Marble Palace** Kolkata, p.74
7 **Rashtrapati Niwas (Viceregal Lodge)** Shimla, p.75
8 **Swapna Bagaicha (Garden of Dreams)** Kathmandu, p.76
9 **Baldha Gardens** Dhaka, p.78
10 **Dutch Period Museum** Colombo, p.79

**Mehtab Bagh
(Moonlit Garden)
Agra**

◆1
Near Taj Mahal,
Dharmapuri, Forest
Colony, Nagla Devjit
Daily: 06.00–19.00
Admission fee

This is the 'lost garden' of the Taj Mahal, the second half of the garden complex that surrounded the mausoleum built in 1632–54 by the Mughal Emperor Shah Jahan for his beloved wife Mumtaz Mahal. On the northern bank of the Yamuna River, the garden was buried in mud by floods and forgotten about until the 1990s, when it was rediscovered and restored. Conforming to the traditional Islamic *chahar bagh* (quadripartite) layout, this verdant garden has orchards, avenues and sweetly scented plantings that are far more authentic than those of its famous counterpart. At the terminus of the axis aligned on the mausoleum and close to the river is a large octagonal pool (now empty) with fifteen fountains. At the full moon, the reflection of the Taj Mahal in the water would have produced the mythical Black Taj. Mehtab Bagh is not only a delicious escape from the hot, bustling Agra, but also offers a superb and less commonly photographed view of the Taj itself. Visit the almost always empty garden in late afternoon, when the sun is on the mausoleum's rear face and the white marble glows gold.

Mughal Gardens, Rashtrapati Bhavan (President's Residence)
Delhi

● 2
President's Estate (enter from Gate 35)
Open: see p.365
Admission fee

This green haven in the centre of Delhi is hidden away behind tall walls and tight security. Publicly accessible only three days a week and requiring advance booking (via the website), it's a bit of a challenge to get into this magnificent, presidential garden – but well worth it. Designed by the world-famous English architect Sir Edwin Lutyens, the geometry, symmetry and quadripartite patterning are strongly inspired by Islamic garden-making, but Lutyens also introduced both Hindu and British traditions. There are in fact three gardens: the Main, Terrace and Long or Purdah, all of which are inventive and playful. The lush green lawns contrast boldly with the rust-red sandstone, while the planting, both structural and with shows of massed seasonal flowers – tulips in spring and salvias, dahlias, chrysanthemums, marigolds and heliotrope in summer – introduces colour, texture and variety. Most charming is the ingenious, uplifting use of moving water: its gentle movement creates a calming murmur and, thankfully on a hot Delhi day, it helps to cool the air, too.

Jantar Mantar
Jaipur

● 3
Gangori Bazaar, JDA
Market, Kanwar Nagar
Daily: 09.30–17.00
Admission fee

Located close to the strikingly beautiful pink and red sandstone Hawa Mahal (Palace of the Winds) and set within clipped hedge-edged lawns that infuse the space with a garden-like feel, Jantar Mantar boasts nineteen bizarre-looking architectural structures. These are in fact masonry-built astronomical instruments, for this is an observatory. One of them – the Brihat Samrat, with its 22.6-metre-tall gnomon arm – is probably the largest gnomon sundial ever built, and it continues to measure local time to an accuracy of two seconds. Climb to the top of it to get the best view of the observatory. The ideal time to visit is when the light is at its softest, at opening time and just before closing. The Jantar Mantar was built by Jai Singh II (1688–1743) as a focal point of his new capital, the first geometrically planned city in India. Jantar Mantar is the most complete and best-preserved great observatory site built in the pre-telescopic Ptolemaic tradition. It is one of five erected by Jai Singh, who was charged by the Mughal Emperor Muhammad Shah with revising the calendar and astronomical tables.

**Chokelao Bagh
(Mehrangarh Fort
Gardens)
Jodhpur**

● 4
Fort Entrance Rd,
Sodagaran Mohalla
Daily: 09.00–17.00
Admission fee

Chokelao Bagh is part of the Mehrangarh Fort complex in Jodhpur, a little to the north of the old town on a rocky promontory that affords lovely views of the city. The intimate garden – often missed by visitors but a great spot to sit and relax – is tucked away below the imposing fort. The now restored garden was first laid out in 1739 by Maharaja Abhai Singh (1702–49), the Raja of Marwar (Jodhpur) Kingdom, in an Islamic-style *chahar bagh* (quadripartite) layout over three terraces. A welcome retreat from the heat, the upper terrace is a shady flower garden with drought-tolerant plants, selected for texture and colour and planted in square blocks. The central well symbolizes the source of the four rivers of life described in the Qur'an. The middle terrace is an equally shady orchard, with banana, dessert apple, orange and pomegranate trees. The lower terrace, the *mehtab bagh* (moonlit garden), was originally designed to be enjoyed at night, when the white-flowered chandni *(Tabernaemontana divaricata)* glows ethereally and the scent of kamini *(Murraya paniculata)* perfumes the air.

South Park Street Cemetery
Kolkata

● 5
184 Acharya Jagadish Chandra Bose Rd,
Park St
Daily: 09.00–17.00
Free

Hidden behind a high brick wall at the intersection of Mother Teresa Sarani (Park Street) and Acharya Jagadish Chandra Bose Road, lined with varied shades of foliage, filtering the sharp sunlight to a verdant glow, this cemetery is darker and cooler than the sweltering city. It is filled with the mortal remains of many pioneers of the British East India Company, and to walk this city of forgotten souls, their monuments suffering the ravages of time, is sobering and melancholic. Perhaps most poignant is the youthful ages engraved on so many of the stones. In use between 1767 and the 1830s – and now, thankfully, being restored – this is one of the world's earliest detached cemeteries, and, at 3.2 hectares, probably the subcontinent's largest nineteenth-century Christian cemetery. The 1,500-plus tombs are a jumbled admixture of styles from European Classical and Gothic to Indo-Saracenic, and among the famous figures buried here are Sir William Jones, founder of the Asiatic Society (his memorial obelisk is the tallest structure), and Robert Kyd, founder of Kolkata's botanic garden.

Marble Palace
Kolkata

📍6
46 Muktaram Babu St
Open: see p.365
Free (permit required)

The whimsical neoclassical Marble Palace epitomizes the opulence and grandeur of nineteenth-century Kolkata. It is surrounded by formal lawns studded with statuary, and in front of the imposing facade stand lofty palms and a very tall stone fountain and pool set in lawn and with formal flower beds, urns and pots filled with seasonal colour. To the west of the house, an ornate stone fountain depicting mermaids and mermen stands in a large formal pool with beds of roses around it. Look out, too, for the Marble Palace Zoo, today a small menagerie and aviary but historically India's first zoo. The palace was built in 1835–40 by Rajendra Mullick, who began the project aged just sixteen and filled it inside and out with artworks. It was given its name by Lord Minto, former Governor-General of India, because the intricate architectural details are picked out using more than 100 types of marble. The estate is still inhabited by Mullick's descendants today, and to visit requires a permit obtained twenty-four hours in advance from the West Bengal Tourism Information Bureau at 3/2 BBD Bag East Road.

**Rashtrapati Niwas
(Viceregal Lodge)**
Shimla

● 7
Observatory Hill
(near Summer Hill
Railway Station)
Open: see p.365
Admission fee

In 1864, Shimla, a picturesque town at an altitude of 2,200 metres, became the cool summer capital of the British Raj and gained some splendid examples of colonial architecture. Without doubt the finest is the imposing Jacobean Viceregal Lodge, now known as Rashtrapati Niwas. Behind the lodge an equally impressive formal garden was created, complete with an innovative rainwater-harvesting and irrigation system. Today the terraces are mostly lawn, and the well-maintained flower beds and topiary produce a good show. Beyond the house, on this 45-hectare estate, are informal wooded grounds, affording splendid views through the trees over the dramatic landscape. There is also a rare *stické* (an indoor racquet sport) court. To visit when the hilltop is shrouded in mist or the garden blanketed in snow is an ethereal experience. Built on Observatory Hill at the western end of this strung-out city as the summer residence of the Viceroy, the palace was designed by the Irish architect Henry Irwin and completed in 1888, and is now home to the Indian Institute of Advanced Study.

**Swapna Bagaicha
(Garden of Dreams)
Kathmandu**

● 8
Tridevi Sadak
Daily: 09.00–22.00
Admission fee

In the midst of busy Kathmandu, next door to the former Royal Palace (Kaiser Mahal) and at the entrance to the notoriously touristy Thamel neighbourhood, it is possible to pass through a gateway and enter what is, to all intents and purposes, a walled garden in the English Arts and Crafts style. It was designed in 1920 by the architect Kishore Narsingh for Field Marshal Kaiser Shumsher Rana (1892–1964). In 2000–7, following decades of neglect and decay, it was restored under the aegis of the Austrian government and the Nepal Ministry of Education. It is also known as the Garden of Six Seasons, and its formal layout focuses on six impressive pavilions, one for each of Nepal's six seasons. Strolling through the grounds, with their sunken areas, grass amphitheatre, pools, verandas, pergolas, balustrades, urns and birdhouses is almost like being in Edwardian England, but for the elephant statues and exotic plants, including palms, bamboos, tree ferns, orchids, angel's trumpet (*Brugmansia* spp.) and bunya pines. The stylistic adaptations are unconventional but effective, once you get over the culture shock.

Baldha Gardens
Dhaka

● 9
Nawab St, Wari
Daily: 09.00–17.00
(Mar–Nov); 09.00–
19.30 (Dec–Feb)
Admission fee

This tropical green haven is a welcome escape from the congested streets of Wari, the old part of Dhaka. A small botanic garden of 1.3 hectares, it houses a collection of 672 taxa, including stately, shade-giving trees. Here, too, are a round lotus pond, a rockery, glasshouses, a collection of orchids, a sundial, a tomb and a cave. The highlight is perhaps the picturesque, waterlily-cloaked rectangular tank with steps leading down to the water's edge. Keep an eye out for the fauna: sleeping Asian fruit bats hang from the tree branches, and there is often a mongoose family or two to be spotted. Now managed as part of Bangladesh's National Botanical Garden (in the Mirpur district, by Dhaka Zoo), this is in fact one of the oldest botanic gardens in Bangladesh. It was established in 1909 by Narendra Narayan Roy Chaudhury, landlord of the Baldah estate, who continued to add to the plant collection until his death in 1943. For more solitude and seclusion, visit the Dhaka Christian Cemetery on nearby Narinda Road, which with its eighteenth-century tombs is very atmospheric.

Dutch Period Museum
Colombo

● 10
95 Prince St, Pettah
Open Tue–Sat:
  09.00–17.00
Admission fee

Part of the excitement to be had from this hidden garden is finding it. It is in Pettah: the oldest, most diverse part of the city, and a warren of business emporia. Don't even think of driving here, but walk or take a tuk-tuk to Main Street and turn off at 2nd Cross Street. Built by Thomas van Rhee, the Dutch Governor of Ceylon (1692–97), as his official residence, this two-storey, red-tile-roofed and many-pillared mansion is possibly the best-preserved Dutch era (1656–1796) building in the city. The museum may appear closed, but simply knock and a caretaker will let you in. Pass through arched wooden doors and the mansion's thick walls smother Pettah's noise and clamour. The ancient hall leads to the city's oldest *meda midula* (courtyard garden), enclosed on three sides by a white-columned veranda. Its main feature is the well-tended lawn and stone well. A cinnamon tree, cannas, ixias and palms make up the planting. Looking around, it is easy to see how this columns-and-courtyard form so inspired the country's most famous architect, Geoffrey Bawa.

1   Lavigerie Garden,
    Church of St Anne
    Jerusalem, p.81
2   Gan Yaakov (Yaakov
    Garden) Tel Aviv, p.82
3   Darat al Funun, Khalid
    Shoman Foundation
    Amman, p.84
4   Madreseye Chahar
    Bagh (Chahar Bagh
    Theological School)
    Isfahan, p.85
5   Khaneh-ye 'Abbasiha
    (Abbasi House)
    Kashan, p.86

6   Naranjestan-e Qavam
    (Qavam Orange Grove)
    Shiraz, p.87
7   Bagh Negarestan (Citrus
    Garden) Tehran, p.88
8   Dubai Park Dubai, p.89

**Lavigerie Garden,
Church of St Anne
Jerusalem**

● 1
Derech Sha'ar
HaArayot
Open: see p.364
Admission fee

A little north of the Temple Mount, just inside the Lions' Gate a short way down the Derech Sha'ar HaArayot, and on the right-hand side, is a doorway in a rather austere wall, above which is daubed 'Birth Place of the Virgin Mary'. This is, in fact, the entrance to the Church of St Anne, dedicated to Anna and Joachim, Mary's parents. The best-preserved Crusader church in the city, this restored Romanesque church was built some time between 1131 and 1138 on the site of a grotto believed to be the Virgin's childhood home. Pass through the church, with its wonderful acoustics, and beyond are not only the Bethesda excavations but also a small, square courtyard garden. The focal point of this delightful space with its cheerfully planted stone-edged beds and planted pots on stone pedestals is a bust of Charles Lavigerie (1825–92), archbishop of Carthage and Algiers and primate of Africa, after whom the garden is named. Rest for a moment on a stone bench shaded by palms, cypress and citrus trees and reflect on the millennia of history this site has seen.

**Gan Yaakov
(Yaakov Garden)
Tel Aviv**

📍 2
Sterot Tarsat 6
Open: 24/7
Free

A ten-minute walk south from the downtown area brings one to this enclave of the arts and the recently revamped, two-tiered Yaakov Garden. The design and structure are playful, and the garden unites yet simultaneously breaks up and softens the rigid Modernist architecture. There are concrete slab and stone crazy-paving paths; trees with branches that weave their way amid the white pillars and beams; a formal pool with fountain jets; and both ground-level and raised beds. The feature plants are the three ancient sycamore fig trees, and new planting has recently added a mixture of shrubs, perennials and ornamental grasses. Scented plants perfume the air, and when in bloom the wisteria covering the high pergola is spectacular. Combined with the shade and splash of fountains, the sweet scents make this a calm place, especially when it is lit up in the evenings. Designed by the architect Yaakov Rechter and built in 1963, the garden was renovated in 2010 and integrated with the new Culture Square by artist Dani Karavan. The funky sunken garden in the new square is worth a visit, too.

Darat al Funun, Khalid Shoman Foundation
Amman

● 3
13 Nadim Al-Mallah St
Open: see p.364
Free

A short walk from both Jabal al-Weibdeh district's Paris Square and King Faysal Square in downtown Amman, Darat al Funun was inaugurated in 1993 as a centre for the arts and artists of the Arab world, in the hope of nurturing creativity and critical discourse. Enjoying broad views over the heart of the city and housed in six renovated historical buildings, interspersed with gardens, Darat al Funun is a stimulating fusion of garden art, architecture and archaeology. The cafe terrace features an ornate raised octagonal pool and burbling fountain. The most striking feature of the southern gardens are the remains of a sixth-century Byzantine church built over a Roman temple and an ancient cave. The ruins occasionally host events and screenings, while the cave is illuminated atmospherically at twilight. Outcrops of white limestone are softened by shrubby plantings including plumbago and bougainvillea; planted terracotta pots introduce form and colour, and tall pines and cypresses give shade. In 2002 Darat al Funun was incorporated into the non-profit Khalid Shoman Foundation.

Madreseye Chahar Bagh (Chahar Bagh Theological School)
Isfahan

● 4
Chahar Bagh
e Abbasi St
Daily: 09.00–20.00
 (closed Fri)
Free

In the seventeenth century Isfahan was world famous as a city of gardens, and it still has many historic green spaces to explore. One of the less well known is hidden in the centre of the city, within the Chahar Bagh Theological School. Pass under the monumental and magnificently ornate entrance gate, adorned with blue, white and gold tiles in complex geometric patterns, arabesques and calligraphy, to an airy, domed, octagonal vestibule with similarly ornate tiling. Beyond is a verdant courtyard garden enclosed by arcades on two levels, off which are the students' rooms. The layout is based on the traditional quadripartite *chahar bagh*, but with subtle differences. Defining the four-square form is a sunken rill running west to east, perpendicular to which is a wide, paved path. At its southern end stands the mosque and to the north a blue-painted, ornate, rectangular pool. Filling the quarters are square lawns edged with tall cypress and plane trees. After soaking up the tranquillity, perhaps walk a little north and visit the large but beautiful Hasht Behesht (Eight Heavens) garden.

**Khaneh-ye 'Abbasiha
(Abbasi House)
Kashan**

◆ 5
Alavi St
Open Sat–Thu:
 09.00–18.00
Admission fee

About 100 metres south along Alavi Street from its T-junction with Fazel Naraqi Street, on the right-hand side, stands one of the grandest examples of late eighteenth-century Kashani domestic architecture. The residence of a wealthy and important citizen, the complex has six courtyards, each of which fulfilled different needs. The serene outer courtyard is the best restored and most impressive. In the centre of the rectangular space stands a handsome turquoise-tinted pool with a single fountain. When the waters are still they reflect the high porticos and intricate stuccowork of the lovely enclosing architecture. On either side of the pool, surrounded by stone paving, is a pair of equally long but wider flower beds, planted with shrubs. Inside the house, look for the enchanting room with a mirror-embedded ceiling. The intention – at night, and when lit by candles – is to give the impression of a glittering starry sky. Also with watered courtyards and meriting a visit are the Taj Historical House on the same street, and four minutes' walk southwest, the Tabatabaei Historical House.

**Naranjestan-e Qavam
(Qavam Orange Grove)**
Shiraz

● 6
Lotf Ali Khan Zand St
Daily: 08.00–19.00
Admission fee

The city of Shiraz is famous for its large, much-visited Persian-inspired Islamic gardens. In contrast, the city's smallest and least-visited garden offers shade, solitude and peace. It was created in the late nineteenth century as part of the *andaruni* (private quarters) of this residential complex, built by one of Shiraz's wealthiest and most influential families. The twenty-room Qavam house, now a museum, is well worth visiting. The rectangular, walled and detached garden was accessed by a tunnel (now closed), and the focal point is the opulent pavilion (1879–86). Its mirrored entrance hall opens on to rooms decorated with stunning inlaid wooden panels, intricate tiling and a kaleidoscope of stained glass. The veranda gives views down over a rectangular pool and along a blue-tiled rill, punctuated by pools and fountains, that runs the length of the garden and is aligned on the pavilion's main axis. Flanking the rill are cheerfully planted beds and a pair of paths. Filling the rest of the courtyard is a shade-giving, dark-green grove of the bitter orange trees that give the garden its name, above which tower rows of tall palms.

**Bagh Negarestan
(Citrus Garden)
Tehran**

📍 7
**Daneshsara, District 12
Daily: 09.00–19.00
(closed Mon)
Admission fee**

This small, pleasant Islamic garden near Baharestan Metro Station and the Iranian Parliament has a great cafe, and water features make it quiet and cool. It is not a typical quadripartite *chahar bagh*, but it is formal and geometric, with terraces linked by steps and paved courts into which are set pools with fountains and gently burbling rills, some lined with potted plants. Tall trees introduce a strong vertical element and soften the sunlight, while benches entice one to sit, relax and admire the floral displays – many of which are in beds set into the lawns. Negarestan was created along with its associated palace by the Qajar king Fath-'Ali Shah (1772–1834) as a summer residence outside the capital. The now greatly reduced gardens narrowly escaped being demolished to make way for a car park and service station in 1971, and again in 1986, and today the palace is an art museum displaying the works of the 'Persian Michelangelo', Mohammad Ghaffari (also known as Kamal-ol-Molk; 1847–1940), and his students. The nearby Masoudieh Palace and gardens also deserve a visit.

Dubai Park
Dubai

📍 8
P3 11A St
Open: 24/7
Free

A gift to the city from His Royal Highness the Aga Khan IV in 2008, this small, serene neighbourhood park is based on the Islamic garden-making tradition. The main axis runs from the entrance to the grand pergola at the far end. On its raised setting this square, pillared structure with a domed lattice roof, echoing the entrance gate, provides a shaded sitting area with a view of the entire park. The main axis itself comprises a series of interconnected formal pools, with arching jets inspired by the Generalife in Granada. The fountains gently stimulate the ears and eyes, generating a tranquil atmosphere that can be enjoyed while resting on one of the stone benches that adorn the paths on both sides of the pools. Either side of the main axis, separated by low walls, is a pair of lawned enclosures planted with tall, shading palms and set with three linked, circular pools with fountains. Savour a moment's peace and harmony out of the sun – and come again at night, when the park is lit.

1 **Listasafn Einars Jónssonar (Einar Jónsson Museum)** Reykjavik, p.93
2 **Arktisk Alpin Botanisk Hage (Arctic-Alpine Botanical Garden)** Tromsø, p.94
3 **Tervasaari** Helsinki, p.95
4 **Slottsträdgården (Castle Garden)** Malmö, p.96
5 **Strömparterren** Stockholm, p.98
6 **Assistens Kirkegård (Assistens Cemetery)** Copenhagen, p.99

7 **Botanisk Have (Botanical Garden)** Copenhagen, p.100
8 **Ny Carlsberg Glyptotek Museum** Copenhagen, p.101

Listasafn Einars Jónssonar (Einar Jónsson Museum) Reykjavik

📍1
Eiríksgata 3, 101
Open: 24/7 (see p.367 for museum times)
Free (admission fee for museum)

In 1909 Einar Jónsson (1874–1954), Iceland's first sculptor in the modern sense of the word, arranged with the country's parliament to provide him with a home and studio in Reykjavik, in return for which he agreed to bequeath all his works to the nation. Set amid the geometry of the concrete paths and lawns of the sculpture garden to the west of the house are bronze casts of twenty-six pieces by Jónsson, as well as relics of the garden he and his wife made while living there. Note the peculiar ring of stones between the office and museum buildings. Many of the works are figurative, with complex symbolism influenced by Jónsson's exposure to the ideas of the Swedish theosopher Emanuel Swedenborg, ideas that led him to become deeply spiritually attuned and reclusive. Benches encourage one to sit and study both the unconventional, indecipherable bronzes and their interesting visual juxtapositions with the modern architecture. The Brutalist building, adjacent to the spectacular Hallgrímskirkja church, was designed by Jónsson and architect Einar Erlendsson, and opened as a museum in 1984.

Arktisk Alpin Botanisk Hage (Arctic-Alpine Botanical Garden)
Tromsø

● 2
Stakkevollvegen 200, 9019
Daily: 09.00–17.00
Free

Nestled at the foot of an east-facing slope with natural forest rising above it, the world's most northerly botanic garden (opened in 1994) offers broad views over the Tromsdalen valley and across the fjord to the Tromsdalstinden mountains beyond. It is planted with taxa from northern polar regions and alpine habitats, and in the spring and the midnight summer sun the garden is a spectacular floral feast of rhododendrons, Himalayan and Arctic poppies, *Lewisia* spp., primulas, saxifrages and much more. Indeed, this small botanic garden punches above its weight; although it is a scientific plant collection, its layout pays close heed to site and aesthetics. The naturalistic design takes full advantage of the rocky topography, and with the gravel paths winding among the attractive plant collections. Each of the twenty-five collections is displayed in a habitat created to provide the plants with their favoured growing conditions, be it by a stream, on a scree slope or nestled among rocks. Set 350 kilometres north of the Arctic Circle, the garden is possible only because the island is warmed – just – by the Gulf Stream.

Tervasaari
Helsinki

📍 3
Tervasaarenkannas 1,
00170
Open: 24/7
Free

The small, C-shaped Tervasaari island is reached by a very pleasant walk from downtown Helsinki along the tree-lined Esplanade Park (Pohjoisesplanadi) via the South Harbour front and the Kauppatori market square. (The open-air market is held daily, all year round, and the heated cafe tents in winter are a treat.) Turn north here, along the Pohjoisranta, with the waters of the harbour on your right, after five minutes' walk a long causeway projects to the right, flanked by marina pontoons. This is Tervasaarenkannas, which leads to the island. Tervasaari translates as 'tar island' and refers to a time when the island was covered in warehouses that stored ships' tar for export. The land was repurposed as naturalistic public green space in the 1990s, and today paths meander through groves of trees and among gentle grassy mounds. In summer the wild roses and seasonal plantings are beautiful, and the island is a relaxing place for a picnic. Find one of the many benches and enjoy the views over the harbour and back to the city, or paddle from the small sandy beach. There is also a play area and restaurant.

**Slottsträdgården
(Castle Garden)
Malmö**

● 4
Malmöhusvägen 8,
211 18
Open: 24/7
Free

Slottsträdgården is a few minutes' walk west of the downtown area of this delightful city, and is part of a larger green space that includes two informally landscaped late nineteenth-century parks of trees, lawns and sinuous waterways. Roughly rectangular, and covering about 1.2 hectares, the garden was established in 1994 with the aim of creating the ambience and appearance of an old-fashioned pleasure garden. At its northern perimeter, the eight Theme Gardens enclosed on three sides by tall yew hedges include the insect garden, the school garden, the perennial garden and the Linnaeus garden. Facing them is the Long Border, some 5 metres wide and 130 metres in length, filled with drifts of bulbs in spring and perennials in summer. Flanked by paths, the border is carefully planned to appear attractive from both sides and in both directions. Between it and the canal that marks the southern boundary are the potager and cut flower gardens. The bounty from both is sold to visitors and used in the kitchen of the organic café, where it is delightful to linger and enjoy a *smörgås*.

Strömparterren
Stockholm

● 5
Norrbro 1, 11128
Open: 24/7
Free

From the must-see Gamla Stan, the historic heart of Stockholm, the wide street of Norrbro offers a picturesque walk north to the modern city. At the eastern end of the small island of Helgeandsholmen is Strömparterren, a splendid spot to rest. Dating from 1832 and re-opened in 2012 after a major facelift, the park is one of Stockholm's oldest. Access is via granite steps down from Norrbro, beside geometrically pollarded linden (lime) trees. Inside the semicircular park, the eye-catcher at the end of a rectangular pool with fountain jets is Carl Milles's statue *Solsångaren* (*The Sun Singer*; 1926). Surrounded by wide gravel paths, he faces east, his arms raised, welcoming dawn. Either side of this composition is a lawn edged with continuous concrete benching, while flower beds and containers introduce seasonal colour. Sit here or on the steps down to the water with a drink from the cafe and contemplate the rapids of the Norrström, watch the fishermen or admire the surrounding monumental architecture of the Royal Palace (south), the Royal Opera House (north) and the Parliament Building (west).

**Assistens Kirkegård
(Assistens Cemetery)**
Copenhagen

● 6
Kapelvej 4, 2200
Open: see p.365
Free

It is a twenty-minute walk from the Botanical Garden (see p.100) through an elegant neighbourhood and across the Sortedams Sø, a canal that once formed part of the city's defences, to the ethnically diverse Nørrebro district. Here, a tall, yellow-painted wall abuts the perpendicular main roads of Nørrebrogade and Jagtveg, behind which lies Assistens Cemetery. Founded in 1760 and still in use today, it is most famous for the graves of the writer Hans Christian Andersen (1805–75) and the philosopher Søren Kierkegaard (1813–55). Yet this is a cemetery with a difference. Its layout is park-like, with the tombs and graves – most of them neatly tended – set in expanses of lawn and hidden among a fine collection of trees and shrubs. As it has been for more than two centuries, Assistens Cemetery is a popular spot for locals to visit, bring their children to play, and even picnic. The cemetery is used recreationally with respect, however. Visit Andersen's grave, wander the paths and the grounds, admire the well-maintained flora, and do sit on the grass and enjoy the serenity of this remarkably peaceful place.

**Botanisk Have
(Botanical Garden)
Copenhagen**

● 7
Gothersgade 128, 1123
Open: see p.365
Free

Covering 10 hectares, the University of Copenhagen Botanical Garden is not small, but it is certainly hidden. Created on repurposed seventeenth-century moat-and-bastion fortifications and opened in 1874, much of the garden is below street level. Even the inconspicuous entrance on the corner of Gothersgade and Øster Voldgade is easily missed. But venture in – and down – and the hubbub of the city stills as you enter a haven of birdsong and flowers. The beautifully maintained yet informally landscaped garden boasts 13,000 plant taxa (including a collection of Danish native species) and twenty-seven glasshouses to explore. There is much for the gardener here, but with its inviting lawns, shady ornamental trees, winding rockery, sinuous lake and hidden nooks there is ample opportunity just to rest weary feet. This is in fact the botanic garden's fourth incarnation after its founding in 1600; it was laid out here by the landscape designer and inspector at the royal gardens Henrik August Flindt, who also designed the nearby public parks Ørstedsparken and Østre Anlæg.

Ny Carlsberg Glyptotek Museum
Copenhagen

📍 8
Stoltenbergsgade,
1576
Daily: 07.30–22.00
(see p.367 for
museum times)
Free (admission fee
for museum)

For most people, the garden associated with the Ny Glyptotek is the lovely Winter Garden inside the building, with its tall palms. The conservatory is certainly attractive and well planted, but it's not all that peaceful, being a thoroughfare for museum visitors. However, the garden behind the building is so secret that it doesn't even have a name. It is an absolute treasure. Laid out in a formal, geometric style and running the width of the classically inspired building are two large lawns, each fringed by narrow, well-planted borders of seasonal colour enclosed by low box hedges ornamented with topiary cones. There are three bronzes, and greeting you at the entrance at the northeastern end of Stoltenbergsgade is Rodin's *The Thinker* (1903). Scattered at the perimeter are wooden benches that allow you to sit and do the same. This little gem is across the road from the Tivoli Gardens but hardly visited, and more often than not you will have it to yourself. Nearby is another hidden green space, a small courtyard within the Rådhus (City Hall) that features a splendid bear fountain.

**Herschel Museum
of Astronomy Garden
Bath**

📍 1
19 New King St,
BA1 2BL
Open: see p.366
Admission fee

In the garden of a typical mid-eighteenth-century house, part of a honey-coloured limestone terrace a mere nine minutes' walk west of the famous Roman Baths, the amateur astronomer William Herschel (1738–1822) discovered Uranus on the night of 13 March 1781. Today the house is a museum to Herschel and his comet-discovering sister, Caroline, and the narrow rectangular town garden has been re-created in Georgian style. The central bed is edged with a low, clipped hedge of box and separated from the two long borders at the foot of the garden wall by gravel paths that lead to the charming quince arbour at the end of the garden. The planting is symmetrical and 'period correct', both in the selection of native medicinal and culinary plants and in the planting style. Ornamental artworks include an armillary sphere, a contemporary metal seed-head installation representing the solar system, and a stone sculpture of William and Caroline mapping the heavens. It is quite something to stand in the spot where, as Herschel observed, he 'looked further into space than any human being did before me'.

The Secret Garden and Discovery Terrace, Library of Birmingham
Birmingham

● 2
Centenary Square,
Broad St, B1 2ND
Open: see p.368
Free

Designed by the Dutch architectural firm Mecanoo with a striking facade of overlapping circles, Birmingham Library (2013) has two integral gardens. On the seventh floor is the rooftop Secret Garden and on the third the Discovery Terrace – both afford panoramas over the city as well as creating a space to relax, socialize and give the brain a break from book work. The planting of the Secret Garden is deliberately dense, creating a quiet space. It forms a tapestry predominantly of flowering perennials and ornamental grasses of different heights in cleverly sloping asymmetric beds (the autumnal show of seed heads is quite lovely), surrounded and pierced by paved and gravel paths. On the Discovery Terrace the silver, fish-scale-shaped raised beds are edged by low hedges and also contain edibles, with the aim of encouraging visitors to learn about healthy eating and growing produce. In both cases, the plant mix is designed to attract wildlife and support the urban ecology, while the gardens themselves are part of the city's drive to reduce carbon-dioxide emissions by 60 per cent from 1990 to 2026.

**College Gardens,
University of Cambridge**
Cambridge

● 3
Fellows' Garden
Clare College,
Trinity Lane, CB2 1TL
**Fellows' Garden
& Darwin Garden**
Christ's College,
St Andrew's St, CB2 3BU
Open: see p.366
Free

Many of Cambridge's colleges have lovely gardens to explore, including Sidney Sussex, Newnham and Emmanuel, but the highlights are the Fellows' Gardens at Clare and Christ's. The former, with its lovely combination of lawns, borders and hidden corners, is on the west bank of the River Cam, accessed via an elegant stone bridge. The sumptuous herbaceous borders are particularly stunning, their planting augmented with seasonal colour. Behind the yew hedge enclosing the sunken garden, with its rectangular pool, is a secret flower garden. The more central Christ's also has sweeping lawns and flower-filled borders, but in combination with a fine collection of trees, including plane, horse chestnut and the venerable Milton's Mulberry, probably planted in the early seventeenth century and named after the English poet, who was admitted to the college in 1625. In front of the New Court Building is a second garden honouring another famous alumnus: the Darwin Garden, containing plants associated with the great man's travels, created in 2009 to mark Darwin's 200th birthday.

**Chester Cathedral
Cloisters**
Chester

📍 4
St Werburgh St,
CH1 2DY
Open Mon–Sat:
09.00–18.00;
Sun: 11.00–16.00
Free

The city of Chester was an important Roman stronghold, and there may have been a Christian basilica here as early as the late Roman period. The oldest parts of the present cathedral date from the late eleventh century. The Perpendicular Gothic-style cloister to the north of the nave had just been completed at the time of the Dissolution, when in 1541 the Benedictine St Werburgh's Abbey was re-consecrated as the cathedral. Restored in the twentieth century, the cloister garth ('garthen' is the plural of 'garth', or enclosed space, hence 'garden') is laid out mostly as lawn, with specimen trees including Chilean fire bush, ginkgo and magnolia, as well as rhododendrons and wisteria. In the centre of this enclosed space, is a sunken, box-hedged pool; steps lead down to the water's edge. At the centre of the pool (and, symbolically, the cloister) stands the bronze sculpture *The Water of Life* by Stephen Broadbent. Installed in 1994 as part of the church's 900-year celebrations, it depicts the encounter between Jesus and the Woman of Samaria, showing their shared bowl overflowing with water.

Dunbar's Close
Edinburgh

● 5
137 Canongate,
EH8 8BW
Daily: from 07.00,
closing times vary
throughout the year
Free

Along the Royal Mile descending towards the Scottish Parliament and between two shops is an archway into one of this ancient street's numerous narrow lanes or 'closes', evidence of the area's medieval origins. Pass under the arch and be transported into the haven of a re-created seventeenth-century garden. It was made just before his death by the biologist, sociologist and pioneering town planner Sir Patrick Geddes (1854–1932), and in 1978, after years of neglect, it was revamped by the landscape architect Seamus Filor. Compact and formal, the garden was designed to be typical of those belonging to well-to-do burghers at a time when this was the city's wealthiest area. The rectangular 3,000-square-metre space comprises eight interlinked 'rooms' divided by clipped yew hedges, wooden fencing and ivy-clad walls. Some contain richly planted flower beds; others are laid out in an arrangement of neat knot beds ornamented with bay topiary; another is shaded by a tall tulip tree (*Liriodendron tulipifera*). Benches are set in suntraps, and there are views of the picturesque Calton Hill.

St Nicholas Garden, Provand's Lordship
Glasgow

📍 6
3 Castle St, G4 0RH
Open: see p.367
Free

Ten minutes' walk from Glasgow's High Street railway station stands the restored Provand's Lordship, the sole surviving house from the medieval city. Built in 1471 by Andrew Muirhead, Bishop of Glasgow from 1455–73, it formed part of St Nicholas's Hospital in the cathedral precinct. Behind it is the St Nicholas Garden, designed in 1997 as an interpretation of a fifteenth-century garden. It is dominated by the square, geometric knot garden, the motifs picked out in low box hedging and ornamented with four yew cones. The visitor can stroll along the granite path to the centre of the square and admire the stone fountain, reminiscent of a Norman font and set around with a curving yew hedge. In the fifteenth century the range of plants available was vastly smaller than that today, and many also had a functional role. The taxa chosen here are those that would have been put to culinary or medicinal use in the hospital. Enclosing the garden on two sides, the modern cloisters offer an elevated perspective of the knot; the walls are embellished with intriguing carved stone faces known collectively as the Tontine Heads.

The Hidden Gardens
Glasgow

● 7
Tramway, 25A Albert
Drive, G41 2PE
Open: see p.366
Free

This award-winning triangular garden was created in 2003 on the site of the former Copelawhill Tram Works (1899), in the diverse area of Pollokshields. It is a place of peace, learning and exchange, but also a space in which to relax on the large lawn and enjoy the lovely rill, sculpture installations, herb border and wildlife area, which aims to enhance local biodiversity. According to the charity that runs the communally developed garden, it 'exists to promote understanding between people of all cultures, faiths and backgrounds. It celebrates the universal spirit of nature'. The design, by City Design Cooperative, was inspired by the site's history. For example, the north–south borders echo the nineteenth-century tree nursery that was once here, and the retained tramlines and chimney indicate the former industrial use. Other influences include Celtic and Asian gardening traditions, especially noticeable in the spatial structure and planting. Taxa significant to various cultures and belief systems occur throughout the garden, including bamboos, ginkgo, hazel, magnolia, rowan and winter-flowering plum.

Jellicoe Roof Garden
Guildford

● 8
House of Fraser, 5th
floor, 105–11 High St,
GU1 3DP
Open Mon–Wed &
  Sat: 09.00–18.00;
  Thu: 09.00–19.00;
  Sun: 11.00–17.00
Free

Hidden away on the top floor of the department store House of Fraser in the centre of Guildford is a wonderful, important example of modern English garden design. Viewed from the Tea Terrace restaurant and to be enjoyed with a pot of tea and slice of cake (sadly it is no longer possible to walk through the garden as originally intended), this rooftop water garden, with its splendid views over the North Downs, was designed in 1958 as the Sky Garden by Sir Geoffrey Jellicoe, arguably Britain's most influential twentieth-century landscape architect. It has an infinity-pool effect and fountain bowls, circular stepping stones, and sinuous islands and promontories planted with architectural species, including ornamental grasses, bamboo, royal fern and corkscrew hazel. Jellicoe's inspiration was the flight of the Russian satellite *Sputnik I* in 1957, and his aim was 'to unite heaven and earth; the sensation is one of being poised between the two'. The garden was restored from a state of dilapidation in 2000 and reduced in size in 2008.

Leeds University Sustainable and Edible Garden
Leeds

📍 9
Between the Roger Stevens Building & Chancellor's Court, Leeds University, LS2 9JT
Open: 24/7
Free

This small, no-dig allotment-and-forest-style edible garden is accessible for all to enjoy some quiet contemplation, and is to be found at the centre of the University campus, next to the Roger Stevens Building. A roughly Y-shaped permeable path of resin-bound recycled glass divides the plot into three areas, with lawn, benches and planting areas. These include the central Pictorial Perennial Meadow, a herb garden in chimney-pot planters, pocket habitat planters for vegetables, bed-grown vegetables, fruit trees, and a lovely edible hedge planted with a mix of black-currant, blackthorn (sloe), elderberry, gooseberry, hazel and red-currant. The garden is a great example of a functioning ecosystem, with wildflower areas and insect houses, and it is an outreach tool. Run collaboratively by the Sustainability Service, the students' union (LUU) and academic staff, LUU's rooted project runs gardening sessions to teach students, staff and the local community food growing skills. Created in 2013, it was based on the Royal Horticultural Society Gold Medal-winning exhibit staged by the university the previous year.

**Church of Our Lady
and St Nicholas**
Liverpool

● 10
5 Old Church Yard,
L2 8GW
Open: 24/7
Free

Close to the River Mersey, a two-minute walk from the famous Royal Liver Building and a stone's throw from Princes Dock, this churchyard is now public green space, an oasis of calm in the heart of the city's business district. It was created in 1361 and used as a burial ground until 1849, but in May 1892 it was decided to repurpose the graveyard as an 'Ornamental Ground'. In true Victorian public-park style, the layout comprised 'walks' and 'beds of shrubs or plants surrounded with turf'. The design has changed little since. Inside the perimeter of iron railings, narrow mixed borders are fronted with a strip of mown grass. The central lawn is fringed with borders of mostly perennials, predominantly maritime species to withstand strong salt-laden winds. Around the lawn is a wide stone-flagged path with west-facing benches. Stop here, enjoy the view over the river and contemplate all the history the docks have seen. Access to the gardens is via a rather splendid and ornate stone arch and steps up from George's Dock Gates, or through gates at the end of Tower Gardens and in Old Church Yard.

**Sir Bobby Robson
Memorial Garden**
Newcastle-upon-Tyne

📍 11
Corner of Gallowgate
& St Andrew's St,
NE1 5SF
Open: 24/7
Free

In the shadow of St James Park – Newcastle United Football Club's stadium – and a little south of the Gallowgate End, this pocket park opened in 2011 as a memorial to the footballing legend Sir Bobby Robson (1933–2009). The square space is mostly lawn, flanked on both sides by flowering cherry trees. Set within the sward, the four long, low stone walls create three grassy terraces, provide somewhere to sit and lead the eye towards the rear of the space, where stand five square, white, carved monoliths by Graeme Mitcheson. Brought into focus by the wooden wall behind them and the four silver birch trees planted between – their silver bark complementing the monoliths perfectly – each work represents an era of Sir Bobby's life. Taken together, the tops of the pieces form a gentle convex curve, suggesting the progress of a full and rich life. Robson was a childhood supporter of the club and, after a career as a player (he won twenty caps for England) and manager of both club and national teams, he managed Newcastle United between 1999 and 2004.

Plantation Garden
Norwich

📍12
4 Earlham Rd, NR2 3DB
Daily: 09.00–18.00
Admission fee

Descend into a 1.2-hectare time capsule of beautifully restored nineteenth-century gardens in an abandoned chalk quarry a short distance from the city centre. This is an engaging and distinctive creation, completely in keeping with Victorian garden-making fashions, which tended towards plundering ideas from the past and then misrepresenting them, using the latest technology and planting arrangements as bold, brassy and clashing as possible. An absorbing mix of formal and informal, the design weaves together – not altogether harmoniously – an 18-metre-long Italianate terrace, a medieval wall, a 9-metre-tall Gothic fountain, a rustic bridge and summerhouse, lawns, shrubberies, carpet bedding (low-growing foliage plants closely massed to create a carpet look) and heated greenhouses. The garden's creator was Henry Trevor, a wealthy cabinetmaker and upholsterer, who between 1856 and 1897 spent much money and effort creating his idiosyncratic paradise. After his death the garden fell into ruin but thankfully its restoration began in 1980. Admire the new iron gates by David Freedman.

College Gardens
University of Oxford
Oxford

● 13
Worcester College
1 Walton St, OX1 2HB
Open: see p.366
Free
New College
96 Holywell St, OX1 3BN
Open: see p.366
Admission fee

Many of the colleges beneath the 'dreaming spires' open their gardens to the public, and those gardens are as diverse as the colleges themselves, for example Corpus Christi, Lady Margaret Hall, St Catherine's and Wadham. Two lovely and more unusual examples are at Worcester College and New College. The former's 11 hectares of award-winning gardens date from the eighteenth century onwards and are a rich mix: bowling-green perfect lawns in the Quad; contemporary 'hot borders' and lush tropical courtyard planting; the meadow-like Nuffield Lawn studded in spring with *Tulipa* 'Queen of the Night'; even a lake in true English landscape tradition. New College gardens are smaller and older. In the midst of a lawn once laid out as knot gardens stands the tree-covered Mound (a viewing mount was a popular feature of Tudor gardens). It is worth the climb for the view from the top; this includes sections of the old city wall that now enclose this part of the college and provide a mellow backdrop for the splendid herbaceous borders. Do take time to visit the lawned cloister and magnificent chapel.

**Addison's Walk,
Magdalen College**
Oxford

● 14
Magdalen College,
High Street, OX1 4AU
Open: see p.365
Admission fee

Walking down the High Street towards Magdalen Bridge, the traffic noise and crowds of jostling tourists can become overwhelming. To escape this chaos, duck under the arch into Magdalen College, pass through a delightful cloister, cross a small bridge and be transported to a world of quietude. With tree branches that arch over the raised path, creating a tunnel-like feel, Addison's Walk is a shaded, picturesque 1.5-kilometre-long footpath encircling the Meadow, an island embraced by branches of the River Cherwell. In spring the path is flanked with daffodils and the Meadow a riot of snake's head fritillary. Enjoy views of Magdalen Tower, Bridge and Deer Park, and think of the luminaries who strolled this way before you. The Walk is named after Joseph Addison, a Fellow of the College between 1698 and 1711 who, through his articles in *The Spectator*, helped to forge the new naturalistic English landscape garden style. The Walk was also a favourite of another Fellow, C.S. Lewis, and it inspired his poem 'What the Bird Said Early in the Year'. He regularly walked this way with Hugo Dyson and J.R.R. Tolkien.

Arundells
Salisbury

📍15
59 Cathedral Close,
SP1 2EN
Open: see p.365
Admission fee

Occupying an enviable position, this Queen Anne house – formerly the home of the British prime minister Sir Edward Heath – dates from the early eighteenth century. Heath bought it in 1985, had the interiors restored by the renowned interior designer Derek Frost, and laid out the 0.8-hectare garden. One of the defining characteristics of this elongated, informal garden is its sublime views. To the east is the cathedral spire, completed c.1330 and, at 123 metres, the second tallest medieval stone spire in Europe; at the western boundary, the bucolic vista of the confluence of the rivers Avon and Nadder and the water meadows beyond is positively Constable-esque. The sweeping lawn enclosed by sinuous borders of perennials, shrubs and tall trees (including American sweetgum, birch, handkerchief tree, magnolia and mulberry) creates secretive nooks and wooded dells. Look out for the rose arbour and statue, the bronze sculpture of a girl by George E. Wade, and the bow of *Morning Cloud III*, one of Heath's yachts. The property is now maintained by the Sir Edward Heath Charitable Foundation.

Bishop's Palace
Wells

📍16
Bishop's Palace,
BA5 2PD
Open: see p.365
Admission fee

Dating from about 1206 and still home to the Bishop of Bath and Wells, this medieval palace boasts 5.7 hectares of gardens hidden behind moated, crenellated ramparts accessed via a drawbridge and an imposing gatehouse. There are in fact seven gardens to explore (free guided tours are offered at 12.00 and 15.00). Nearest to the palace, the East Garden is a true plantsman's paradise with its St Andrew's Cross border, masses of perennials and roses, a 'hot border' with fiery flowers and exotic foliage, and the formal parterre. At the centre of the parterre is an urn, an artefact from the former parterre laid out in the mid-1800s. From here, pass through a doorway in the walls and over a bridge to the Wells Gardens. The man-made pools accommodate the natural springs that gave the city its name. Climb the ramparts for spectacular views over the gardens (the other five are the Arboretum, Community Garden, Dragon's Lair, Garden of Reflection and South Garden), out to Glastonbury Tor and the Mendip Hills, and to the splendid cathedral, which was begun in the late twelfth century.

Treasurer's House
York

● 17
Minster Yard, YO1 7JL
Open daily: 11.00–16.30
(late Mar–early
Nov only)
Admission fee

In 1897–8 the wealthy industrialist and antiquarian Frank Green purchased three-fifths of a property just north of York Minster. The architect Temple Lushington Moore altered and restored it to create what Green named the Treasurer's House; in 1930 Green donated everything to the National Trust. Laid out by Green, the garden with its sunken lawn, trees, old stone and statuary is formal and tranquil. The muted tones and simple design are in deliberate contrast to the opulence inside the house (which is said to be haunted, most famously by Roman soldiers in the cellar). The raised borders along the walls were added when the property was opened to the public in the 1930s. With its soft tones and pastel shades, the flower display – which lasts from February until the first frosts – perpetuates Green's subtle approach. Crocuses, irises and tulips are followed by delphiniums, peonies and wisteria, and later agapanthus, asters and fuchsias. Another quiet, hidden space a mere three-minute walk south is the leafy churchyard of the lovely, mostly fifteenth-century Holy Trinity Church at 70 Goodramgate.

Dubh Linn Garden
Dublin

● 18
Ship Street Little,
Opposite Dublin Castle
Open daily: 08.00–
  18.00
Free

Legend has it that the *dubh linn* or 'black pool' that gave the city its name was on this site. Today, to find this hidden green space to the south of Dublin Castle, walk east along Ship Street Little and look for a gateway in the stone wall on the right-hand side. Pass through it and be confronted with a big circular lawn that is also a helipad (parts of the Celtic patterning picked out in bricks set into the lawn contain landing lights). Created in the mid-1990s, meticulously maintained and with the benches spaced sufficiently far apart for privacy, this is an unexpected and peaceful place. The raised boundary border is deep, and planted densely with flowering trees, shrubs, climbers and bulbs. Here too is the occasional modern sculpture, including a glass snake, and two memorial gardens. One is dedicated to the fallen of the Garda Síochána, the country's police force; the other to Veronica Guerin, the murdered investigative journalist who was played by Cate Blanchett in the eponymous film of 2003.

An Gairdín Cuimhneacháin (Garden of Remembrance) Dublin

● 19
Parnell Square East, Rotunda
Daily: 08.30–18.00 (Apr–Sep); 09.30–16.00 (Oct–Mar); 11.00–13.00 (Christmas Day)
Free

Designed by Daíthí Hanly, this is a small, subtle, moving garden just north of the city centre, intended as a place of quiet remembrance and reflection. Declared open on a symbolic day, Easter Monday 1966, it is dedicated to the memory of 'all those who gave their lives in the cause of Irish Freedom'. From street level at the Parnell Square East entrance, two flights of steps separated by planters and benches descend to the sunken garden in the form of a non-denominational cross. A path with more benches and planters surrounds the raised pool, and at its head steps ascend to the focal-point sculpture *Children of Lir* by Oisín Kelly, symbolizing rebirth and resurrection, at the end of the garden. It was placed there in 1971, and in 1976 the poem 'We Saw a Vision' by Liam Mac Uistín was added on the wall behind it. Picked out in blues and greens, the wavy mosaic pattern of the pool floor is punctuated with a broken swords and shields motif: an echo of the Clannish tradition that symbolized the end of a conflict.

●N

0 400 800 1200
yd.

King Henry's Walk Garden
London

📍 20
King Henry's Walk,
N1 4NX
Open Sat: 12.00–16.00
(except Christmas
Day & New Year's
Day); Sun: 12.00–
16.00 (May–Sep only)
Free

This very successful community garden in Islington is tucked away behind an adventure playground and accessed by a cul-de-sac on the left of the latter as you face it from King Henry's Walk. Follow the pavement to the entrance at the end. The garden was established in 2007 by a group of volunteers who decided to transform a derelict site into an organic, sustainable garden. Run by local residents for local residents who wish to garden or just come to chill out, the garden is announced by a bespoke gate commissioned from the artist Heather Burrell. The area along the south-facing wall is made up of raised beds split into plots in which individual members grow their own produce. Complementing these are collectively maintained areas of lawn and borders planted to encourage wildlife. The eye-catching teardrop-shaped wildlife pond is traversed by a low bridge that also enables children to go pond-dipping. A composting area, a rainwater harvesting system, a communal greenhouse and building, and – unusually for this part of London – a patch of woodland make up the rest.

Skip Garden
London

📍 21
Tapper Walk, N1C 4AQ
Open Tue–Sat: 10.00–
16.00 (lunch served
12.00–14.00)
Free

King's Cross is a hotspot of exciting small gardens. Set amid the glass and steel of the King's Cross development site, the Skip Garden at the northern end of Lewis Cubitt Park is a few minutes' walk from the railway station, the Dan Pearson-designed Handyside Garden nearby and the wild Camley Street Natural Park (see opposite). This deliciously innovative, eye-catching 'guerrilla' garden is a container garden with a difference, constructed from brightly painted recycled rubbish skips and scaffolding-board planters. The design is also canny and practical: the whole garden is transportable and currently on its third 'incarnation'. The objective is urban food growing, and much of the cornucopia is used in the Skip Garden Kitchen – in itself a reason to visit as the unusual sight of vegetables, herbs and wild flowers erupting out of a skip. It is the flagship of the educational charity Global Generation, which works to create healthy, integrated and environmentally responsible communities – and with great success: since 2004 it has created twenty-six community and commercial gardens.

**Camley Street
Natural Park**
London

📍 22
12 Camley St, N1C 4PW
Open Mon–Sat:
  10.00–17.00 (summer);
  Mon–Sat 10.00–
  16.00 (winter)
Free

At 8,300 square metres it is small, but this thriving patch of urban nature reserve squeezed in beside Regent's Canal and between King's Cross and St Pancras stations boasts woodland, grassland meadow and wetland habitats, including ponds, reed beds and marsh. It is an oasis for wildlife and an escape from the nearby regenerated and bustling urbanity. Wander the paths and board-walks, and, surrounded by birds, butterflies and over 300 plant taxa (as well as bats and amphibians), it is possible to pretend for a charming, calming and educational while that you are in the rural wilds. Do visit the excellent educational centre and also the funky Viewpoint – a pontoon on the canal, intended to bring architecture and nature closer together. It is the perfect hideaway to enjoy the peace and views. The site, once a coal yard for the railway, was returning to nature by the 1970s, and after several years of cam-paigning by locals and the London Wildlife Trust to conserve the new landscape, it was declared a Local Nature Reserve in 1986. It is lovely in all seasons, but best in spring and summer.

Geffrye Museum Gardens
London

📍 23
136 Kingsland Rd,
E2 8EA
Front Gardens
Open: see p.366
Free

The fascinating Geffrye, in a former almshouse in east London's Shoreditch, is dedicated to the home from 1600 to the present, and – as is proper in any exploration of living space – it includes the garden. In fact, the museum has six gardens. The Front Gardens are laid out according to the almshouse records, with large lawns either side of a path leading to the chapel and bordered by magnificent century-old London plane trees. Opened in 1982, the walled Herb Garden is traditional and formal, the twelve brick-edged beds planted with more than 170 different taxa with interpretation boards explaining their utilitarian, culinary and medicinal uses. Each of the four Period Gardens is representative of a town-house garden in each century from the seventeenth to the twentieth. The two older gardens are interpretive re-creations, but the Victorian garden with its bright bedding is based on photographs and descriptions of an 1880s garden in Hackney. The twentieth-century garden shows the influence of the Arts and Crafts movement and of the celebrated designer Gertrude Jekyll.

Inns of Court
London

● 24

Inner Temple, 1 Pump Court, Elm Court, EC4Y 7HL; Middle Temple, Middle Temple Lane, EC4Y 9BT; Lincoln's Inn, WC2A 3TL; Gray's Inn, 8 South Square, WC1R 5ET
Open: see p.366
Free

Near the Royal Courts of Justice in the old City of London, the four Inns of Court are the professional associations for barristers in England and Wales. Each is a complex of buildings and gardens, with the latter a mix of historic charm and contemporary urbanity. The Inner Temple gardens feature several 70-metre-long mixed borders planted for year-round interest, spring bulbs galore and a Wars of the Roses border (legend has it that the conflict started here). The Elm Court (pictured) links the Inner and Middle Temple. The latter's Elizabethan Hall is fronted by a formally planted terrace, while the Fountain Court has four Millennium Beds, an ancient mulberry and boasts what is likely London's first permanent fountain (1681). Lincoln's Inn, the oldest of the four (1422), has 2.9 hectares of gardens with expanses of lawn, ancient trees and a recently restored border. Laid out by Sir Francis Bacon in 1606, 'the Walks' at Gray's Inn are today more informal, with an avenue of American red oaks (*Quercus rubra*) and a fine collection of other trees. In spring the northern bank of the Walks is a mass of daffodils.

Barbican Centre
London

● 25
Silk St, EC2Y 8DS
& Beech St, EC2Y 8DE
Open: see p.365
Free

Designed in Brutalist architectural style and opened in 1982, the Barbican Centre is the largest performing-arts centre in Europe and contains several garden areas. A little to the west are the Beech Gardens, publicly accessible but provided for the residents of the surrounding towers. They are characterized by shining brick paths and raised beds, and underwent a facelift in 2012; the monochrome geometry of the architecture is now softened and cheered by colourful, naturalistic plantings by Nigel Dunnett. This is in fact a roof garden, and the plantings were designed to thrive in the challenging conditions. The most hidden garden is a tropical oasis within the Centre itself, on top of the theatre's fly tower. Home to more than 2,000 taxa of tropical plants and with pools of exotic fish, the Conservatory is London's second largest, covering an area of 2,100 square metres. It is even possible to book afternoon tea amid the jungle. Southwest of the horseshoe-shaped Centre is the Lake Terrace, abutting a long canal and connected to it through a line of water features.

Postman's Park
London

📍 26
King Edward St,
EC1A 7BT
Daily: 08.00–19.00
or dusk, whichever
is earlier (closed
Christmas Day,
Boxing Day & New
Year's Day)
Free

This shady pocket park is tucked away in the City of London, a short stroll north of St Paul's Cathedral and wedged between King Edward Street and St Martin's-le-Grand (with an entrance on both). It opened in 1880 on the site of the former churchyard of St Botolph's Aldersgate, expanded over the next twenty years and acquired its name because of its popularity with workers from the former General Post Office next door. There are lawns, a sundial, a small circular pool and fountain, and stone-flagged paths. Highlights of the permanent planting include the tree ferns and a handkerchief tree that looks spectacular when in spring bloom. The park's main feature, however, is the emotive Memorial to Heroic Self Sacrifice erected by George Frederic Watts in 1900. It is composed of a series of glazed Doulton tablets, each commemorating an act of bravery undertaken by an ordinary person who died saving the life of another. The park featured in the award-winning film *Closer* (2004) and remains an unassuming, tranquil and charming spot in which to sit and enjoy the seasonal flower colour that fills the beds.

St Dunstan-in-the-East
London

♦ 27
Entrances via Idol Lane
& St Dunstan's Hill,
EC3R 5DD
Daily: 08.00–19.00
or dusk, whichever
is earlier (closed
Christmas Day,
Boxing Day & New
Year's Day)
Free

Well provided with wooden benches, the interior of this ruined church now has paved and cobbled paths, a lawn and shading trees, oleanders and palms where once the congregation gathered. It is truly a secluded and verdant haven, the sense of tranquillity heightened by the plash of the delightful circular fountain. The church was built in about 1100, and a new south aisle added in 1391. Severely damaged for the first time during the Great Fire of London in 1666, the church was restored and a steeple and tower added by Sir Christopher Wren in 1695–1701. The church suffered again during the Blitz of 1941, and although Wren's additions survived, the gutted building was not reconstructed. In 1967 the City of London decided to turn the shell into a public garden, which opened in 1971. Replanting and maintenance works took place in 2015, and although the climbers will take a few years to swathe the inner walls once more, those that wind through the glassless windows from the outside – in particular the vine *Vitis coignetiae*, a splash of scarlet in the autumn – give the space a Gothic feel.

**Japanese Roof
Garden, School of
Oriental and African
Studies**
London

📍 28
Brunei Gallery, School
of Oriental and African
Studies, Thornhaugh
St, WC1H 0XG
Open: see p.366
Free

Accessed via the first floor of the Brunei Gallery (which hosts changing contemporary and historical exhibitions from Asia, Africa and the Middle East), the garden designed by Peter Swift in 2001 is Japanese-inspired yet adapted to a British climate. Within its rectangular, mostly horizontal form, the dominant material is stone. Various types are used: sandstone and green slate for the perimeter paving; a central area of raked silver-grey granite chippings ornamented with worked slabs of basaltic rock, alluding to a bridge over flowing water; and raw 'island' stones of Norwegian larvikite. Planting is minimal, with lemon thyme in a chequerboard pattern with dark-grey pebbles and a formal granite edging at the northern end, and along the west a wisteria-covered pergola offering a 'purple rain' of scented blooms in spring followed by shade in summer. The garden was intended as a practical addition to the gallery and a peaceful retreat from the bustle of London's streets, and is dedicated to forgiveness, which is the meaning of the *kanji* character engraved on the granite water basin.

Phoenix Garden
London

📍 29
21 Stacey St,
WC2H 8DG
Daily: 08.30 until dusk
Free

The West End of London can be a crazy place, but it is possible to escape it all, if only for a while. The Phoenix Garden is an urban jungle in the best possible sense of the words. With lawns and benches (both wooden and rough-hewn blocks of stone) it is the perfect hideaway in which to eat a picnic, bask in the sun's warmth or let the kids play (but please do be vigilant as there are pools and other potential hazards). Stroll along the brick paths and enjoy the informally, richly and artfully planted beds and borders – some raised and mulched with brick rubble. Cultivated using sustainable techniques and planted with wildlife-friendly, drought-tolerant taxa this is a refuge for *Homo sapiens* and for urban wildlife which finds a welcome home within the range of different habitats. Run by volunteers and funded by donations, this lovely little community garden was established in 1984 and it is to be found between Soho and Covent Garden: north of Shaftesbury Avenue and east of Charing Cross Road, nestled behind (and northeast of) the Phoenix Theatre.

The Roof Gardens
London

● 30
99 Kensington High St,
W8 5SA (accessed via
Derry St)
Open: see p.367
Free

A 6,000-square-metre roof garden is not perhaps what one might expect to find 30 metres above one of central London's busiest streets, but take the lift and discover not one but three themed gardens, invisible from the street below. A wisteria-clad stone-arched walk leads to the three courtyards of the Tudor Garden, which are covered in the cold months and planted as a winter garden. There is an English woodland, with more than 100 trees, and a stream and pool that are home to ducks and four flamingos; this garden is a delight when the spring bulbs bloom. The colourful Spanish garden is the most flamboyant: taking inspiration from the Alhambra, with its formal layout, fountains, geometric beds, vine-covered paths and palms, the design has a decidedly Islamic feel. The gardens (now listed Grade II) were designed by the landscape architect Ralph Hancock and opened in 1938, when the building was the Derry & Toms department store. Now owned by Sir Richard Branson, the Roof Gardens is an event space and restaurant. It is closed when hired privately, so do phone ahead to check.

**Wildlife Garden
at the Natural
History Museum**
London

● 31
Cromwell Rd, SW7 5BD
Daily: 10.00–17.00
  (1 Apr–early Nov)
Free

Southwest of the museum itself is its first living and working exhibition: the 4,000-square-metre Wildlife Garden. Created on what was once an ecologically barren lawn, and opened in 1995, the L-shaped garden was designed by Adam Loxton Partnership. Now fully mature and winner of the London in Bloom Meadows Award in 2016, it offers a lovely contrast to its urban setting. Sinuous paths snake around pools covered with waterlilies, the trees are full of birdsong, and exploring the range of British lowland habitats represented here – including deciduous woodland and heathland – makes one realize just how biodiverse Britain is. Indeed, in this small garden in the middle of this great city, more than 3,130 taxa of plants and animals have been recorded to date. The garden is a wild yet tranquil spot in which to escape the craziness of Cromwell Road, and to sit and reflect on the wonders seen inside the museum. More than that, it is an educational and inspiring demonstration that inner-city wildlife conservation can be successful, and that a small garden can make a big difference.

Chelsea Physic Garden
London

● 32
66 Royal Hospital Rd,
SW3 4HS
Open: see p.366
Admission fee

Although founded in 1673, this well-kept secret first opened its gates to the public in 1983. Established by the Worshipful Society of Apothecaries of London for the purpose of cultivating medicinal plants to teach apprentices their pharmacological uses (hence its name), the garden continues its educational role. The trapezoidal, 1.4-hectare walled plot is home to about 5,000 different edible, medicinal and historic taxa, and highlights today include the glasshouses, Historical Walk, the Garden of Ethnobotany, the Garden of Medicinal Plants and, created in 2015, the World Woodland Garden. The layout retains much of the late nineteenth-century design by the botanist Professor John Bretland Farmer and the garden's curator William Hales, which itself preserved aspects of the original plan. This was an attractive arrangement of rectangular beds with plants grouped according to a pre-Linnaean classification by use. Look out for one of Europe's oldest rock gardens, constructed in part from Icelandic lava brought to the garden by Sir Joseph Banks in 1772; his bust graces the structure.

**Abbey Gardens,
Westminster Abbey**
London

📍 33
20 Deans Yard,
SW1P 3PA
Open Tue, Wed &
   Thu: 10.00–18.00
   (summer);
   10.00–16.00
   (winter)
Free

Much of the present abbey was built by Henry III in 1245–72, but the first 'west minster' (the 'east minster' being St Paul's) was erected by Edward the Confessor on the site of a small Benedictine monastery and consecrated on 28 December 1065. Within the abbey itself is the Garth, 'only' a grass square within cloisters but redolent with Edenic symbolism. Yet few visitors to this iconic landmark realize that there are another three gardens waiting to be discovered to the south of the church. Accessed by a separate entrance, the College Garden (pictured) was, 1,000 years ago, the monastery's infirmary garden. Today the space, dominated by two large plane trees, is the country's oldest continuously cultivated garden. Within it, the Rose Garden celebrates Queen Elizabeth II's accession to the throne in 1952, and the Herb Garden (2010) the monks who once gardened here. From here one can explore the Little Cloister, with scented borders and a fountain (1871), and St Catherine's Garden, created in the ruins of the medieval chapel where in 1253 Henry III swore to observe the mandates of the Magna Carta.

**Bonnington Square
Pleasure Garden**
London

● 34
11C Bonnington
Square, SW8 1TE
Daily: dawn–dusk
Free

Bonnington Square became famously bohemian in the 1980s, when all the houses were squatted. In 1990 the residents – including the garden designer Dan Pearson – established the Bonnington Square Garden Association to develop a community garden on the 'wasteland' of seven Blitzed houses. Construction of the Pleasure Garden – named after its famous predecessor at Vauxhall about 100 metres to the north – began in 1994. Grab a coffee from the excellent Bonnington Cafe and follow the winding hoggin paths among beds and patches of lawn, where topsoil now covers the house foundations. Rest on a bench and enjoy the unexpected and refreshing planting. Designed by Pearson and the New Zealand garden designer James Frazer, it is a mix of classic English and exotic, with many New Zealand natives and a predominance of foliage textures, both delicate (ornamental grasses) and architectural (bananas and palms). The 9-metre-tall iron slip wheel from the 1860s, rescued from a nearby marble factory, adds drama, and there is even a children's play area.

Queen Elizabeth Hall Roof Garden
London

● 35
Southbank Centre,
Belvedere Rd, SE1 8XX
Daily: 10.00–22.00
(closed winter)
Free

Hiding on top of the Queen Elizabeth Hall, part of the Southbank Centre complex of artistic venues that opened in 1951 as part of the Festival of Britain, is this award-winning roof garden. The angular C-shaped space is a mix of paving and decked paths, lawn and log-edged meadow beds full of trees and perennials, fruit trees in round white concrete tubs and an allotment of blue-painted wooden planters with vegetables. It offers an attractive, purposeful yet soft contrast to the surrounding Brutalist concrete architecture. The garden also has a super bar and cafe. Relax on the lawn and pretend you are in the Cotswolds, or enjoy the beautiful river views and vistas north over the city. The garden was created in 2011 in partnership with the Eden Project, and was built and continues to be maintained by Grounded EcoTherapy, a volunteer recovery charity for adults who have experienced homelessness, addiction or mental health problems. A donation is always welcome from those who have enjoyed this lovely, therapeutic garden.

**The Sackler Garden
at The Garden Museum**
London

📍 36
Lambeth Palace Rd,
SE1 7LB (enter through
the Garden Cafe)
Open: see p.367
Free (admission fee
for musuem)

Exploring and celebrating the art, history and design of British gardens and gardening, the museum is located next to Lambeth Palace, which also has a lovely garden. Housed in the former Church of St Mary-at-Lambeth, the 2017 major redevelopment included the front garden designed by Christopher Bradley-Hole; and at the east end of the church, the Sackler Garden by Dan Pearson. This courtyard garden draws inspiration from the metaphysical concepts of 'Eden' and 'oasis'; it is enclosed by a 'woodland' boundary and joined to the new inside/outside space of cafe, orangery and classroom. Its centrepieces are the tombs of Captain William Bligh (of HMS *Bounty* infamy) and the famous horticulturists John Tradescant, father and son. The planting takes advantage of London's munificent microclimate to provide richness, seasonal flux and ephemerality with an emphasis on horticultural curiosities. The delightful tapestry of trees, shrubs and perennials is a mix of the sensual (*Hedychium* spp. jasmine), symbolic (acanthus, fig), utilitarian (asarabacca, cimicifuga) and edible (lemon, wild strawberry).

1 **Hof Meermansburg (Meermansburg Almshouse)** Leiden, p.143

2 **Basiliek van Sint Servaas (Basilica of St Servatius)** Maastricht, p.144

3 **DakAkker** Rotterdam, p.145

4 **Begijnhof (Courtyard of the Béguinage)** Antwerp, p.146

5 **Rubenshuis (Rubens House)** Antwerp, p.148

6 **Rockoxhuis (Rockox House)** Antwerp, p.149

7 **Botanische Tuin (Botanic Garden of the Royal Zoological Society)** Antwerp, p.150

8 **Godshuizen De Meulenaere and Sint-Jozef (De Meulenaere and St Joseph Almshouses)** Bruges, p.151

9 **Onze-Lieve-Vrouw Sint-Pieterskerk (Our Lady of St Peter's Church)** Ghent, p.152

10 **Le Cloître Lucien Wercollier (Lucien Wercollier Cloister), Neumünster Abbey** Luxembourg, p.153

11 – 15 See **Amsterdam Map**, p.154

**Hof Meermansburg
(Meermansburg
Almshouse)**
Leiden

● 1
Hof Meermansburg
Oude Vest 159, 2312 XW
Pieter Loridanshof
Oude Varkenmarkt 1,
2311 VN
Samuel de Zee's Hof
Doezastraat 14, 2311 HB
Daily: 08.00–22.00
Free

The old city centre boasts thirty-five sets of almshouses, mostly built in the seventeenth and eighteenth centuries by wealthy philanthropists. *Hof*, Dutch for almshouse, also translates as 'courtyard', and these collections of small houses surround a communal inner yard or garden, usually rectangular. Today the rules for occupancy have changed, but the gardens are still idyllic. Walk through the entrance passage and you enter a realm of historical beauty, where time seems to have stood still. The gardens vary in design; three of the most lovely are Pieter Loridanshof (1655), Hof Meermansburg (1683) and the illustrated Samuel de Zee's Hof (1723). Here are two small courtyards: together the embodiment of simple, peaceful elegance and each with a geometrical knot garden. The first has a circle-within-a-square motif and the second a quartered circle, the beds planted with seasonal colour and ornamented with topiary. A walking map, featuring twelve *hofjes*, is available from the visitor centre. Be considerate: the courtyards are private gardens and several still close their gates before 19.00.

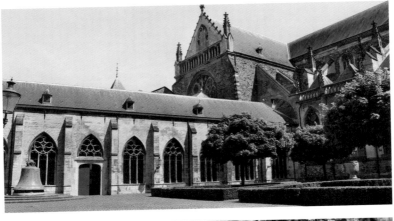

**Basiliek van Sint
Servaas (Basilica
of St Servatius)
Maastricht**

◆ 2
Keizer Karelplein 3,
6211 TC
Open: see p.365
Admission fee

Erected on the site of the grave of St Servatius (d.384), Maastricht's patron saint, the basilica was built in a hybrid of Romanesque, Baroque and Gothic styles over several hundred years from the tenth century. To the north is a square cobbled cloister, the southern part of which, next to the nave, is a four-square garden. In the centre stands an ornate font-like fountain of white marble with four heads that jet water into a circular pool. Four surrounding beds are defined by low, clipped box hedges. From within each rises a clear-trunk maple underplanted with massed lavender. The flowers scent the air, while both flowers and foliage contrast perfectly in colour with the greens and the church's limestone walls. The result is a simple, elegant garden that – given its setting – is symbolic of the Fountain of Life and the four rivers running out of Eden. In the northwest corner stands the massive 'Grameer' ('Grandma') church bell. It weighs 6.6 tonnes and was cast in 1515, but fell silent some time before 1983 because a crack in the bronze damaged its voice.

DakAkker
Rotterdam

📍 3
Schiekade 189, 7th
floor, 3013 BR (take the
lift to the 6th floor)
Open: see p.366
Free

Hidden away on top of a building six minutes' walk north of the Stadhuis (Town Hall), 22 metres above Schiekade, a major arterial road running into the very heart of Rotterdam, is the DakAkker, the city's first – and Europe's largest – rooftop farm. This is an active and proactive garden growing vegetables, herbs and flowers, and with beehives too. The fresh bounty is used by local restaurants, and of course here, in the appropriately named restaurant Op Het Dak (On the Roof). Serving breakfast, lunch and drinks, it is an excellent place to sit and admire the serried ranks of vegetables before taking a stroll to explore the garden. The DakAkker (literally 'rooftop field') was created as an experiment in 2012 by Binder Groenprojecten and partners as part of the city's Fifth International Architecture Biennale to explore the possibilities of both urban rooftop farming and positively repurposing and energizing unused inner-city rooftop spaces. The results speak for themselves, for not only does the roof farm create benefit from its harvest, but it brings the community together through the very act of gardening.

**Begijnhof (Courtyard
of the Béguinage)**
Antwerp

● 4
Rodestraat 39, 2000
Open: 24/7
Free

The Béguines were devout women who did not take holy orders but lived in a community, making them something between laywomen and nuns. Built in 1545 inside the city walls and nestled in the north of the city centre, close to the university, this Béguinage survives little altered. The last Béguine died in 1986 and the forty or so small houses are now residences, but the character and tranquillity of the complex and its garden – the Begijnhof – have been preserved. The homes and an elegant church (rebuilt in 1827) overlook a delightful, truly hidden green space. Surrounded by a narrow cobbled road, the trapezoidal courtyard dates from the founding of the Béguinage. This informal garden offers plenty of benches on which to pause and soak up the calm while taking a break from exploring this lovely city. A large lawn is pierced by paths, graced with patinated statues and shaded by mature trees, the bases of their trunks painted white (in spring the flowering cherries are ethereally pretty). A rockery of sorts surmounted by a statue of Christ on the Cross reminds one of the garden's religious history.

**Rubenshuis
(Rubens House)**
Antwerp

⬤ 5
Wapper 9-11, 2000
Open: see p.367
Admission fee

Peter Paul Rubens (1577–1640) is widely held to have been the most influential Flemish Baroque painter. This impressive residence, a few streets and a ten-minute walk from that of one of his important patrons (see Rockoxhuis, opposite), is mostly to his own design. Rubens bought it in 1610 and lived there until his death, considerably remodelling and expanding it in the Baroque style and also creating a garden. The house was bought by the city in 1937, and as part of the subsequent restoration the garden was remade. Rubens's design for the latter is unknown, but the layout and planting style are based on his paintings and on evidence from contemporary gardens; the taxa are 'period correct'. The dominant feature on the eastern wall and aligned on the main axis of the path is the ornate pavilion, while on the southern perimeter a climber-clad wooden gallery leads to a raised circular pool and fountain. Low yew hedges define four compartments, which are entered through gates and contain low, slate-edged beds. Hornbeam hedges, statuary, topiary and planted containers give extra interest.

Rockoxhuis (Rockox House)
Antwerp

● 6
Keizerstraat 10–12, 2000
Open: see p.367
Free (admission fee for museum)

Burgomaster Nicolaas Rockox (1560–1640) was a leading citizen of Antwerp and a wealthy intellectual, humanist and antiquarian. He was also a patron of the arts, in particular of Peter Paul Rubens (see Rubenshuis, opposite). His substantial residence, with its wonderful interiors, art collection and inner courtyard garden, has been managed by the Nicolaas Rockox Foundation since 1970. Enclosed by the house's brick walls and surrounded by a graceful colonnade, the garden is formal and geometric. Although it is of the Baroque period and an example of early seventeenth-century city garden art, its uncomplicated layout feels distinctly medieval. The cobbled space is punctuated by a four-square geometric arrangement of narrow, rectangular tile-edged beds separated by honey-coloured gravel and complemented by specimens in barrels and pots. The planting is 'period correct' and appears more a collection than an ornamental assemblage. Many of the plants grown here are those Rockox is known to have received from the French humanist Nicolas-Claude Fabri de Peiresc in 1609 and 1610.

**Botanische Tuin
(Botanic Garden of
the Royal Zoological
Society)**
Antwerp

● 7
Leopoldstraat 24, 2000
Daily: 08.00–20.00
   (summer); 08.00–
   17.30 (winter)
Free

Close to the city's historic centre, this small, charming garden is also known as Den Botaniek or Kruidtuin (Herb Garden). It contains about 2,000 taxa, including notable collections of trees and cacti, and thankfully the plants are labelled. Walk through the entrance in the balustraded wall. The layout is informal, with gravel paths flowing between lawns and flower beds, and the planting arrangements are as much for ornament as a collection. There are pools, a rockery-cascade and the fun, attention-grabbing sculpture *Greening II* by Monique Donckers, of heads set into the lawn. Along the northern boundary is the eye-catching glasshouse, while the former gardener's lodge in Swiss chalet style on the southern perimeter is now a decent brasserie. The statue here is of the local Renaissance botanist-physician Peeter van Coudenberghe. Founded in 1804 as a teaching tool for students of the School for Surgery, Chemistry and Botany at the nearby St Elisabeth hospital, the garden became an official scientific botanic establishment later in the century, and today it is managed by the city council.

Godshuizen De Meulenaere and Sint-Jozef (De Meulenaere and St Joseph Almshouses)
Bruges

📍 8
Nieuwe Gentweg 24, 8000
Open: 24/7
Free

The *Godshuis* ('God's house') is a type of almshouse found throughout Bruges. There are about fifty in the city, many with gardens, but this particular example with its pretty court is especially worth visiting. Located south of the Groeningemuseum, it is an agglomeration of the De Meulenaere (established here in the 1620s) and Sint-Jozef (1699) almshouses, the latter of which moved here from Oostmeer in 1905. The wall between the adjacent properties was demolished in 2001 and a communal garden established. Entered through an ornate stone doorway and enclosed by the picturesque almshouses, the trapezoidal courtyard is formal in layout. The asymmetrical arrangement of its geometric beds is defined by low, clipped hedges of box and yew, separated by earthen paths. In spring, the garden boasts a fine display of irises, and in summer a mix of roses and perennials results in a riot of texture, colour and form, while cloud topiary and standard rowan introduce sculptural elements. Please remember that the houses are still inhabited, so respect the peace and quiet.

Onze-Lieve-Vrouw Sint-Pieterskerk (Our Lady of St Peter's Church)
Ghent

● 9
Sint-Pietersplein, 9000
Open: see p.367
Free

Built on the site of a seventh-century Benedictine monastery, the imposing Baroque church also known as St Peter's Abbey was rebuilt from 1629 after periods of both decline and destruction during the Reformation in the sixteenth century. Today it is home to a museum and exhibition centre, and behind it is a splendid hidden garden. The roughly triangular plot is mostly a curvaceously contoured lawn, and the plants pay homage to the site's monastic history. The north is shaded by lofty trees, while in the southwestern corner is an orchard of apple, pear, plum, medlar and peach, with various fruiting shrubs and wall-trained figs. The apple blossom is a picture in spring, and in season visitors are welcome to try the fruit. The garden also contains the remains of the medieval infirmary, and the aromatic herb garden nearby is filled with types the monks would have used. The organic vineyard is planted with 'Muller Thurgau', 'Johanitter', 'Phoenix' and 'Sirius', which yield a quantity of 'abbey wine' each year. This is the perfect place to enjoy a picnic, soak up the tranquillity or enjoy the occasional art installations.

Le Cloître Lucien Wercollier (Lucien Wercollier Cloister), Neumünster Abbey
Luxembourg

🌱 10
28 rue Münster, 2160 Luxemburgo Cidade
Open Mon–Fri: 13.00–18.00; Sat: 11.00–18.00; Sun & public holidays: by appointment only
Free

Cloisters have always been places of meditation, but this is a garden for questioning. It is part of a former Benedictine monastery with a dark history. Closed by Napoleonic decree in 1796, it became a prison on and off until the end of the Second World War. During the Nazi Occupation, political prisoners interned here included Luxembourg's best-known sculptor, Lucien Wercollier (1908–2002). In May 2004, following extensive renovation works, Neumünster was opened to the public as the Cultural Centre of Encounter. As part of the revamp, a new garden was made in the cloister by the visual artist and landscaper Agnès Daval. It houses a permanent exhibition from Wercollier's private collection, and is a study in contrast. Oblique lines are set off by the square geometry of the space and the arches of the colonnade. The grey stone highlights the flowers, mostly purple (including ornamental onions, irises and crocuses, according to the season), and the pale mustard-yellow walls; the long, narrow slate beds contrast with the horizontal paving and the linear patches of rounded cobbles.

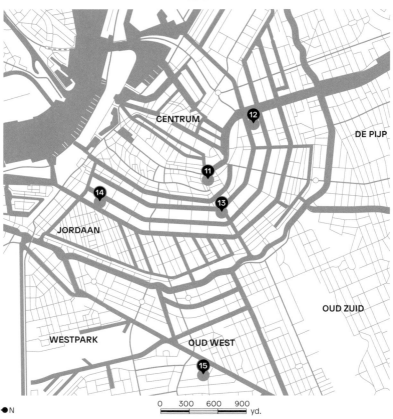

Begijnhof (Courtyard of the Begijntjes)
Amsterdam

● 11
Gedempte
Begijnensloot 13A,
1012 PP
Open: 24/7
Free

Spui is a roughly rectangular plaza in the heart of Amsterdam. Yet until the fifteenth century, when the Singel canal was constructed as a moat around the city, the area was underwater and marked the medieval settlement's southern boundary. To the north of it today stands the English Reformed Church, and behind, accessed via tiny lanes and encircled by a path, is a raised lawn punctuated by trees. At first glance this expanse of sward may be unprepossessing, but it is a rarity – a piece of tranquil public green space in the centre of a city with very little. This communal courtyard was enclosed in the fifteenth century by the wooden buildings of an almshouse-like complex belonging to the Begijntjes, a Catholic sisterhood who took no monastic vows but lived in the manner of nuns. The less flammable brick houses on the site now, with their tiny, colourful gardens, date from the seventeenth and eighteenth centuries (note they are still private dwellings). But Number 34 is Het Houten Huis, Amsterdam's oldest house (c.1420), a rare survivor of the wooden-fronted houses that made up the medieval city.

Museum Willet-Holthuysen
Amsterdam

📍12
Herengracht 605,
1017 CE
Open: see p.367
Admission fee

The best view of this sumptuous eighteenth-century-style Dutch Baroque city garden is from the octagonal conservatory on the first floor of the house. Laid out below are ornate *parterres de broderie*, statuary, topiary and narrow flower beds. The original design is unknown; the current incarnation (from 1972) is larger, extending over the demolished stables, and so immaculately maintained that one feels somewhat ill at ease walking it lest a shoe should inadvertently scuff the gravel. Built towards the end of the Golden Age, in 1687, the large, double-fronted town house on one of the most-sought after canals has always been home to the wealthy. From 1861 it was occupied by Abraham Willet and his wife, Louisa Holthuysen, and at her death in 1895 Louisa bequeathed the house and art collection to the city as a museum. A contrasting garden just ten minutes' walk east is the Hortus Botanicus, founded in 1638 and famous for the plants introduced to it by the Dutch East India Company. It was from a single coffee plant brought here from Java that the Central and South American coffee industry began.

**Cromhouthuis
(Cromhout House)
Amsterdam**

📍13
Herengracht 366,
1016 CH
Open Tue–Sun: 10.00–
17.00
Admission fee

Designed by seventeenth-century architect Philips Vingboons, the Cromhouthuis is a museum telling the story and displaying the art collection of the wealthy merchant Cromhout family, which commissioned and lived in this tall, Golden Age canal house. It is also home to the Bijbels (Bible) Museum, and behind the house is a snug cafe and a compact, modern courtyard garden. The Dutch do small gardens with great panache, filled with inventive features and artful plantings all carefully choreographed, blending new and old, and creating balance and harmony. Designed by landscape architect Arend Jan van der Horst when the Bible Museum moved here in 1975, the formal garden melds Baroque tradition, modern inventiveness and inspiration (and plants) from the Bible. The geometric framework is of pools, surfaces, spaces and of beds assembled from materials that include wood, stone, brick and plantings of both ground cover and architectural specimens. The pool with its stepping stones is allegorical of the parting of the Red Sea and the sculpture by Martie van der Loo represents the Apocalypse.

Van Brienenhofje (Van Brienen Courtyard)
Amsterdam

📍 14
Prinsengracht 89–133, 1015
Open Mon-Fri: 06.00–18.00
Free

Fifteen minutes' walk west from Centraal Station, this charming *hofje* with its elegant clock tower is also known as De Star Hofje, recalling the Star Brewery that once stood here. A brick path runs around the rectangular courtyard ornamented with pots of plants put out by the residents. The *hofje* is privately owned, so do visit with consideration. In a central cobbled circle stands a brick water pump topped with an ornate ironwork lamp. Surrounding it are four beds edged with low, clipped box hedges planted with massed white hydrangeas and shaded by a tall magnolia and inviting benches. White gravel paths lead to a stone bench within a semicircular clipped yew hedge and beds of perennials. The complex was founded as an almshouse in 1797 by the wealthy merchant and banker Arnoud Jan van Brienen; designed by the architect Abraham van der Hart in Empire style, the brick buildings were erected in 1804–6. Amsterdam has a number of such *hofjes*, including Begijnhof (see p.155), Bossche Hofje and Raepenhofje. Similar establishments are found in Leiden, too (see p.143).

**Natuurtuin Slatuinen
(Nature Garden
Slatuinen)**
Amsterdam

📍 15
Slatuinenweg 45,
1057 KB
Open Thu: 09.00–16.00
(April–Sep); 09.00–
17.00 (Oct–Mar);
First Sun of the
month: 13.00–16.00
Free

Strolling down the seemingly ordinary Slatuinenweg in Amsterdam-West (a twenty-minute walk from Anne Frank's house), with its modern, low-rise, red-brick terraces, there is a surprise. Behind a large dark-green gate emblazoned with 'Natuurtuin Slatuinen' in big bronze letters lies a hidden gem, a 3,000-square-metre wild garden-cum-nature reserve enclosed on its other three sides by apartment buildings. To walk along the overgrown paths through this beautiful and peaceful garden is to be translocated from the surrounding city. Tall trees impart a woodland feel, the pools and boggy areas are alive with plants and insects, and the air is filled with birdsong and the croaking of frogs, while the ever-changing scenes are enlivened by the blooms of many taxa, including orchids, snake's-head fritillaries, thistles, cranesbills and yellow monkshood. The aim is to encourage biodiversity while creating a communal space for both social and educational purposes. At local residents' request, construction began on this former park and plant nursery in 1992.

**Comenius-Garten
(Comenius Garden)
Berlin**

● 1
Richardstrasse 35,
12043
Open: see p.366
Admission fee

Neukölln, in southeastern Berlin, is one of the city's most dynamic and hip neighbourhoods. A pleasant contrast is to be able to escape to this 1.2-hectare quaint and engaging garden with its lawns, meadows, wild flowers, ornamentals and fruit bushes. Visit in autumn and help yourself to windfalls from the many fruit trees. Named after John Amos Comenius, a seventeenth-century Czech philosopher, pedagogue and theologian, the garden was laid out by local resident Henning Vierck as a metaphysical interpretation of Comenius' teachings. A specific route and architectonic elements trace the phases of man's life. The medicine garden, for example, represents knowledge gained for the survival of the individual and the community. But you doesn't need to know the allegory to enjoy this lush and tranquil spot, with its formal and informal ponds, gazebo and clipped hedges, winding paths and statue of Comenius (1992) by the sculptor Josef Vajce. The garden project began in the early 1980s on derelict land once covered with tenement housing. To open the gate, look for the tiny silver button on its inside.

98 Potsdamer Strasse
Berlin

● 2
Potsdamer Strasse 98,
10785
Open: 24/7
Free

South of the huge Grosser Tiergarten park and a little north of Kurfürstenstrasse U-Bahn Station in the Tiergarten district, it is easy to miss the small archway with the number 98 in gold above it. But peer in and be surprised with a view of grass, ivy-clad walls, low, clipped hedges and a tall, dark conifer in front of which stands a white statue of Venus. Venture down the passageway and be transported from the bustling street into a secluded, verdant garden, as picturesque as it is unexpected, and surprisingly large. Created in the midst of a grand, nineteenth-century apartment block and a fortunate survivor of Second World War bombings, the garden is a rare find. With its tall trees and lawns, the feeling of tranquillity is palpable, heightened by the gentle trickle of water from the statue fountain that stands at the head of a formal pond, and the splash of the fountain jets in the circular pools. Potsdamer Strasse itself was originally constructed as part of the route to the royal palaces of Sanssouci and Neue Palais in Potsdam; both have large gardens that are also well worth visiting.

Prinzessinnengärten (Princess Gardens)
Berlin

📍 3
Prinzenstrasse 35–38, 10969
Open Mon–Sat: 10.00–22.00; Sun: 10.00–20.00 (closed every second Sun)
Free

A twenty-minute walk almost due east from Checkpoint Charlie, and next to the Moritzplatz U-Bahn Station in the Kreuzberg district, lies an urban cornucopia of vegetables, flowers and herbs waiting to be discovered. Everything is cultivated organically, and vegetables may be purchased at the kiosk; try to visit at lunchtime, because the cafe is not to be missed. As well as making fullest use of the fresh, delicious produce, it helps to fund the project. Prinzessinnengärten itself has a very organic feel, too, especially in its construction. This is thanks in large part to the land lease, which the city renews annually, meaning that this must be a mobile garden with everything grown in moveable containers. But with the distinctive style comes a healthy sense of community, of garden as social hub – integrating, educating and entertaining. Prinzessinnengärten began in 2009, when, inspired by the urban farms he had seen in Cuba, the co-founder Robert Shaw established the not-for-profit company Nomadisch Grün (Nomadic Green) and transformed this former wasteland site.

**Liebieghaus
(Liebieg House)
Frankfurt**

📍4
Schaumainkai 71,
60596
Open Tue–Sun: 10.00–
18.00 (Thu: 21.00)
Admission fee

Southwest of the city's green belt of former fortifications, this palatial villa stands on the Museumsufer (Museum Embankment) of the River Main. A splendid example of the Historicist style, it was completed in 1896 as a retirement home for the Bohemian textile magnate Baron Heinrich von Liebieg (1839–1904). Sadly he did not live to enjoy it for long, and, in accordance with his will, the city acquired the building in 1908, repurposing it as a public sculpture gallery. The informal garden occupies the remaining part of the city-block-sized plot, its informal, gently undulating lawns studded with vegetation from all over the world. Of particular note are the mature trees: plane, paulownia, black walnut, red and white horse chestnut, magnolia and Japanese pagoda tree (*Styphnolobium japonicum*). Island beds offer points of colourful interest, as do a number of sculptures, including a replica of Johann Heinrich von Dannecker's *Ariadne on the Panther* (c.1814). Most of the time one can lounge in peace on the lawns with something from the excellent cafe, but during events the garden can become crowded.

**Marco-Polo Terrassen
(Marco Polo Terraces)**
Hamburg

📍5
Grosser Grasbrook 14,
20457
Open: 24/7
Free

There is a lot of water but little green space in the old city of Hamburg. But twenty minutes' walk south from the Rathaus (Town Hall) brings one to the western end of HafenCity (Harbour City), a former warehouse district in the port, recently redeveloped for housing. At the head of the Grasbrookhafen basin, and enjoying views over and beyond it to the Norderelbe River, are the 6,400-square-metre Marco Polo Terraces. This open space creates an interface between the water and the filled spaces of the buildings. From the street-level terrace a ramp and broad flight of steps descend to an elegantly paved, curvilinear esplanade punctuated by trees and mounded lawns. Nearest to the river and with views of the constantly rising or falling water are three small terraces: some parts paved, with wooden benches, others covered with lawn, with wooden platforms suitable for sitting or lying on. Across Grosser Grasbrook at the southern end of the Terraces is the larger Grasbrookpark, with lawns and a fun kid's play area boasting a sandy 'beach' and a stream.

Kabinettsgarten (Cabinet Garden)
Munich

📍 6
Residenzstrasse 1,
80333
Open: 24/7
Free

The great Munich Residenz was the seat of government and residence of the Bavarian rulers from 1508 to 1918. Nine of the complex's ten courtyard gardens charge an entrance fee; the tenth, the rectangular, 1,000-square-metre Kabinettsgarten beside the Church of All Saints, is free to visit (as is the large Hofgarten, to the north). Both church and Kabinettsgarten were badly damaged during the Second World War, and it was not until 2002 that the garden was redesigned, to an axially symmetrical plan by the landscape architect Peter Kluska. The central path of white limestone harmonizes with the warm honey tones of the walls that enclose this peaceful garden entirely. Set into the path at its eastern end is the bronze sculpture *Flora III* (1971) by Fritz Koenig, and at the western end a low fountain pool in a paved square is canopied by four clipped plane trees. Either side of the axial path and backed by strips of lawn are shallow pools lined with black granite and geometric mosaics in white, red and green glass. The path that traces the perimeter of the courtyard is set with benches.

Hesperidengarten and Barockgarten (Garden of the Hesperides and Baroque Garden)
Nuremberg

📍 7
Johannisstrasse 13 & 43–47, 90419
Daily: 08.00–20.00 (Apr–Oct only)
Free

Beginning in the Middle Ages, wealthy citizens moved a little outside the western walls of the old city of Nuremberg, to the St Johannis area, where they built grand houses with rich gardens. Most have vanished, but in the early 1980s a handful of seventeenth-century gardens were restored and opened to the public. Five minutes apart along Johannisstrasse are the small Barockgarten, tucked away behind no.13, and the larger Hesperidengarten, behind nos 43–47. The former (pictured here) is geometrically formal, intimate and charming, with its playful statues, neatly clipped hedges, yew topiary, four lawns around a central circular fountain and delightful little orangerie. The Garden of the Hesperides is also geometrically laid out, with statues, fountains, a topiary sundial and citrus trees in large terracotta pots. While not as ornate or extravagantly planted as it once would have been, it does suggest the grandness and formality of the gardens of the time. The beautiful cemetery of the nearby St John's Church contains the grave of Albrecht Dürer (1471–1528; his house/museum is at Albrecht-Dürer-Strasse 39).

Alter Botanischer Garten (Old Botanic Garden)
Zurich

● 8
Pelikanstrasse 40,
8001
Daily: 07.00–19.00
(Mar–Sep); 08.00–
18.00 (Oct–Feb)
Free

Bounded on two sides by the Schanzengraben (defensive moat), the former university botanic garden was created in 1837. After it moved to a larger site in 1976, this garden became a pretty public park with a fine arboretum. At its highest point is the Gessner Garden, which opened in 1997 and celebrates the life and work of the Swiss scientist and physician Conrad Gessner (1516–65). Stone-edged beds are laid out within gravel paths in replication of a period physic garden and planted with fifty commonly used medicinal taxa; interpretation boards offer insight into sixteenth-century use of the plants. Gessner was also known as a classical linguist and the author of a 4,500-page encyclopaedia of animals (1551–8). However, he was best known in his time as a botanist, and indeed it was his descendant, Johannes Gessner, who founded Zurich's first botanic garden in 1746. The elegant octagonal palm house – a wooden structure from 1851 was replaced by cast iron in 1877 – is used mainly for concerts, performances and exhibitions. The garden also contains the university's Ethnographic Museum.

**Petersfriedhof
(St Peter's Cemetery)
Salzburg**

📍 9
Sankt-Peter-Bezirk 1,
5010
Daily: 06.30–20.00
  (Apr–Sep); 06:30–
  18.00 (Oct–Mar)
Free

St Peter's Abbey – a Benedictine monastery founded by Rupert, a Franconian missionary, in 696 – is the world's oldest Christian monastery with a continuous history. Enclosed by elegant wrought-iron fences, probably laid out at the same time and still in use is the Petersfriedhof or St Peter's Cemetery. The lovingly maintained graves also feature beautiful wrought iron, and most have their own little garden. This is one of the world's prettiest cemeteries, but its location is dramatic, at the foot of the Festungsberg, atop which sits Hohensalzburg Castle. The ambience is reflective rather than sad, and as a whole the cemetery offers a contemplative respite from the city, be it in summer, when the little gardens are blooming and at their most touching, or in winter, when the graves are blanketed in snow. The Baroque porticoes house the chapels of Salzburg's old wealthy families, and Crypt 54 contains the remains of Mozart's sister Nannerl. The cemetery appears in the film of *The Sound of Music* (1965): the fight scene during the Von Trapps' flight from Salzburg was filmed here.

Biblioteka Uniwersytecka w Warszawie (Warsaw University Library), Roof Garden Warsaw

📍1
Dobra 56/66, 00-312
Daily: 09.00–20.00
(Apr–Oct); 09.00–
15.00 (Nov–Mar)
Free

Warsaw University Library boasts one of Europe's largest and most beautiful roof gardens. Designed by Irena Bajerska and opened in 2002, it comprises two areas connected by a stream and cascades. The smaller, upper area, of 2,000 square metres, is the roof garden itself. It is accessed from the lower space by a ramp flanked by massed ground cover of ivy and greater periwinkle (*Vinca major*), ornamented by towering, sculptural pergolas covered with silver lace vine (*Fallopia baldschuanica*). With sweeping views of the skyline and the River Vistula, the roof garden is divided into four colour-themed compartments, each richly planted. To the north is the Golden Garden, to the south the Purple Garden, to the west the Green Garden and to the east the Silver Garden. Sinuous catwalks wind over the roof and the glass atrium roofs, affording glimpses of the interior, while an intricate system of cascading streams and ponds collects rainwater. The 1.5-hectare lower garden is planted in a blue and pinkish-white theme. It contains a large fish pond and a series of granite sculptures by Ryszard Stryjecki.

**Cmentarz Żydowski
(Jewish Cemetery)
Warsaw**

📍 2
Okopowa 49/51,
01-043
Open Mon–Thu:
  10.00–17.00;
  Fri: 09.00–13.00;
  Sun: 09.00–16.00
Admission fee

Established in 1806, covering 33 hectares and containing more than 250,000 marked graves, this is one of Europe's largest Jewish cemeteries. To visit is a poignant experience and a tangible reminder of never-to-be-forgotten atrocities. But make a personal visit rather than joining a guided tour, and venture further than the entrance area, which is still used for burials. The cemetery was neglected during Communist rule; overgrown with weeds and shrouded by a dense canopy of self-sown trees in which ravens perch, the dilapidated tombstones – some still standing, others toppled and tumbledown – are silent witnesses to a bygone era. To walk here is to feel a palpable aura of sorrow, of abandonment, and yet it is heartening to see among the ruination nature and new life. Knowing that this rare surviving reminder of Warsaw's once-thriving Jewish community was the scene of mass executions and burials by the Nazis challenges one to reflect on what happened in the city and to what was in 1939 Europe's largest metropolitan Jewish community. The cemetery is encouragingly being restored.

**Františkánská Zahrada
(Franciscan Garden)
Prague**

📍 3

Vodičkova 2108/39a,
Nové Město, 110 00
Daily: 07.00–22.00
  (15 Apr–14 Sep);
  07.00–20.00 (15 Sep–
  14 Oct); 08.00–21.00
  (15 Oct–14 Apr)
Free

The Franciscan Garden is about ten minutes' walk south of the old city, and directly south of Kostel Panny Marie Sněžné (Church of Our Lady of the Snows), with access via Jungmannovo Square or passages from Vodickova Street or Wenceslas Square. The first garden was made here in 1348 by Carmelite monks, before the Franciscans took over in 1604. It was returned to them after a period of confiscation by the Communists, and the modern garden is a delightful place to picnic or rest from culture-vulturing. The trapezoidal space is essentially two gardens. The northern part has a distinctly medieval monastic feel. Surrounding a small yellow-painted building (a boutique) is an arrangement of thirty-six mostly rectangular, stone-edged beds set in gravel, in the manner of a herb garden, but planted with massed ornamentals. Positioned along the enclosing black metal fence are white benches, some lovely rose arches, a rather good cafe and a children's play area. Look out also for the sculptures in the garden's southern part, with chest-high yew hedges enclosing (inaccessible) lawns.

**Vrtbovská Zahrada
(Vrtba Garden)
Prague**

● 4
Karmelitská 373/25,
Malá Strana, 118 00
Daily: 10.00–19.00
(Apr–Oct only)
Admission fee

This small, unusually shaped Italian-influenced garden reopened in 1998 after major restoration and enchants once more. Created for Jan Josef, Count of Vrtba, in 1715–20 by the architect František Maxmilián Kaňka and the sculptor Matthias Bernard Braun, it boasts all the features one would expect in a fine Baroque garden. Three terraces rise up the steep northeastern slope away from the building. On the lowest, between the ornate Sala Terrena (garden pavilion) and the aviary, four beds surround a pool containing a statue of a sea monster, while against the high, balustraded retaining wall of the middle terrace are statues and ornamental vases. All beds are *parterre de broderie*, their embroidery-like patterns picked out in clipped box, filled with bright seasonal colour and ornamented with yew cones. At the top the garden narrows to two triangular lawns, where the shell grotto work and the super view over the old city can be enjoyed. Do also visit the three larger Baroque gardens on the hillside: Vratislav, Schönborn and Lobkowicz.

The Writers' House of Georgia
Tbilisi

📍5
13 Ivane Machabeli St
Open Mon–Fri:
11.00–19.00
Free

The Writers' House is near central Tbilisi's Freedom Square, and the lush, bohemian courtyard hidden behind this splendid bourgeois mansion is the perfect spot to stop for an invigorating coffee – available from the on-site Cafe Littera – and spend an hour or so in convivial conversation or lost in a book. Beneath the lofty cedar and Chusan palm, the beds are cloaked with ivy, and benches and tables are scattered in a most welcoming way. Popular with locals, the courtyard is illuminated and makes a cosy, atmospheric space even on a winter's afternoon. The white mansion, with a splendid wooden wraparound balcony and a balustraded terrace, was designed between 1903 and 1905 by the German architect Carl Zaar for the chemist and philosopher David Sarajishvili, founder of the Georgian brandy industry. When Georgia was Sovietized, in 1921, the house was seized and used by the writers' and artists' unions. Since 2008 it has been home to the Writers' House, a proactive organization that aims to popularize Georgian literature through national and international cultural activities and events.

**Taynitskiy Sad
(Taynitsky Garden)
Moscow**

⬤ 6
Spasskaya ulitsa,
103073
Open Fri–Wed: 10.00–
18.00 (15 May–30
Sep); 10.00–17.00
(1 Oct–14 May)
Admission fee

To visit the Kremlin, with its glittering museums and historic churches, is an absorbing experience, but the sheer press of people can be overwhelming. It's pleasant, then, to take a break and decompress before launching oneself into Red Square, St Basil's Cathedral and the queue to see Lenin. Few visitors take advantage of the peaceful, pretty park tucked away inside the Kremlin's southern walls; they just walk on by towards the Spasskaya Tower. But do pause and enjoy the Taynitsky Garden. The mature trees imbue the area with a sylvan feel – not something one expects in such a location, with its scattering of fountains and ornamental urns. Paths cross manicured lawns set (in true Victorian style) with geometric beds filled with bright, cheerful displays of seasonal flowers – the tulips in spring are a picture. Do also look for the oak tree named 'Cosmos', planted by Yuri Gagarin on 14 April 1961, just two days after his return to Earth. The garden occupies the site of a late fourteenth-century church dedicated to saints Constantine and Helena, and destroyed by Bolsheviks in 1917.

**Aptekarsky Ogorod
(The Apothecaries'
Garden)**
Moscow

📍 7
Prospect Mira 26,
129090
Open: see p.365
Admission fee

Founded by Peter the Great in 1706 (a larch tree planted by him still stands here), this is Russia's oldest botanic garden still on its original site. A twenty-five-minute ride by public transport north of Red Square, it is hidden behind the street frontages of shops and housing blocks, and planted with a vast number of plant taxa, so there is much variety to be discovered and enjoyed. Roam the paths beneath the trees, relax on the lawns and enjoy the plant collections. It is most rewarding to visit in spring and summer, when highlights include the quadripartite arrangement of narrow raised beds filled with about 160 taxa of medicinal herbs, inspired by the garden's original layout. The modern glasshouses contain collections of waterlilies, palms and succulents. Most photogenic is the canal, flanked by borders of shrubs and perennials. As with the Chelsea Physic Garden in London (see p.136), the garden's original purpose was to cultivate medicinal plants for educational purposes. In 1805 it became a botanic garden, and today it is managed by the Botanic Gardens of Moscow State University.

Mozaichny Dvor (The Mosaic Courtyard)
St Petersburg

● 8
ulitsa Chaykovskogo 2/7, 191187
Daily: dawn–dusk
Free

As well as the spectacular Hermitage Museum, this beautiful Baroque city is home to another, less well-known masterpiece. Unusual and charming, the 'Mosaic Universe', as it is known to locals, is not easy to find, but is well worth the effort. Look for an alley on Tchaikovsky Street (ulitsa Chaykovskogo) to reach building 2/7. On entering the courtyard, one is struck by the vivacious and funky tilework in a rainbow of bright colours. The walls are covered with murals – of angels, dancers and children flying on the backs of geese – some of which flow on to the ground. There are also raised beds (planted with seasonal colour), a sundial, statues, benches in the shape of lions and even a children's jungle gym, all covered entirely with mosaic. The project was started in 1984 by Honoured Artist of Russia Vladimir Lubenko, a local resident, who decided to bring a splash of colour to the outside of his workshop. The workshop became a children's art school and Lubenko, his staff and students have now covered just about every available space to create a cheerful and welcome escape.

Volkonsky House Museum
Irkutsk

📍 9

pereulok Volkonskogo
10, Irkutsk, 664007
Open Tue–Sun:
10.00–18.00
Admission fee

Painted lavender grey-blue and white, this small wooden mansion stands opposite the Church of the Transfiguration and Saviour, and close to the central bus station. Built by Count Sergei Volkonsky in nearby Urik in 1838, it was moved here in 1846 and became the centre of Irkutsk cultural life until the Volkonskys returned west in 1856. In summer the beds in front of it are filled with peonies, the remains of the large garden that was diligently cultivated here by Volkonsky himself. The Count was especially proud, however, of the delightful wood-and-glass conservatory that is integrated with the house on its south-facing side. In it he grew tender taxa and even a lemon tree (its descendant continues to thrive) – quite an achievement in a city where winter temperatures can sink to -40°C. A nobleman and general, Volkonsky was exiled to Siberia because of his involvement in the Decembrist revolt of 1825. After his release from the mines, he became a pioneer of Siberian horticulture and glasshouse cultivation. The story of these exiled nobles – in particular that of the women – is truly fascinating.

1   Square Vinet
    (Vinet Square)
    Bordeaux, p.181
2   Square des Ducs
    (Dukes' Square) Dijon,
    p.182
3   Jardin du Palais
    Saint-Pierre (Garden
    of St Peter's Palace)
    Lyon, p.183
4   Jardin Rosa Mir
    (Rosa Mir Garden)
    Lyon, p.184
5   Jardin Benedetti
    (Benedetti Garden)
    Marseille, p.185

6   Jardin du Monastère
    de Cimiez (Cimiez
    Monastery Garden)
    Nice, p.186
7   Hôtel Le Vergeur
    Museum (The Vergeur
    Museum Hotel) Reims,
    p.188
8   Jardin St-Martin
    (St Martin Garden)
    Monte Carlo, p.189
9 – 16 See **Paris Map**, p.190

**Square Vinet
(Vinet Square)
Bordeaux**

● 1
rue Vinet, 33000
Open: see p.368
Free

Less than ten minutes' walk from the cathedral, in the midst of the city's commercial and tourist activities – yet hidden away down a small side street squeezed between rue du Cancera and rue Maucoudinat – is this modern pocket park. Created in 2005, it provides a striking yet harmonious contrast with the quaint old buildings that surround it. One of the reasons it fits in so well is that the landscape designer, Michel Desvigne, used gravel in the same colour as the limestone of the buildings. Shaded by six mature plane trees, the central area of this delightful space contains a pair of long, parallel benches that embrace a small rubber-surfaced play area for children. However, the feature of note is the L-shaped vertical garden or green wall by the botanist Patrick Blanc. It fills this simple park with different shades of green, varying textures and, in spring and summer, colourful flowers, creating an ambience of relaxing calm in the centre of Bordeaux. This is the perfect spot to sip a *café au lait* while munching on a sinful *pain au chocolat*.

**Square des Ducs
(Dukes' Square)
Dijon**

● 2
place des Ducs de
Bourgogne, 21000
Open: 24/7
Free

Tucked away behind the impressive limestone Palace of the Dukes of Burgundy, parts of which date to the fourteenth century and which today is home to both Dijon's town hall and its fine arts museum, is this small park. Redesigned in 2013, it stands on what was once a vast menagerie, part of the long-lost gardens created by Margaret of Flanders (1350–1405). A statue of her husband, Philip the Bold (Duke of Burgundy 1363–1404), now overlooks the 975-square-metre garden. Enclosed by ornate iron railings backed with plantings of shrubs and perennials, and well provided with wooden benches, the space is mostly lawn, through which runs a winding concrete path and another of rectangular slabs. The focal feature is a pool into which water falls from a rockwork cascade, a restored relic of an informal nineteenth-century landscape that occupied the site. Of similar date are the splendid specimen trees, including a silver lime, a copper or purple beech and a Japanese pagoda tree (*Styphnolobium japonicum*).

Jardin du Palais Saint-Pierre (Garden of St Peter's Palace)
Lyon

● 3
20, place des Terreaux, 69001
Open Wed–Mon: 10.00–18.00 (Fri opens 10.30)
Free (admission fee for museum)

The Musée des Beaux-Arts – which is well worth a visit – is housed in what was the seventeenth-century Royal Abbey of the Sisters of St Pierre. One of the oldest convents in France, the abbey was first constructed in about the sixth century and Benedictine nuns lived here until the Revolution in 1792. The museum was founded in 1801, and the garden occupies what was the cloister. Its present layout of low, clipped hedges, flower beds and lawns pierced by wide paths dates from 1884, the work of the architects René Dardel and Abraham Hirsch, who successively worked on the garden, the latter conceiving the space as a sculpture garden. The circular central fountain featuring an antique sarcophagus and crowned with a small statue of Apollo, the god of arts, is however a new addition. This is a truly pleasant refuge, with benches that encourage you to admire the bronze statues displayed under the leafy branches of the specimen trees (among them oak, linden, weeping willow, birch and *Paulownia* spp.). Note the two major works by Auguste Rodin: *The Age of Bronze* (1876) and *The Shadow* (1904–5).

Jardin Rosa Mir
(Rosa Mir Garden)
Lyon

📍 4
87, grande rue de la
Croix-Rousse, 69004
Open Sat: 14.00–17.30
 (1 Apr–31 Oct only)
Free

Created by Jules Senis (1913–83), a Spanish anarchist who fled his country's Civil War, this quirky 400-square-metre courtyard garden hidden behind a row of ordinary town houses has echoes of architect Antoni Gaudí's distinctive style. To walk through this grotto-like space, between shade and sun, is a thought-provoking and delightful experience, akin perhaps to exploring a somewhat kitsch Roman ruin. The walls, columns and cross-beams that give the garden structure are encrusted with thousands of shells and tufa. The contrastingly ebullient plantings smother the beams and the planters crowning the columns, and fill the ground-level beds. Succulents (particularly agaves and sempervivums) dominate and are complemented a framework of perennials (including daylilies and geranium) and plantings of seasonal colour. A testament to an ordinary man's passion for life and his artisanal skill. In the 1950s Senis, a stonemason, vowed to build a garden if he survived treatment for cancer. He did both, and devoted the last twenty-five years of his life to this place, dedicated to his mother.

**Jardin Benedetti
(Benedetti Garden)
Marseille**

● 5
10, rue Félix-Fregier,
13007
Open: 24/7
Free

There is not much green space in central Marseille. The Jardin des Vestiges is just lawn, with a scattering of Greek and Roman archaeological remains; west of downtown, the Parc Émile Duclaux in front of the Palais du Pharo (the palace built in 1858 by Napoleon III and now a conference centre) is also just lawn, with modern Cor-Ten steel U-shaped sculptures and a view of the harbour. Jardin Benedetti is not central, but it is a small, hidden and quiet retreat southwest of the main harbour, half-an-hour's walk or a ten-minute bus ride (no.83, every eight minutes from Canebière Vieux Port; alight at Corniche Fregier). Enclosed by trees, the sloping, informally laid-out garden nestles into the hillside. The small terrace enjoys splendid views westwards to the Mediterranean, and at the bottom of the garden is a fenced-in children's play area. Gravel, concrete and paved paths wind past wooden benches and a picnic area with tables, around patches of grass punctuated by palms and among natural rock outcrops, which are planted naturalistically with Mediterranean taxa.

Jardin du Monastère de Cimiez (Cimiez Monastery Garden)
Nice

📍6
place Jean-Paul-II
Pape, 06000
Daily: 08.00–18.00
 (Oct–Mar); 08.00–
 19.00 (Apr, May &
 Sep); 08.00–20.00
 (Jun–Aug)
Free

This is the oldest garden on the Côte d'Azur, and offers a peaceful atmosphere as well as a stunning view over Nice to the Mediterranean. Originally the Franciscan monks' vegetable garden and orchard – legend has it that the mesclun mixed salad was invented here – the garden is laid out in eight roughly rectangular sections, a concept that has not changed since 1546. Today these are lawns studded with square flower beds, ornamented with domed citrus and shaded by specimen *Magnolia grandiflora*. West of these beds, the long borders that flank the path are planted with colourful and carefully coordinated displays, and there is a rose tunnel that is breathtaking in summer. At the apparent end of the garden, a pergola-covered viewing platform looks out over the city to the south, and down on to a hidden garden below. Reached via a flight of steps, it has two pools, a central bowl fountain and geometric box-edged beds planted ornamentally with vegetables. The artists Henri Matisse and Raoul Dufy and the writer Roger Martin du Gard are buried in the monastery's cemetery.

Hôtel Le Vergeur Museum (The Vergeur Museum Hotel) Reims

◆ 7
36, place du Forum, 51100
Daily: 14.00–18.00 (closed 1 May, 14 July, 1 Nov, 24 Dec–1 Jan)
Admission fee

Facing the northern corner of the place du Forum, this thirteenth-century turreted building has an unusual and moving garden of architectural remembrance. Reims was shelled by the German army for four years during the First World War, and largely destroyed. Hugues Krafft, a wealthy traveller, photographer and antiquarian, had acquired this property in 1910, and after the war devoted much of his fortune to restoring it and installing his collections. He also mourned the destruction of the historic city, and set about saving what he could from the rubble, salvaging doorways, lintels, facades, columns, archways and tombs from private mansions and religious institutions. While the splendid beds of roses sound a contrastingly cheerful note, the ivy-clad walls and evergreen shrubs and ferns poking from between the stones give the garden the melancholic feel of a forgotten cemetery – only here, ruins are tombstones to a lost city. After Krafft's death in 1935, the property was bequeathed to the Société des Amis du Vieux Reims (Friends of Old Reims); the museum has a collection of Albrecht Dürer prints.

**Jardin Saint-Martin
(St Martin Garden)**
Monte Carlo

● 8
9b, avenue Saint-Martin, 98000
Daily: 07.00–20.00
(Apr–Sep); 07.00–18.00 (Oct–Mar)
Free

Given the value of land in the principality, it is surprising that there is any green space at all, yet Monaco boasts several gardens. Arguably the most surprising is the hidden Jardin St Martin, which seems to hang from the southwestern face of 'The Rock'. This 62-metre-tall monolith rises above the harbour and is also home to the Prince's Palace, the cathedral and the Oceanographic Museum. The garden stretches along the clifftop adjacent to the palace, with small paths winding among manicured lawns, occasional sculptures and pools. The highlight, however, is the mix of native Mediterranean taxa and introduced exotics that creates a luxuriant floral show of colour, form and scent. Tall Aleppo pines make this a place of shady repose and a spot to enjoy the beautiful views of the small Fontvieille harbour and the azure Mediterranean. A couple more gardens well worth exploring are the large Jardin Exotique de Monaco, with its collection of prickly succulents, and the hidden Princess Grace rose garden, created as a monument to the actress and royal wife, with some 8,000 bushes of 300 cultivars.

N

0 300 600 900 yd.

**Square du Vert-Galant
(Vert-Galant Square)**
Paris

● 9
15, place du Pont-Neuf,
75001
Open: 24/7
Free

It's all about location, and for pure wow-factor the Square du Vert-Galant is hard to beat. This small, triangular garden is in the middle of the River Seine, on the western tip of the Île de la Cité. Interestingly, the garden is at the original level of the island, some 7 metres below today's streets; during high floods it is submerged. It is accessed via a double flight of steps from place du Pont-Neuf. The equestrian statue here is of Henri IV (1553–1610), whose nickname Vert-Galant ('sprightly'), acquired because of his many mistresses in spite of his advanced age, gives the garden its name. The lawn with its beds of seasonal planting is surrounded by a charming collection of trees and shrubs, including ginkgo, horse chestnut, Japanese maple, tamarisk, walnut and weeping willow. The garden was created in 1607, when two islets were joined to the main island; the current layout dates from 1884, when the City acquired the land. Enjoy the splendid river views, and look out for the memorial plaque recording the execution here on 18 March 1314 of the Grand Master of the Knights Templar, Jacques de Molay.

**Jardin Anne-Frank
(Anne Frank Garden)
Paris**

⬤ 10
14, impasse Berthaud,
75003
Open: see p.367
Free

The mid-thirteenth-century Marais district has long been aristocratic and, as well as its many architectural treats, has a number of atmospheric gardens and parks. Jardin Anne-Frank is one of the best of the larger, more secluded retreats. Opened in 2007 as a memorial to Amsterdam resident and diarist Anne Frank, perhaps the most discussed Jewish victim of the Holocaust, the 2,200-square-metre garden has three parts. Just north of the Centre Pompidou, a shady, contemplative, contemporary space is planted with camellias and a small horse chestnut tree – a graft from the one that stood in front of Frank's home and is mentioned in her diary. The open central area was once part of the gardens of a seventeenth-century mansion, which now houses the Museum of Art and History of Judaism. Here a beautiful semicircular, Baroque-inspired, rose-planted pergola, set with benches, overlooks a circle of grasses set in gravel. And beyond a wall are a lawn, mixed borders, a small vegetable garden and a children's play area shaded by ornamental cherries, their blossom exquisite in spring.

Clos des Blancs Manteaux
Paris

📍 11
21, rue des Blancs-Manteaux, 75004
Open: see p.366
Free

This hidden garden is a challenge to find. Walk rue des Blancs-Manteaux in the direction of the traffic and look for two green planters on the left-hand side. A red watering-can-shaped sign is placed by the entrance arch during opening times (weekends only). Behind the primary school is a 1,000-square-metre, two-tiered garden. The lower, entrance level is shaded by trees with plenty of welcoming benches. The upper level, at the far end, is a medieval-style formal garden of small hedge-edged beds separated by concrete paths and planted with over 250 taxa of edible, domestic and medicinal plants. The little vegetable garden is a community project and cultivated by local inhabitants. Opened in 2001 and dedicated to the memory of Diana, Princess of Wales, this is a peaceful spot in the busy Marais. Close to the Centre Pompidou, it is a verdant, natural remedy to a surfeit of modern art and architecture, or simply a place to rest and read. Five minutes' walk southeast is the Jardin des Rosiers-Joseph-Migneret, and seven minutes northwest is Jardin Anne-Frank (see opposite).

Square Saint-Gilles-du-Grand-Veneur (St-Gilles-du-Grand-Veneur Square)
Paris

● 12
12, rue Villehardouin,
75003
Open: see p.368
Free

Behind the seventeenth-century Hôtel du Grand Veneur ('hunter'; so named because it was home to Marquis d'Ecquevilly, Louis XV's Master of Hounds), in the middle of the Marais district, this small, serene, romantic garden remains unknown even to most Parisians. To find it, take rue de Hesse where the rue Villehardouin makes a right-angle turn by no. 12; or rue du Grand Veneur, where rue des Arquebusiers does the same by no. 5. With its backdrop of elegant architecture, the rectangular courtyard has four symmetrical, iron-railed and box-edged lawns around a gravel circle set with four stone benches that entice the visitor to pause for a rest; a rectangular lawn fills the southern end. The perimeters of the lawns have narrow borders of mixed planting and a delightful profusion of roses that smother the fine ironwork pillars and framework. Thus the best time to visit this hideaway is when it is filled with rose blossoms and their scent, making it a delightful picnic spot. That said, the autumnal show of golden-yellow maple leaves is very attractive too.

**Square Roger-
Stéphane (Roger
Stéphane Square)**
Paris

📍 13
7, rue Récamier, 75007
Open: 24/7
Free

On the Left Bank in the 7th arrondissement, not far from the famous Bon Marché department store, this quiet, enclosed pocket park is to be found at the top of rue Récamier, a small pedestrianized lane running north from rue de Sèvres. The natural topography of the site – a mere 1,438 square metres – has been enhanced by raised beds and level changes, while the mature mixed planting of perennials and shrubs heightens the hidden, private feeling. Notable specimens include lilac, magnolia and rhododendron, and there is an immense weeping beech in the central island bed, around which benches are arranged. The sound of water tumbling over the ivy-clad stone cascade into a pool adds to the tranquillity, and there is also a small children's play area. The design of the park has not changed significantly since it was created in 1933, when it was named Square Récamier, in honour of the nineteenth-century socialite Juliette Récamier, who ended her days in a convent here. The park was renamed in 2008 after the Resistance fighter, writer, journalist and gay rights activist Roger Stéphane.

**UNESCO Garden
of Peace (Japanese
Garden)
Paris**

📍 14
7, place de Fontenoy,
75007
Open by appointment:
see p.368
Free

To the east of the Y-shaped UNESCO headquarters in the Faubourg Saint-Germain area of Paris, the Garden of Peace was designed by the Japanese-American sculptor Isamu Noguchi (1904–88) in 1952–55. UNESCO describes the garden as 'of great historical significance, being the first created by a sculptor rather than a gardener'. However, Noguchi was assisted by the highly regarded Japanese garden master Toemon Sano, who also oversaw a revamp of the garden in 1999–2000. The 1,700-square-metre plot reflects Noguchi's personal design aesthetic and heritage. A synthesis of abstract sculptural form, modern minimalism and Zen tradition, it comprises a stream, a lake, a bridge, rocks, imported Japanese trees (flowering cherries, plums, pines and magnolias) and sculpture. A highlight is Noguchi's granite *Fountain of Peace* (1957), carved in reverse with the Japanese characters for the word 'peace', which reflect correctly in the water. The composition is a study in balance and serenity, and perfect for quiet contemplation.

Jardin de la Nouvelle France (Garden of New France)
Paris

📍15
Opposite 1, avenue Franklin-Delano-Roosevelt, 75008
Open: 24/7
Free

Central Paris is so grand that sometimes one has to flee the ostentation, the noise, the tourists. This small haven (just 0.7 hectares) near the Champs-Élysées is a perfect antidote. Yet it is easily missed, being hemmed in by the Grand Palais and two streets, cours la Reine and avenue Franklin Delano Roosevelt. The 'main' entrance is on the latter street, between the white marble *Dream of the Poet* (1910) by Alphonse de Moncel and a pair of stone busts. This charmingly overgrown sunken wilderness, designed in the late nineteenth century by the engineer Jean-Charles Adolphe Alphand and previously called the Jardin de la Vallée Suisse, is said to be of French/English inspiration. However, the picturesque, informal, miniature landscape with its sinuous plant-lined paths, rustic bridge, rock garden and rockwork arch, pool (fed by the river Seine) and fountain has a hint of the Japanese strolling garden – but more richly planted, with a tapestry of perennials, shrubs and trees. Highlights include bamboo, citrus, lilac, Japanese maple and a century-old weeping beech overhanging the pool.

Jardins Renoir, Musée de Montmartre (Renoir Gardens, Montmartre Museum)
Paris

📍16
12–14, rue Cortot, 75018
Daily: 10.00–19.00 (Apr–Sep); 10.00–18.00 (Oct–Mar)
Admission fee

The district of Montmartre is touristy, but it is still possible to escape into small streets and soak up the village-like feel. It is particularly famous for the artistic community that lived and worked there during the Belle Époque (1871–1914), when rents were low and the creative atmosphere congenial. Notable residents included Degas, Matisse, Picasso, Toulouse-Lautrec and Van Gogh. Housed in several seventeenth-century buildings on the Butte (hill of Montmartre), this museum reveals the district's rich culture and history, and its three charming Renoir gardens are named in honour of the artist, who lived on the site in 1875–7. They offer delightful views of the northern cityscape and the nearby vineyard (vines have been cultivated here since medieval times and, according to the *New York Times*, the Clos Montmartre produces the most expensive bad wine in the city!). With their cobbled and gravelled paths and verdant lawns, mix of flowering shrubs, trees and luscious borders, pools, pergolas and gazebos, the gardens have been reconstructed according to the works Renoir painted here.

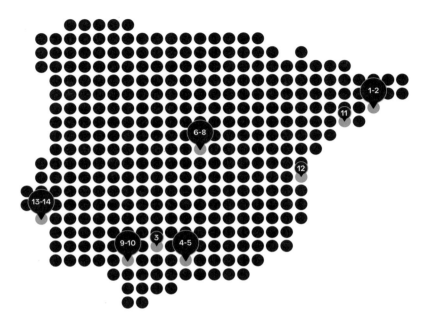

Jardins de la Torre de les Aigües (Torre de les Aigües Gardens)
Barcelona

♦ 1
Between Carrer de
Roger de Llúria 56 &
58, 08009
Daily: 10.00–21.00
(Apr–Oct); 10.00–
19.00 (Nov–Mar)
Free (fee for pool)

Many who visit Barcelona will stop to marvel at Gaudí's eclectic Casa Milà, but few know that a garden lies waiting to be discovered a mere ten minutes' walk away. In fact, even if you know it's there, it can be a challenge to find because the inconspicuous entrance is part of a building. The reference to water (agua) in the sign above the dark alleyway – Manantial del Agua de la Asociación de Propietarios – gives a hint of what is to come. Stroll through into the interior of the street block to find a red-brick-paved courtyard planted with red hibiscus and with benches shaded by rows of clear-trunk *Magnolia grandiflora*. At the far end, large concrete bleachers provide somewhere to sit, lounge or lie. The dominant feature, though, is the 30-metre-tall hexagonal brick water tower, the Torre de les Aigües. Built in 1870, it provided drinking water for some of the first houses in the district. In keeping with its history, the space in front of the tower has been converted into a swimming pool and artificial sandy beach, which in the hot Spanish summer are very popular with children.

Jardins del Palau Robert (Palau Robert Gardens)
Barcelona

📍 2
Passeig de Gràcia 107, 08008
Open Mon–Sat: 10.00–20.00; Sun & public holidays: 10.00–14.30 (closed Christmas Day, Boxing Day, New Year's Day & 6 Jan)
Free

This small, tranquil garden on the corner of the busy Passeig de Gràcia and Avinguda Diagonal was designed in the early twentieth century by Ramón Oliva (who later designed the gardens at Plaça de Catalunya, a fifteen-minute walk down Passeig de Gràcia). Gravel paths wind past shaded benches and among informally shaped beds filled with exotic plants. The towering Canary Island palms (*Phoenix canariensis*) were transplanted from the Universal Exhibition of 1888; other highlights include the Senegal date palm (*Phoenix reclinata*) and the blue fan palm (*Brahea armata*), two enormous laurel-leaved snail trees (*Cocculus laurifolius*), Japanese pagoda trees (*Styphnolobium japonicum*) and bitter oranges. Contrasting with the exotic plants are contemporary sculptures, including *The Moon* (2001) by Kiku Mistu. Now home to the Catalan Information Centre, the neoclassical palace was built in 1903 for the influential financier and regional politician Robert Robert i Surís. It had rather a chequered history until it was acquired by the government of Catalonia in 1981.

**Palacio de Viana
(Viana Palace)**
Cordoba

● 3
Plaza de Don Gome 2,
14001
Open Tue–Sun: 09.00–
 15.00 (Jul–Aug);
 Tue–Sat: 10.00–
 19.00; Sun: 10.00–
 15.00 (Sep–Jun)
Admission fee

Ten minutes' walk northeast of Plaza de las Tendillas, this stunning Renaissance palace is set around twelve beautiful courtyards (or *patios*). It dates from 1492, when it was built as a family estate by the nobleman Gómez Suárez de Figueroa. From then until the mid-twentieth century, the palace and gardens grew almost organically, expanded by successive owners, until 1980, when the estate was acquired by the Provincial Savings Bank of Cordoba. It currently belongs to the CajaSur Foundation. The gardens, where homage is paid to plants, flowers, light and water, are a cornucopia of styles and influences: Roman, Arabic and Spanish. The tone is set by the Courtyard of the Gate (pictured), with its pebble-mosaic floor, bougainvillea and Arabic fountain. The rustic Courtyard of the Cats is the oldest documented community courtyard in Cordoba. The shady Courtyard of Oranges has Islamic echoes, while the Romano-Arabic Courtyard of the Columns with its pots, pool and jets was constructed in the 1980s but feels ancient. The stunning seventeenth-century colonnaded Reception Courtyard is idyllic.

**Carmen de los
Mártires (Carmen
of the Martyrs)
Granada**

● 4
Calle de Antequeruela
Alta 1, 18009
Open: see p.365
Free

The Alhambra and Generalife are without doubt Granada's 'must-sees', but there are a couple of splendid gardens near by that are almost unvisited. This is one; the other is the Rodríguez-Acosta Foundation (see opposite). Just south of the Alhambra, the Carmen de los Mártires has a long and interesting history. The nineteenth-century house and garden occupy the site of the first church to be built following the *reconquista* in 1492 and a Barefoot Carmelite convent established in memory of Christian captives who were imprisoned in caves on the site. The charming garden is generous – some 7 hectares – and perhaps best described as romantically dishevelled. With many of the original architectural elements integrated into the nineteenth-century design, this is not an Islamic garden but one in a mixed style, inspired by Spanish, French and English gardens. The shaded paths pass various features including a three-tier fountain, parterres, a grotto, statues, a pool, a sinuous lake, a sunken courtyard garden under the shade of ancient palms, a vegetable garden and, of course, wonderful views across the city.

**Fundación
Rodríguez-Acosta
(Rodríguez-Acosta
Foundation)**
Granada

📍 5
Callejón Niños del
Rollo 8, 18009
Daily: 10.00–18.30
(1 Apr–14 Oct);
10.00–16.30 (15
Oct–31 Mar); closed
Christmas Day & New
Year's Day
Admission fee (book
in advance)

In spite of its proximity to the Alhambra, that most famous Islamic palace complex, this formal garden borrows from classical design. It is laid out in a cascade of terraces, verandas and courts. The central terrace below the towering form of the house offers sweeping views over the garden and city beyond. Beneath it, the cryptoporticus with its circular pool connects the Courtyard of Venus to the west and the Garden of Bacchus to the east. The goddess emerges from the former's rectangular pool, which has four columnar fountains. In the latter are two square pools and a statue of the god, backed by an exedra of columns. Large, clipped cypress hedges reinforce the architectural framework in both areas. Below this level is the cypress-lined Funeral Walk and the Lower Garden with its low-hedged flower beds, large trees, fountains and colonnades that frame views out. The house and gardens were designed in the early twentieth century in large part by their wealthy owner, José María Rodríguez-Acosta (1878–1941), a passionate painter; the house now holds his collection.

**Museo Sorolla
(Sorolla Museum)
Madrid**

● 6
Paseo del General
Martínez Campos 37,
28010
Open Tue–Sat: 09.30–
20.00; Sun & public
holidays: 10.00–15.00
(closed New Year's
Day, 6 Jan, 1 & 6 May,
24 Dec, Christmas
Day, 31 Dec)
Admission fee

The artist Joaquín Sorolla y Bastida (1863–1923) was actively involved in the design of his house (by Enrique María de Repullés y Vargas, completed in 1911), and also laid out the garden, which reveals strong Mudéjar (Islamo-Hispanic) influences. There are in fact three formal garden rooms, all of which are delightful, displaying a rich use of geometric tiles, fountains and rills, pelargoniums in terracotta pots and lush shades of green from the clipped bushes and trees. Here, insulated from the noise of surrounding streets by the high brick wall, you can enjoy the intimate, sensuous environment: the burble and murmur of fountains and jets, the multi-coloured tilework and white marble statuary, the heady perfume of scented flowers. The 'room' in front of the house was inspired by the Garden of Troy in the Alcázar of Seville, and the long rill and arching jets by the Generalife in Granada; the third room features a 'Fountain of the Secrets' (because of the sculptures that decorate it) and a shady pergola. In 1925 the house and its contents were bequeathed by Sorolla's widow to the state.

Jardín del Príncipe de Anglona (Garden of the Prince of Anglona)
Madrid

● 7
Calle Príncipe Anglona, 28005
Daily: 10.00–22.00
  (only until 18.30
  from Oct–Feb)
Free

Set in a brick wall in the historic area of Madrid de las Austrias at the northern end of Plaza de la Paja – once the city's economic centre – is a narrow, inconspicuous gate that you can easily pass without noticing. Through it is the secret Garden of the Prince of Anglona. Redesigned by Javier de Winthuysen in 1920 and restored by the municipality in 2002, the garden takes its name from the illustrious seventeenth-century tenant of the adjacent royal palace. Entering through the gate really is like stepping back in time, into the Madrid of Goya. Though not adhering to its original layout, this is a rare surviving example of an eighteenth-century aristocratic garden. The calming, intimate space is shaded by tall trees, and in the centre stands a small stone fountain that is approached on a brick path. Around the fountain are four small, formal lawns edged with low hedges, an arrangement that gives the garden a distinctly Moorish feel. Running along the side facing the entrance gate is an arched tunnel covered with roses. Bring a book and relax. Four minutes' walk north is the Huerto de las Monjas (see opposite).

Huerto de las Monjas
Madrid

● 8
Calle del Sacramento
7, 28005
Open Mon–Fri:
    10.00–17.00 (closed
    weekends)
Free

A little southwest of the Plaza de la Villa (Town Hall Square), this small, square garden is enclosed on two sides by tall brick walls and accessed down steps via a gateway that opens on to Calle del Sacramento. With its brick paths, beds edged with low hedges and planted with ground cover, and trees that cast welcome shade in summer, it is a peaceful place to sit a while. The tranquillity is heightened by the gentle burbling of the central octagonal pool, edged in brick and featuring a Baroque bronze cherub fountain that once graced the Dukes of Montellano's garden El Castañar near Toledo. It was originally laid out in the early seventeenth century as a productive garden for the Convento del Sacramento (its name means 'Orchard of the Nuns'). In 1976, however, the convent was demolished and new government offices and housing erected. Thankfully, the orchard was saved and has become this pretty, public ornamental garden, its new design incorporating the old walls and the general layout of the original.

**Casa de Pilatos
(Pilate's House)
Seville**

📍 9
Plaza de Pilatos 1,
41003
Daily: 09.00–18.00
(Nov–Mar); 09.00–
19.00 (Apr–Oct)
Admission fee

Dating from the fifteenth century, the Casa de Pilatos is the prototype Mudéjar Andalusian palace. In the sixteenth century it pioneered Italian Renaissance architecture in Spain, and in the nineteenth it was altered according to Romantic fashions. Two courtyard gardens open off the gorgeous Main Patio, with its ornate stucco columns and coloured *azulejos* (ceramic-tiled) walls, patterned floor, sculptures and dominant central stone fountain. The neatly clipped orange trees of the Large Garden hint at the garden's origins as an orchard. The Renaissance architect Benvenuto Tortello added three loggias overlooking the now enclosed garden, complete with central fountain and grotto. In the early twentieth century two courtyards were amalgamated to form the shady Small Garden. It has formal beds, swags of bougainvillea and plumbago, tall palms and massed *Zantedeschia aethiopica*, but the highlight is the pool with its fountain of a young Baco and rows of rose-planted terracotta pots. The water here is a reminder of the palace's ancient privilege of *agua de pie* (running water).

**Casa de los Pinelo
(Pinelo House)
Seville**

📍10
Calle Abades 14, 41004
Open Tue & Thu:
11.00–13.00
Admission fee

Once 'wowed-out' by the size and splendour of the magnificent cathedral and equally impressive Alcázar, take a short walk northeast and discover another National Monument of enchanting contrast. The contrast is only in size, however, because for sheer elegance and grace the beautiful patio of the sixteenth-century Casa de los Pinelo can compete with the biggest and best. Architecturally, the garden courtyard was deliberately designed to be the centrepiece of the house, and it is still a pleasure to sit on a bench here and soak up the atmosphere and quietude. In the ornate, graceful stucco columns, geometrically patterned tiled floor, centrally positioned scalloped marble fountain bowl and four citrus trees, the Mudéjar (Islamo-Hispanic) influence is clear. Built by the rich Pinelo family, who came to Seville from Genoa in the fifteenth century, the house has had many owners and the City of Seville acquired it in 1966. Today it is home to the Royal Seville Academy of Humanities and the Royal Academy of Fine Arts of St Isabel of Hungary. If visiting in June and July, check the website for events.

**Tarragona Cathedral
Cloister**
Tarragona

◆ 11
Plaça Pla de la Seu 1,
43003
Open: see p.368
Admission fee

With its impressive octagonal dome, Tarragona Cathedral was begun
in 1184 in the Romanesque and then Gothic style. Its hilltop site, long
considered sacred, was previously occupied by a Christian basilica,
a tenth-century mosque, a Visigoth cathedral and a first-century
temple to the Roman emperor-god Augustus. The large, airy, light
cloister is west of the apse, and is laid out in traditional quadripartite
form (symbolic of the Garden of Eden and the four rivers flowing from
it), defined by paved paths. The large, circular waterlily pool in the
centre is surrounded by clipped *Abelia* spp. and box, and contains an
ornate stone fountain. Each of the four quarters of this serene garden
is a lawn set with small rose beds and paths leading to a circular
papyrus-planted pool with a columnar stone fountain. The dark
greens of large *Magnolia grandiflora*, cypresses and orange trees
are set off by the pale stone of the surrounding peristyle walkway; its
round, under-pointed relieving arches provide a calming rhythm that
echoes that of this contemplative space.

**Jardines de Monforte
(Monforte Gardens)**
València

◆12
Carrer de Montfort 1,
46010
Daily: 10.30–20.00
(21 Mar–20 Sep);
10.30–20.30
(21 Sep–20 Mar)
Free

A stone's throw from the old city and near both the famous but large Jardines del Turia and Jardines del Real (Royal Gardens), are the Monforte Gardens. Hidden behind high walls, this is a quiet, lush realm of 1.1-hectares. Pass through the gate and back in time. They were created in the mid-nineteenth century for Don Juan Bautista Romero Almenar, Marquis of San Juan, by the local architect Sebastián Monleón Estellés, and is considered to be the last historic-artistic garden of their age in the city. Immediately west of the attractive pink-and-yellow pavilion and entered through an imposing arch is a small, formal sunken garden enclosed by cypress, with pools, fountains and neatly planted beds. To the north are six neatly clipped parterres ornamented with classical statues, and a circular pool and statue fountain align on the main axis. A bougainvillea-cloaked pergola leads to the wider garden, which comprises well planted and shady compartments including a formal orange grove (the site was originally an orchard), a shaded mount and a large pool.

**Jardim do Torel
(Torel Garden)**
Lisbon

● 13
Rua Júlio de Andrade 3
Open: 24/7
Free

Part of the fun of visiting this garden, named after the Dutch settlers who once lived in the area, is getting to it. Like Rome, Lisbon is a city of seven hills, and Jardim do Torel sits atop one of them, to the east of the wide, elegant and plane-tree-shaded Avenida da Liberdade. Walking uphill from the Monumento dos Restauradores, take the first right into Largo da Anunciada, then jump on the funky funicular, the Ascensor do Lavra. From the top, it's a short walk to the garden, which originally belonged to a mansion built by Count Manuel de Castro Guimarães in 1886. The garden opened to the public in 1930 and was renovated in 2000. With a splendid panorama over the rooftops to the River Tagus, and well shaded during the day and interestingly illuminated at night, it contains a statue of the composer José Vianna da Motta, water features, a playground, a small cafe and surprisingly comfortable reclining seats. In summer the swimming pool, which is on a lower terrace, is temporarily turned into an 'urban beach', and is very popular with families.

**Estufa Fria
(Greenhouse)
Lisbon**

● 14
Parque Eduardo VII,
1070-051
Daily: 10.00–19.00
(Apr–Oct); 09.00–
17.00 (Nov–Mar)
(closed New Year's
Day, 1 May &
Christmas Day)
Admission fee

The Estufa Fria is in fact three delightful gardens that are easy to miss: looking down into the former basalt quarry that houses them, all that's visible is a scruffy grey roof. This is in fact a lath roof made of slats of wood wired together, and at just over 1 hectare it is the largest in the world. It covers the Cold House (1933), the largest and oldest of the three gardens, providing unheated shelter and shade for moderately hardy subtropical plants. Meandering paths of stone and sand afford ever-changing views of the lush plantings, which include ferns, palms, *Ficus* spp. and *Philodendron*. The jungle-like atmosphere is heightened by streams and pools, while the unusual light cast by the roof and the mix of green foliage is brightened by a diverse understorey of foliage and flowering taxa, including ornamental gingers, hydrangeas and azaleas. The heated Hothouse was added in the 1970s against the back wall of the former quarry. Tall and airy, with a glass dome, it is home to many tender tropical taxa; the third garden, the Sweet House, is a smaller glasshouse filled with a collection of cacti.

Italy

**Palazzo d'Accursio
(Palace of Accursius)
Bologna**

📍1
Via IV Novembre 16,
40123
Open Mon: 14.30–
20.00; Tue–Fri:
10.00–20.00; Sat:
10.00–19.00 (closed
public holidays)
Free

Leave the car park that is the city's central Piazza Franklin Delano Roosevelt in an easterly direction, and about 20 metres along Via IV Novembre, on the left-hand side, is a stone-and-red-brick arched gateway protruding from the massive walls of the Palazzo d'Accursio (former Town Hall, and now home to the civic art collection). Down a short tunnel is an enclosed courtyard recently graced with a small, modern garden centred on a large, ornate, ancient *pozzo dei desideri* (wishing well). The small car park detracts somewhat from the calm ambience, but the simple, elegant garden is a rare quiet escape in the centre of this busy city. Stepped wooden decked seating surrounds a geometric arrangement of four formal beds defined by low box hedges, planted with seasonal colour and ornamented with topiary domes. Set into the decking and providing a contrast with the orange-painted walls are clear-trunk Japanese maples, which are pleasantly green in spring and summer and turn a stunning scarlet in autumn. The Palazzo d'Accursio itself is also well worth a visit.

Palazzo Medici Riccardi (Medici Riccardi Palace)
Florence

● 2
Via Camillo Cavour 3, 50129
Daily: 09.00–19.00
(closed Wed)
Admission fee

A three-minute walk north of Filippo Brunelleschi's magnificent Duomo, this innovative palazzo is now an art gallery hosting temporary exhibitions focusing on the building's Renaissance and Baroque identity and artistic context. The rectangular garden enclosed by tall, crenellated outer walls is accessed westwards from the palazzo's central arched courtyard. Remade in the early twentieth century, the space is divided into four square lawns fringed with marble statues and citrus trees in decorated terracotta pots. At its northern end stands a statue and fountain of Hercules, and at the southern a lawn-girt circular pool. Commissioned by Cosimo de' Medici in 1444 (he chose the architect Michelozzo di Bartolomeo after rejecting a design by Brunelleschi as being 'too lavish and magnificent'), the square stone building was purchased and revamped by the Riccardi family from 1659. Do not miss the gem of a chapel, which contains Benozzo Gozzoli's famous frescoes showing the procession of the Magi (1459) – in which many of the followers are depicted as members of the Medici family.

Palazzo Corsini al Prato (Palazzo Corsini)
Florence

📍 3
Il Prato 56, 50123
Daily: 09.00–dusk
(by reservation)
Admission fee

Concealed in the western part of the old town is a Renaissance garden of tranquil loveliness and formal beauty. Best of all, you are likely to have it almost to yourself. Designed for Alessandro Acciaiuoli in 1594 by the architect Bernardo Buontalenti (who, legend has it, also invented Italian *gelato*), the garden of medicinal plants and the unfinished palazzo were sold in 1620 to Filippo Corsini, who entrusted the garden to Gherardo Silvani. The core of Silvani's garden – the wide path flanked by classical statues on plinths – remains. Do look carefully at the statues; they are deliberately of graded sizes, a perspective effect that is intended to make the garden appear larger. Enjoy the geometric knot beds either side of the path, picked out in clipped box, planted with low shrubs, roses and perennials, and ornamented with about 180 citrus trees in large terracotta pots. Admire the two *limonaia* (orangeries for lemon trees) and the pool full of turtles, and get lost in the shaded laurel labyrinth. In mid-May the garden hosts a three-day fair celebrating Florentine artisanship and traditions.

**Giardino dell'Iris
(Iris Garden)
Florence**

● 4
Viale Michelangelo 52,
50125
Open: see p.366
Free

The view from the Piazzale Michelangelo northwards over the river Arno to the Renaissance city beyond is spectacular. But if visiting between late April and late May, be sure to venture to the eastern end of the terrace and visit the Iris Garden below. The iris is said to have inspired the fleur-de-lis – symbol of Florence for centuries – and on this site since 1954 the world's best cultivars have vied for the coveted annual Florence Prize, awarded by the Società Italiana dell'Iris. The garden was designed by the architect Giuliano Zetti in 1957, and at the entrance is a small terrace with formal beds planted with this glorious flower. Beyond, many more colourful beds weave among the olive trees down the slope – which also offers an attractive view of distant Florence – to a pool. To stroll amid this enchanting multicoloured tapestry of 1,500–2,500 cultivars is unforgettable. Take care: the steep paths are slippery when wet. To the west of the Piazzale is the Giardino delle Rose (Rose Garden), planted with over 350 cultivars. It is open all year but looks – and smells – its best in early summer.

**Palazzo Podestà
(Podestà Palace)
Genoa**

📍5
Via Garibaldi 7, 16124
Open first Sat of the
month: 10.00–18.00
Admission fee
(includes house
and guided tour)

Named after the family that bought it in 1865, and whose heirs live there still, this magnificent palace is also known as the Palazzo Nicolosio Lomellino. It is one of forty-two built by aristocratic Genovese families along what is now the Via Garibaldi. It was designed by the Lombard architect Giovanni Battista Castello (Il Bergamasco) and built in 1563–9. At ground level its rear wings enclose a courtyard with a magnificent Baroque nymphaeum, added in the eighteenth century by Domenico Parodi. Above it, the balustraded terrace garden built into the hill is accessed from the top floor. In the centre of the first terrace is a pool and fountain. The surface here is a geometric mosaic in black and white pebbles edged with marble benches and four white marble urns. Surrounding it are four symmetrical agapanthus-edged lawns. To the west is a wisteria tunnel and to the east a palm and several large *Magnolia grandiflora*. The upper terrace – with another, smaller nymphaeum – is similarly quadripartite but laid out perpendicularly; its notable feature is a tall white tower.

Villa Necchi Campiglio
Milan

📍 6
Via Mozart 14, 20122
Open Wed–Sun:
 10.00–18.00
Free (admission fee
 for villa)

Tucked discreetly away in the centre of Milan lies a beautiful garden waiting to be discovered, its design formal and its layout subtle. Take, for example, the azure swimming pool. More often than not, such pools impose, and appear jarring and domineering. But this one, with its stepped surroundings of crazy-paved paths and flower beds filled with seasonal colour backed by low, clipped hedges, is a focal point that enhances the whole composition. Stroll the lawns, then retire to the tree-shaded patio ornamented with large terracotta storage jars that now double as planters. Take a seat on the wrought-iron furniture and enjoy the unexpected but welcome atmosphere of calm. Built by Piero Portaluppi in 1932–5 for the wealthy Lombard industrialist Necchi Campiglio, the villa is in Rationalist – and, let's be honest, Fascist – style. Now a museum holding a collection of decorative arts and furnishings, it offers a fascinating insight into the zeitgeist. The villa also 'starred' in the film *I Am Love* (2009), with Tilda Swinton. The garden is free to visit and gives access to the cafe.

**La Vigna di Leonardo
(Leonardo's Vineyard),
Milan**

📍7
Corso Magenta 65,
Milan
Open Mon–Sun:
  09.00–18.00 (by
  guided tour only,
  see p.368)
Admission fee

Few visitors who gaze in wonder at Leonardo da Vinci's *Last Supper* (1495–98) at Santa Maria delle Grazie then cross the Corso Magenta to visit the late fifteenth-century Casa degli Atellani and its delightful – and unique – garden beyond. This shady, lawned space is ornamented with Japanese maples and roses, statues and a circular pool and fountain. Sitting on a bench here is a pleasure in itself, but venture further in and you discover 'Leonardo's Vineyard'. Don't expect the original hectare of vines: fire, war and ill-considered urban development have destroyed and covered much of the vineyard that was given to Leonardo by Ludovico Sforza, Duke of Milan, in 1498. But archival research has revealed that this is the site of the vineyard that Leonardo loved so much, and for Expo 2015 it was replanted in accordance with photographs taken in 1920. The vine cultivar is 'Malvasia di Candia Aromatica', which was shown by DNA testing to be as close as possible to what Leonardo grew. It is quite something to imagine Leonardo standing proudly in this quiet garden and savouring his vines.

**Orto Botanico
di Padova (Padua
Botanic Garden)**
Padua

● 8
Via Orto Botanico 15,
35123
Open: see p.367
Admission fee

Founded in 1545 by the Venetian Republic on land belonging to the Benedictine monks of St Justine, the University of Padua Botanic Garden – now a UNESCO World Heritage Site – is the world's oldest botanic garden still in its original location. Covering 2.2 hectares and in use since 1546 as a teaching facility, the walled garden originally contained medicinal plants. Preserving its original layout, the garden is today home to about 6,000 taxa, arranged according to taxonomic, utilitarian and historical standards. The design is commonly attributed to the architect Andrea Moroni, but the real mastermind was the learned Venetian nobleman Daniele Barbaro. His design was inspired by medieval *horti conclusi* (enclosed gardens), and the geometric layout is a perfect square within a perfect circle, divided into quarters by perpendicular paths. The oldest plant in the garden is the Goethe Palm (1585), so called because the poet referred to it in an essay in 1817. A recent addition to the south are the five conservatories of the Biodiversity Garden, which contain a cross-section of the world's flora from pole to pole.

Chiesa di San Giovanni degli Eremiti (Church of St John the Hermit) Palermo

📍 9
Via dei Benedettini 20, 90134
Open Mon–Sat:
09.00–19.00; Sun
& public holidays:
09.00–13.30
Admission fee

The small, cool and peaceful church of St John the Hermit dates from the sixth century. It was converted into a mosque in the aftermath of the Islamic invasion (AD 827) and re-consecrated in about 1136 by the Normans, who had taken the island in 1061; Roger II of Sicily entrusted the church then to the Benedictine monks of St William of Vercelli. The building has been extensively modified over the centuries, but a late nineteenth-century restoration attempted to bring it back to its medieval appearance. Today the red-domed church is empty, and the real reason to visit is the diminutive rectangular cloister. With its small double columns, their capitals decorated by vegetable motifs and supporting ogival arches, it is the best-preserved part of the ancient monastery. The quadripartite garden with its Arabic cistern is symbolic of both *Jannah* (the Islamic Paradise) and the Christian Garden of Eden. Cobbled paths divide the space into four flower beds, in each of which grows a bitter orange tree, underplanted with flowers. Rest awhile and reflect on all the history the walls have seen.

**Orto Botanico di Pisa
(Pisa Botanic Garden)**
Pisa

📍10
Via Luca Ghini 13, 56126
Open Mon–Sat:
09.00–17.00 & Sun:
09.00–13.00 (Oct–
Mar); Daily: 08.30–
20.00 (Apr–Sep)
Admission fee

Founded in 1543 by the celebrated Pisan physician and botanist Luca Ghini under the patronage of Duke Cosimo I de' Medici, this was the first university botanic garden in Europe. It moved twice during the next half-century, before arriving at its present location in 1591. The 3-hectare walled garden includes fountains, ponds, a library, greenhouses, herb gardens, one of the oldest iron-framed hothouses in Italy and the building that housed the original botany institute (1591–5), its facade ornamented with seashells. The layout of the garden is much simpler than that of its Paduan cousin (see p.227): the 148 rectangular beds are arranged in pairs either side of an axial path, interspersed with pools. Unusually, the beds are grassed, and the specimens cultivated in little squares set into the sward. Look for the large gingko tree (*Ginkgo biloba*), planted in 1787, and the exceptional collection of aquatic plants, some of them extinct in the wild. The fascinating museum is heir to the ancient gallery of 'natural objects' set up in 1591 by the Grand Duke of Tuscany, Ferdinando I de' Medici, to collect the 'works of nature'.

Chiesa del Santissimo Redentore (Church of the Most Holy Redeemer)
Venice

📍 11
Sestiere Giudecca, 30133
Open: see p.366
Admission fee

Built on the island of Giudecca by Doge Alvise I Mocenigo in thanks for the city's deliverance from an outbreak of plague (1575–7), Il Redentore was designed by Andrea Palladio and consecrated in 1592. It is also the centrepiece of one of the city's most important public celebrations, the Feast of the Redeemer, held on the third Sunday of July. This charmingly unpretentious productive garden belonging to the Capuchin monastery is behind the masterpiece of Renaissance architecture (which from this aspect looks a lot like a mosque), creating an engaging juxtaposition. The roughly rectangular garden is enclosed to the east by a wall and on the other three sides by rows of honey-coloured brick buildings. Providing a relaxing contrast with the narrow streets of tourist-filled Venice, it is a simple pleasure to stroll over the large, empty lawns and stone-flagged paths, to enjoy the vines and kiwi fruit, the small olive grove and the orchard of apple and cherry trees, and to admire the beds with their serried ranks of delicious-looking vegetables. It is also possible to visit the monastery's small cloister.

Fondazione Querini Stampalia (Querini Stampalia Foundation)
Venice

📍12
Santa Maria Formosa,
Castello 5252, 30122
Open Tue–Sun:
 10.00–18.00
Admission fee

This magnificent sixteenth-century residence in the central district of Castello is the only palazzo to have survived the end of the Venetian Republic unaltered. In 1869 it was opened to the public at the behest of Conte Giovanni, the last descendant of the Querini Stampalia family. The unmissable museum also boasts a garden created in 1961–63 by the acclaimed Venetian architect Carlo Scarpa, in a rectangular courtyard that formerly contained a barn. It is conceived as a flowing, unified space with no visual interruptions from the palazzo's facade to the end wall, and this is achieved through the use of vertical architectural elements in wrought iron and glass. The main lawn is planted with Japanese flowering cherry, a Judas tree (*Cercis siliquastrum*) and a *Magnolia* x *soulangeana*; drapes of evergreen ivy clothe the walls. A waterlily rill terminates at the eastern end in a square, mosaic-surrounded pool with a complex fountain. The space is liable to flooding, so the design incorporates channels and even areas that water may pass through and into – including the atrium of the building itself.

Ca' Morosini del Giardino
Venice

📍 13
Sestiere Cannaregio
4629, 30121
Open by appointment:
   see p.365
Free

Open only by appointment, this garden is completely hidden behind high walls, tucked away alongside the Rio dei SS Apostoli. In the mid-seventeenth century the Morosini family bought and renovated a complex of buildings – including the one that still bears their name – during which the original garden was paved over to create a rectangular court. At the start of the eighteenth century, the courtyard housed a menagerie before being redesigned once more as a garden in 1829. The L-shaped garden is now run by Dominican sisters and retains the characteristics of Venetian gardens: a charming formal mix of edibles and ornamentals. Structured geometrically, its paths run between rectangular stone-edged beds, some planted with vegetables. A statue of the Virgin Mary stands in a small grotto, and numerous ironwork pergolas are smothered variously with wisteria, roses and Virginia creeper. The collection of fruit trees includes apricots, figs, medlars and pomegranates, while the mix of ornamentals includes hydrangeas, mimosa, dahlias, irises and a Carolina allspice (*Calycanthus floridus*).

Patsy R. and Raymond D. Nasher Sculpture Garden, Peggy Guggenheim Collection
Venice

● 14
Palazzo Venier dei Leoni, Dorsoduro 701, 30123
Open Wed–Mon: 10.00–18.00 (closed Christmas Day)
Admission fee

Trees cast dappled shade over this hidden sculpture garden, while geometrically clipped hedges and rocket-like pencil cypress introduce organic structure. The texture, shape and varied greens of the perimeter foliage create a backdrop for some sculptures, while others emerge from beds of ferns. Nestled in the midst of the mid-eighteenth-century Palazzo Venier dei Leoni, by the architect Lorenzo Boschetti, this asymmetrical courtyard once housed a lion – or so legend has it. The sculpture garden that Raymond Nasher (see p.308) helped design opened in 1995, and today the patterned paving and sculptures suggest a free-flowing extension of the architecture and the exhibits within. For thirty years from 1949, Peggy Guggenheim transformed this palace on Venice's Grand Canal into a cultural heaven. It now contains her collection of twentieth-century art, and most of the works in the other outdoor spaces are from the permanent collections (by Arp, Goldsworthy, Hepworth, Moore and Richier, to name just a few). Before departing, pay your respects to Guggenheim, buried in the garden.

**Palazzo e Giardino
Giusti (Giusti Palace
and Garden)**
Verona

📍15
Via Giardino Giusti, 2,
37121
Daily: 09.00–20.00
(Apr–Sep); 09.00–
19.00 (Oct–Mar)
(closed Christmas
Day)
Admission fee

Across the River Adige east from the old city, among the crumbling facades of the Via Giardino Giusti, is an arch through which a hint of green is visible. Enter and be immersed in an oasis of calm named after the noble family that bought the land in the fourteenth century and that has tended the garden since creating it in the late sixteenth century. The garden, immediately juxtaposed to the palazzo, comprises nine squares arranged three by three. This highly formal garden was laid out in 1570 and restored in the 1930s. With its rocket-like Italian cypresses (*Cupressus sempervirens*), topiary and hedged mazes, neat lawns and statues, grotto and waterworks, it is considered a masterpiece of Renaissance garden art. Although fairly large, it is not overwhelming, and being of perfect scale and harmony it is always tranquil: a place of old-fashioned refinement away from irascible drivers and honking horns. It is always possible to find a hidden corner, especially in the more informal area to the east, where paths weave among trees and the belvedere offers a lovely view out over the city.

● N

0   300   600   900
━━━━━━━━━━━━━━━ yd.

Palazzo del Quirinale (Quirinal Palace)
Rome

📍 16
Piazza del Quirinale, 00187
Open Tue–Sun: 09.30–16.00 (closed Thu & Aug)
Admission fee (guided tour only)

Some hidden gardens one simply stumbles across, others – such as this one – require planning to visit. But do, because, perched like an island atop the highest of Rome's seven hills, this 4-hectare garden is a magnificent blend of seventeenth-century formality and eighteenth-century romance. Be impressed by the wide Palm Tree Avenue and twelve adjacent, richly planted geometric flower beds, and enjoy the fountains and pools, and the elegant coffee house. Particularly special is the enclosed Boschetto, a formal grove with straight paths, dense planting and arbours, that was restored in the twentieth century. It was made in 1560 by Ippolito d'Este (of Villa d'Este fame), who rented the estate that became the Quirinal Palace. Eighteen times the size of the White House, and the official residence of the President of Italy, the palazzo was designed by Ottaviano Nonni for Pope Gregory XIII and completed in 1585. Reservations for the long tour must be made at least five days in advance; book via the website, arrive at the Porta Giardini on Via del Quirinale fifteen minutes beforehand, and bring ID.

Villa Aldobrandini
Rome

📍 17
Via Mazzarino 11, 00184
Daily: dawn–dusk
Free

This villa, now an international institute headquarters, enjoys an enviable location in central Rome near Trajan's Market. It was built in the early seventeenth century by Cardinal Pietro Aldobrandini, the nephew of Pope Clement VIII, who in 1598 had given Pietro another Villa Aldobrandini in the town of Frascati, renowned for its famous garden. The grounds of this Roman garden were dramatically reduced to their current 8,000 square metres by the construction of the Via Nazionale in the late nineteenth century; and in 1926 the Italian state bought the gardens and opened them to the public. Yet the walled garden hidden some 10 metres or so above street level is almost always empty. The staircase up to the informal garden features second-century archaeological ruins from the site, and at the top rough gravel paths meander between amorphic, boulder-edged, mounded lawns enlivened by a scattering of headless classical sculptures and burbling fountains. The planting is mainly of camellias, citrus and palms; notable trees include a ginkgo tree and a cockspur coral tree (*Erythrina crista-galli*).

Orti Farnesiani sul Palatino (Farnese Gardens on the Palatine)
Rome

📍 18
Via di San Gregorio 30, 00186
Daily: 08.30–1 hour before sunset (closed Christmas Day & New Year's Day)
Admission fee

Near the Arch of Titus, and affording a commanding view of the ruins of the Roman Forum below, this small yet pleasant formal garden occupies the northern part of the Palatine Hill (the entry ticket covers both Forum, Palatine and the Colosseum, and is valid for two days). With its circular pool, moss- and fern-encrusted *Fontanone*, cool, watery grotto and rose-planted, box-edged beds, it offers a welcome break from the surrounding rocky, bricky archaeology. It is but a small remnant of the great formal terraced garden created by Cardinal Alessandro Farnese in 1550 over the ruins of the first-century Palace of Tiberius. Unfortunately, though understandably, most of what had been the first private botanic garden in Europe was destroyed by archaeological excavations in subsequent centuries. However, as well as offering splendid views, the garden is a cool and serene rest stop, a place perhaps to contemplate the significance of the Palatine Hill, for it was here that Rome – and hence the whole of the Roman Empire – was founded under the direction of Romulus.

Villa Celimontana
Rome

● 19
Via della Navicella,
00184
Daily: 07.00–dusk
Free

The verdant lawns of this charming yet slightly tumbledown and little-known garden, just ten minutes' walk south of the Colosseum or east from the Baths of Caracalla, are the perfect place to enjoy a picnic or take a shady break from sightseeing. Walk the winding pathways through the greenery that covers most of the valley between the Caelian and Aventine hills, enjoy the tree-framed vistas, and discover the scattering of ancient marble artefacts and features, including an Egyptian obelisk, fountains and a fishpond. This 'archaeological landscape' is nineteenth century, but the villa and garden were originally designed in 1580 by Jacopo del Duca, a student of Michelangelo, for the nobleman Ciriaco Mattei. The obelisk, a gift from the Capitular magistrates in 1582, became a focal point of the innovative Baroque gardens made in 1645–8 by Ciriaco's nephew Girolamo, who also commissioned fountains from Bernini. There are two entrances: one near the Basilica Minore di Santa Maria in Domnica alla Navicella, and a more attractive, hidden one near the basilica of SS Giovanni e Paolo, on the Clivo di Scauro.

**Parco Savello
(Savello Park)
Rome**

📍 20
Piazza Pietro D'Illiria 1,
00153 (main entrance
Via di Santa Sabina 37)
Daily: 07.00–18.00
(Oct–Feb); 07.00–
20.00 (Mar & Sep);
07.00–21.00 (Apr–
Aug)
Free

Set on the Aventine Hill, the attractive Basilica of Santa Sabina all'Aventino was built in AD 422 and is widely considered the best example of an early Christian church in Rome; its fifth-century carved wooden doors are not to be missed. It is also famous as the motherhouse of the Dominican order, having been presented to St Dominic by Pope Honorius III in 1219. Beside it to the northeast, hidden behind a high brick wall, is the Parco Savello, also known as the Giardino degli Aranci (Orange Garden). Overlaying the monastery's vegetable garden, the 7,800-square-metre garden is now mostly lawn and, as its name suggests, planted with bitter orange trees; in spring, the perfume from the blossoms is heady. According to legend, St Dominic planted the first orange tree here, a sapling he had transported from Spain. The present design, by the architect Raffaele De Vico (from 1932), is formal, with an umbrella pine-shaded path aligned on a terrace at one end. From this belvedere is a beautiful view of the Eternal City. Romantics come for the sunset, which can be spectacular.

**Giardini Vaticani
(Vatican Gardens)**
Rome

● 21
00120 Vatican City
Daily: 09.00–18.00
  (guided tours only)
Admission fee

The Vatican, the world's smallest state (covering 44 hectares), must also be the richest in gardens: the nearly 23 hectares occupied by the Vatican Gardens is more than half the entire area. Hidden behind walls north and west of St Peter's Basilica, the private gardens – perhaps landscape would be a better word – cover the Vatican Hill and parts were famously laid out by Donato Bramante in the early sixteenth century, during the pontificate of Julius II. Baroque, English landscape and contemporary additions create a congruous mix of styles and an enlivening visit. Much of the sloping site is lawn, peppered with various trees and buildings. Here and within the landscape are the Rockery Wall, the Lourdes Grotto, the Eagle Fountain, the formal parterres of the Italian Garden (pictured) shaded by tall cedars, the elegant French garden with its views, and the sylvan English Garden with its classical sculpture scattered among the trees. Access is possible only on an official tour, which lasts about two hours (book via the website). The day issue ticket also includes entry to the Vatican Museums and Sistine Chapel.

1   Franjevački samostan
    (Franciscan Monastery)
    Dubrovnik, p.245
2   Galerija Meštrović
    (Meštrović Gallery)
    Split, p.246
3   Numismatic Museum
    Athens, p.247
4   Sofia University
    Botanic Garden
    Sofia, p.248

Franjevački samostan (Franciscan Monastery)
Dubrovnik

📍 1
Placa 2, 20000
Daily: 09.00–18.00
Admission fee

Dubrovnik's Franciscan monastery, just inside the city's historic Pile Gate, dates from 1317 and is still active. Its primary role has always been to tend the sick, and so the monks established a profitable pharmacy. Now housed in the Old Pharmacy Museum, it is the world's third-oldest functioning apothecary. To supply ingredients, a physic garden was planted in the cloister, which was built in 1360 in late Romanesque style by master mason Mihoje Brajkov. It is one of Croatia's most beautiful, with its harmonious colonnade of slim double columns each boasting a different geometric, plant-, human- or animal-like capital. The central space is divided in two by a paved path lined with stone benches, backed by a low hedge, and at the terminus is an ornate bowl fountain (now dry). Sit on the cool stone, enjoy the delicious contrast between the green foliage and the white limestone walls, luxuriate in the shade cast by palms and inhale the aromas of the two raised herb beds. The cloister of the Dominican monastery at Ulica Svetog Dominika 4 in the city's northeast is another green retreat four minutes' walk east.

**Galerija Meštrović
(Meštrović Gallery)
Split**

● 2
Šetalište Ivana
Meštrovića 46, 21000
Open Tue–Sun: 09.00–
   19.00 (May–Sep);
   Tue–Sat: 09.00–
   16.00 & Sun: 10.00–
   15.00 (Oct–Apr)
Admission fee

Ivan Meštrović (1883–1962) is not as well known as he should be: he was a student of Rodin, who thought him the 'greatest phenomenon among sculptors of the world'. This museum, about twenty minutes' walk west of the Riva (Split's downtown promenade), displays a stellar collection of his lovely works. With its pleasant formal gardens and stunning views south over the Adriatic, the imposing marble villa was designed by Meštrović as a residence, studio and gallery in 1931. The gardens are complementary – geometric and uncomplicated, yet with hints of classical influence. A paved path leads from the entrance gate, on either side of which is a lawn displaying a sculpture. Ascending to the villa, the imposing flight of steps is flanked by four narrow terraces, each mass-planted with low shrubs, including lavender; white-columned pergolas on either side mark the garden's edges. Shade is cast by palms and tall cypress. The admission price includes access to the Kaštilac, a former fortress that Meštrović converted into a private chapel. It contains twenty-eight beautiful wooden reliefs by the sculptor.

Numismatic Museum
Athens

● 3
Panepistimiou 12,
106 71
Open Tue–Sun:
  08.30–15.30
Free (admission fee
  for museum)

The Greeks have never been great ornamental garden-makers. It is a treat, then, to discover a little green hideaway a four-minute stroll north of the Parliament building and Syntagma Square. Look for the elegant, pale-yellow three-storey mansion in neoclassical-cum-Renaissance Revival style, built by Ernst Ziller in 1880. Behind, protected from the noisy street, is an elegant, peaceful garden courtyard and cafe. Pass through the side gate and be greeted by a statue of Diana in a circular bed of roses flanked by shrubby borders and clipped citrus trees. A flight of balustraded steps overarched by a vine-clad pergola to the rear of the building leads to a stone-flagged patio edged with statues and informally shaped beds. The planting is mostly of citrus and lantana. Have a Greek coffee and reflect on the house's history. Named 'Iliou Melathron' (Palace of Troy), it was built for the archaeologist Heinrich Schliemann, who famously excavated Mycenae and Troy, and it was considered Athens' most magnificent private residence. Today it is home to one of the world's most important collections of coins.

247

**Sofia University
Botanic Garden
Sofia**

● 4
49 Moskovska St, 1000
Open Mon–Fri: 09.00–
    17.00; Sat & Sun:
    09.00–18.00
Free

Directly northwest of the Vasil Levski Monument roundabout, and a two-minute walk northeast of St Alexandar Nevski Cathedral in the east of the city centre, this is the oldest of three botanic gardens attached to Sofia University. Square and bijou, it covers about 0.5-hectare, including 500 square metres of glasshouses, home to collections including aroids, bromeliads, cacti and other succulents, cycads and orchids. Outside, the lawns, pale honey-coloured gravel paths, statuary and flower beds are laid out artistically and informally. A lovely touch is the arrangement of tiny brick- or cobble-edged beds set into the wide gravel path. Highlights include the Mediterranean, Rock, Rose and Water gardens, and a delightful country-house kitchen garden in miniature. The garden, which continues to pursue its scientific, educational and cultural mission, was founded in 1892 by the university's first professor of botany, Dr Stefan Georgiev. At its inauguration, King Ferdinand I planted an oak tree that thrives still; sit under its branches and think that the region was once covered by dense oak forests.

Africa

**Bayt Al-Suhaymi
(Al-Suhaymi House)**
Cairo

● 1
9 Al Tambaksheyaa,
El-Gamaleya
Daily: 09.00–17.00
Admission fee

The graceful courtyards are integral to the beautiful and ingenious architecture of this, the best example of a seventeenth-century wealthy Cairean residence, and now a museum. On entering the house you reach, via a zigzag corridor, the central flagged courtyard or *sahn*, with its palm- and cycad-fringed lawn. The north-facing *takhtabush* – a sort of portico – is a cool place to sit in the morning, while the *mashrabiya* windows overlooking the garden enabled women of the household to enjoy the view without being seen by guests. The *sahn* also had a functional purpose – to circulate cool air. The second, larger courtyard is mostly paved and features wooden pergolas, clipped shrubs and borders of bougainvillea, palms and ancient trees. The domed structure pierced with coloured glass is a sixteenth or seventeenth-century mausoleum, moved here in 1952. Built in 1648 by Abdel Wahab el Tablawy, the house was bought in 1796 by Sheikh Ahmed al-Suhaymi, whose family expanded it. It offers a truly remarkable insight into how the elite lived during the Ottoman period.

**Genenet El Asmak
(Aquarium Grotto
Garden)**
Cairo

● 2
El Gabalaya St, Al
Gabalayah, Zamalek
Daily: 09.00–16.30
  (closed Tue)
Admission fee

On the west of Gezira island, just north of the German Embassy,
is the 3.8-hectare, triangular Aquarium Grotto Garden. Wide paths
lead between lawns dotted with oleander and shady palms, and
there are beds of shrubs and a lake crossed by a bridge. But the
most striking feature is the grotto, a warren of bridges and steps,
caverns and tunnels that appear to be made of adobe but are
actually concrete. Trees and palms poke out here and there, the
view from the top is worth the climb, and former fish tanks in
the naturally lit caverns contain somewhat bizarre natural history
exhibits. Completed in 1867 and filled with a collection of exotic
plants from all over the world, as well as a menagerie of African
reptiles, the garden – with the rest of the island – was part of the
private estate of Khedive Ismail (1830–95). The garden was opened
to the public in 1902 by the English army officer and zoologist
Stanley Flower, who added the aquaria to house a collection of
rare African fish. The garden is not as glorious as it once was, but
renovations began in 2000 and are ongoing.

**Hadikat Al-Andalus
(Andalusian Garden)
Cairo**

● 3
El Andalos Park,
Zamalek
Daily: 07.00–22.00
Admission fee

Registered on the list of Islamic and Coptic monuments, and located across the Qasr El Nil Bridge from Tahrir Square on Gezira island, in the affluent district of Zamalek, this 0.84-hectare park is only a few minutes from bustling downtown Cairo. But here, away from the city's frenetic traffic, you can take a quiet promenade along the riverbank and watch the feluccas, stroll among the formally landscaped gardens and admire their features, or simply relax on a palm-shaded bench. Established in 1929 by Zulfugar Pasha as a present to his wife, this formal garden was formerly part of the Gezira Palace Garden and has three parts. The Andalusian Garden is intended to resemble the Moorish gardens of southern Spain and features mosaic-edged grass steps descending to a large pool and fountain. The Pharaonic Garden is home to a number of replica artefacts, including several sphinxes and obelisks, while the turquoise Fayrouz, or Al-Fardus, features an arabesque design. A public park since the 1940s, it is a favourite with Cairenes, a great place to people-watch or simply enjoy the sunset.

Dar Si Said (Museum of Moroccan Arts)
Marrakech

● 4
8 rue de la Bahia
Open Wed–Mon:
  09.00–16.45
Admission fee

Just north of the Bahia Palace, hidden away in a lane, the Museum of Moroccan Arts occupies the former residence of a brother of the Grand Vizier of Marrakech, Ba Ahmed (1840–1900). The elegant two-storey Mudéjar-style building, with its delightful interior features including intricately decorated ceilings, tiling and carved cedar woodwork, is charming in its own right, as is the small, shady courtyard garden. Its form, as you might expect of an Islamic garden, is quadripartite, with the four beds divided by perpendicular paths tiled in zigzags of green and white; they intersect at an ornately carved open wooden pavilion. The structure covers a geometrically tiled raised platform in which is an octagonal pool with fountain. Trees cast welcome shade, and the beds are enlivened with angel's trumpet, banana and *Crinum* spp. The effect is one of understated elegance and grace, wonderfully tranquil and cool. It is also worth asking the watchman for the 'harem': he may show you another pretty tiled courtyard that is not generally open to the public.

El Bahia Palace Garden
Marrakech

📍 5
5 rue Riad Zitoun
el Jdid
Daily: 08.00–17.00
Admission fee

Stylistically a blend of Moroccan, Andalusian and Islamic, El Bahia (the name means 'brilliance') was built piecemeal by a father and son, both Grand Viziers to successive Alawid Sharifs (Moroccan sultans). As a result, the palace and garden complex has a charmingly irregular, almost haphazard layout. The oldest (smaller) part, built by Si Moussa in 1859–73, is lavishly decorated with beautiful and intricate stuccowork, painted, inlaid woodwork and *zellige*, a form of polychrome tile mosaic. Yet the decor is refined, with ambience. The highlight of the garden is the *chahar bagh* (quadripartite) courtyard. Enclosed by richly stuccoed walls and surfaced with *zellige*, the four beds surrounding a marble fountain are lushly planted with exotic taxa including bold-foliaged banana, evergreen citrus and ornamental ginger. The new parts of the palace were built by Ba Ahmed in 1894–1900. His aim was simply to surpass the achievements of his father. Here the highlight is the large peristyle courtyard with *zellige* paths defining the quarters of white marble and ornamented by three fountains on the main axis.

**Le Jardin Secret
(The Secret Garden)
Marrakech**

● 6
121 rue Mouassine
Open: see p.368
Admission fee

Following seventy years of neglect, this mid-nineteenth-century complex of two *riads* was restored in the 2000s. Le Jardin Secret opened in 2016 and features two courtyard gardens with general layout and planting by the British garden designer Tom Stuart-Smith. The larger Islamic Garden has been returned to its eighteenth-century *chahar bagh* layout, but with contemporary planting. A central scalloped bowl and fountain feed a rill that runs towards the boundary pavilion, and paths made of turquoise brick delineate the four beds (or gardens), each with a central pool and fountain. The perimeter planting is of palms and olive trees, while the beds are a carpet of ornamental grasses from which rise citrus trees. Beside the paths the greens are enlivened by splashes of flower colour. The smaller Exotic Garden comprises a central rill fed by a formal pool and an arrangement of mostly rectangular beds divided by herringbone brick paths. The lush planting is a deliberately global mix, echoing the experimental nature of Marrakech's great gardens of the past. For a great view, climb the tower.

Andalusian Gardens
Rabat

● 7
Kasbah les Oudaias
(at the southeastern
tip of the kasbah
complex, near
ave Al Masa)
Open: 24/7
Free

At the southern edge of Rabat's historic citadel – the Kasbah les Oudaias – stands the seventeenth-century palace built by Ismail Ibn Sharif. Today it is a museum of Moroccan art and culture, and the Andalusian Gardens created during the French protectorate (1912–56) occupy a courtyard enclosed by thick, crenellated walls. A series of geometric beds is defined by a grid of straight, ornately patterned pebble paths interspersed with the occasional fountain bowl. The long pergola is smothered with vines, and a combination of raised beds, stone benches and steps navigate the slopes. The beds are filled with exotic trees and flowers, including angel's trumpet, banana, citrus, marigolds, marvel of Peru, oleander, palms and roses, while swathes of cheerful bougainvillea and morning glory add vibrantly to the show. This is a lovely spot and relatively unvisited; take a shaded seat and prepare yourself for the hectic streets of the Kasbah. While in the citadel, do climb to the Plateforme du Sémaphore, the plaza at the high point, and enjoy the splendid views over the Bou Regreg River and the Atlantic Ocean.

**Dar el-Makhzen
(Sultanate Palace)
Tangier**

● 8
Place de la Kasbah
Open Wed–Mon:
    10.00–18.00 (closed
    public holidays)
Admission fee

The Dar el-Makhzen was constructed outside the medina in the seventeenth century by Sultan Moulay Ismail and is now home to the Kasbah Museum, containing collections of Moroccan arts and archaeological finds. Enjoy the palace's two lavishly tiled courtyards decorated with wooden ceilings, marble fountains and arabesques; and once you are done with the exhibits, enter into the lush Andalusian garden behind its high walls. With its white-pillared, blue-beamed wisteria and vine-smothered pergola over four perpendicular brick paths meeting at a marble bowl fountain, the layout is clearly Islamic-inspired. The four hedge-edged beds are planted with diverse taxa including bougainvillea, cabbage tree, canna, citrus, hydrangea, jacaranda, lantana, loquat and oleander, while additional ornament is a somewhat eclectic mix of terracotta pots, Roman columns and cannon. But the result is a shaded and tranquil haven, the perfect spot in which to cool off. The palace is on one of the city's highest points, with spectacular views over the medina and across the Straits of Gibraltar to Spain beyond.

Tangier American Legation Institute for Moroccan Studies
Tangier

📍9
8 rue d'Amerique
Open Mon–Fri:
   10.00–17.00
   Sat: 10.00–15.00
Admission fee
   (museum)

Offering repose for those exploring the maze of the old medina is this shady courtyard within the sprawling compound of what was the first American public property purchased outside the United States, and is still the only US National Historic Landmark on foreign soil. Formerly known as the American Legation Museum, this lovely example of Islamic-inspired architecture is in the Bni Idder quarter. The original building – of which little remains – was given by Sultan Mulay Suleiman (1766–1822) to the United States in 1821 to serve as a diplomatic presence in Morocco (the first country to recognize the fledgling United States, in 1777). The structure was rebuilt in 1848 and repeatedly expanded during the nineteenth and twentieth centuries, and today houses a museum, a library and cultural facilities. Rest a while in the restored trapezoid east courtyard garden with its citrus trees, fountain and octagonal pool. Then climb the steps to the orange-tiled patios, find a shady nook and enjoy the view over the courtyard, its paving pattern and varied materials defining the quadripartite *chahar bagh* form.

Oranjezicht City Farm
Cape Town

📍 10
Upper Orange St,
Oranjezicht
Open Mon–Fri:
 08.00–16.00
 Sat: 08.00–13.00
Free

Oranjezicht means 'Orange View', and the story of the Oranjezicht City Farm (OZCF) is one of history turning full circle: an urban farm where once was the Upper Table Valley's largest farmstead. On arriving, take in the stunning views north towards downtown and south to Table Mountain, then explore the beautiful, productive garden. The diversity of well-cultivated vegetables and fruits set within twelve beds defined by cobbled paths is a picture. Wander through the geometrically asymmetrical layout to the eye-catcher, an oval pool on the main axis fed by a long rill and set within a square pattern of beds. The original farmstead was worked by the Van Breda family for seven generations before the homestead was demolished in 1957. The land was subsequently levelled for a bowling green, and in 2009, after years of neglect, the site was cleaned up. In 2012–13 the green was converted into the OZCF, which is also a volunteer project that celebrates local food, culture and community while performing a vital educational role, teaching both horticulture and how to improve diet through good eating.

The Company's Garden
Cape Town

📍 11
19 Queen Victoria St
Daily: 07.30–20.30
  (Sep–Mar); 07.00–
  19.00 (Apr–Aug)
Free

This delightful green refuge in the city centre dates from 29 April 1652, when the master gardener Hendrik Boom of the Dutch East India Company (VOC) sowed the first seeds of a new productive garden. Its purpose was to feed the settler community and revictual Dutch ships on their way to and from Southeast Asia. Within ten years the garden had grown to its present size. In 2014, in acknowledgement of its origins, the VOC Vegetable Garden was made next to the Rose Garden in the southwestern corner of the garden. Delightful, Baroque-inspired and formal, with neat wooden divisions, plant supports and serried ranks of heritage varieties of fruit, vegetables and herbs, the garden is beautiful, educational and evocative. After enjoying this corner, do venture further and explore the wider garden. It was redesigned as an ornamental garden by the British and became a botanic garden after 1848, before evolving gradually into a pleasure park. Head for the Public Garden with its green lawns, refreshing fountains and fine collection of plants and display gardens.

The Old Fort Garden Durban

📍12
208 K.E. Masinga Rd
Daily: 09.00–15.00
(museum closed weekends & public holidays)
Admission fee

From the road a wooden lychgate marks the entry into a shady, quiet and informal haven brimming with a diverse mix of trees and shrubs, ground cover and flowers. Winding among the lush flora, lawns and defensive earthworks that are now interestingly shaped landforms are stone-flagged paths and steps. Here and there tile plaques give helpful information about the memorials and other historical features. The complex contains a museum (well worth visiting), a small chapel (once the arms and ammunition store) and a military cemetery. As a whole, the Old Fort – a National Monument – affords a fascinating insight into the history of Durban and KwaZulu-Natal, for it was here in 1842 that the Dutch besieged a contingent of British troops as part of a failed attempt to establish the Republic of Natalia. The British rebuilt the fort in 1858 and it was in use until 1897, after which it fell into decay. Its saviour was Brigadier General G.M.J. Molyneux (1873–1959), who revamped the buildings and made the garden. Many of the trees and cycads still thriving here were grown from seed collected by him.

North America

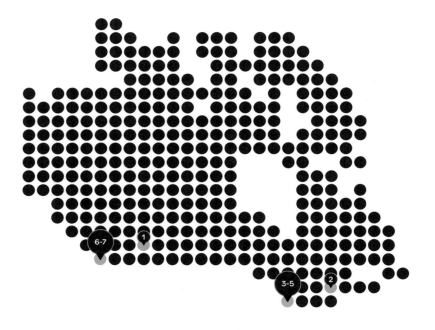

Devonian Gardens
Calgary, AB

📍1
Fourth floor, CORE
Shopping Centre,
333 Seventh Ave
SW, AB T2P 1B5
Open: see p.369
Free

On the fourth floor of the downtown CORE Shopping Centre, this tropical conservatory and botanic garden was donated to the city of Calgary by the Devonian Group of Charitable Foundations and Calford Properties. Originally designed by J.H. Cook Architects and Engineers, it opened in 1977. In 2012 the 1-hectare conservatory underwent major renovations by Janet Rosenberg & Studio, resulting in this linear, informal, well-lit garden. Bright and vibrant, the plantings of tropical taxa are of horticultural significance, and there is also a large 'living wall'. The hard landscaping features elegant wooden and black stone-flagged paths meandering among large raised beds. Among the flower beds are geometric raised pools in the same dark colour as the flagged floor, filled with koi and enlivened with computer-controlled fountains. Here and there, contrasting with the verdant jungle of the planting, are pieces of sculpture by local artists. This is also a family-friendly garden with flexible seating, an adjacent food court, a well-equipped kids' play area and climbing wall.

Château Ramezay
Montreal, QC

📍 2
280 Notre-Dame East
St, QC H2Y 1C5
Daily: 09.30–17.30
(1 Jun–Canadian
Thanksgiving only,
see p.369 for
museum times)
Free (admission fee
for museum)

The garden of this unprepossessing stone building (1705) with red shutters, opposite City Hall, was inaugurated in 2000 as part of a comprehensive restoration. The original garden (some 3,900 square metres) has been lost to urban development, and the Governor's Garden behind the house, a vignette of 750 square metres, is a reconstruction in the formal French Colonial style. Descend the steps behind the museum that now occupies the building, or enter the walled garden through the gateway obscured by the trees of Place de la Dauversière, and you are met with a formal rectangular garden of three compartments, each divided into square beds. To the north is the *verger* (fruit garden), the *jardin ornemental* (pleasure garden) is in the middle and the *potager* (vegetable garden) to the south. Herbs and medicinal plants fill beds surrounding the compartments and against the long wall. The historic taxa cultivated are as close as possible to those grown by Claude de Ramezay, the French governor, whose house it was. This hidden city garden is as unexpected as it is likeable.

**Cloud Gardens
(Bay Adelaide Park)**
Toronto, ON

● 3
14 Temperance St,
ON M5H 1Y4
Open Mon–Fri:
10.00–14.30 (closed
public holidays)
Free

Nestled beneath the high-rise towers of the busy downtown area, between Richmond Street West and Temperance Street (with entrances on both), there is both an indoor and an outdoor garden to explore. The small, award-winning conservatory reopened after a revamp in 2015, and the environment inside imitates a cool, moist cloud rainforest. The flora includes tree ferns, palms and other exotic taxa to provide year-round interest; for the full visual and 'cloud' experience, take the ascending walkway and exit near the waterfall. The elaborate outdoor landscape was designed by Baird Sampson Neuert Architects and the MBTW Group/Watchorn Architect in association with two artists: Margaret Priest and Tony Scherman. The eastern section features a zigzag walkway that rises past the waterfall and Priest's monument to Toronto's construction workers. To the west the pathways are integrated with a small grove of trees set around a semicircular lawn. The whole park looks particularly attractive illuminated at night.

**Sheraton Centre,
Toronto Hotel**
Toronto, ON

● 4
123 Queen St West,
ON M5H 2M9
Open: 24/7
Free

Across Queen Street West from Toronto City Hall stands the Brutalist Sheraton Centre. However, hidden within the complex, between the hotel's three-storey entrance on Queen Street and the eleven-storey block behind, is an open-air courtyard. The green and peaceful garden within, by the Modernist landscape architect J. Austin Floyd, opened in 1972. Terraced on three levels, it features naturalistic rockwork, two waterfalls (the water system recycles condensate from the hotel's heating and cooling system) and naturalistic, woodland-like planting. Sit in the plaza on the uppermost level in the shade of silver birch trees growing in concrete planters and enjoy the sound of moving water in the pool, which is backed by borders of woodland taxa. Flowing out, water falls over the upper rocky waterfall into a middle pool crossed by a bridge and surrounded by tall stone wall planters. From there the water cascades over staggered rocks to the lowest pool, which is edged with rough stones and borders of shade-tolerant taxa, including hostas and ferns.

**Podium Green Roof,
City Hall**
Toronto, ON

📍5
100 Queen St West,
ON M5H 2N2
Open Mon–Fri:
07.30–21.30; Sat, Sun
& public holidays:
08.00–18.00
Free

In his Modernist design for the podium level of Toronto City Hall in 1965, the Finnish architect Viljo Revell envisioned a raised public plaza, but his scheme never came to fruition and the space was left a dull expanse of concrete. However, as part of the revitalization in 2009 of Nathan Phillips Square in front of City Hall, and with the intention of both reducing the building's environmental impact and contributing to urban sustainability, Revell's concept was realized, albeit in a contemporary way. Inaugurated in 2010 and often called the Podium Green Roof, Canada's largest publicly accessible roof garden is a retreat for residents and visitors alike all year round. Reached by a ramp, it features large flower beds planted with bold drifts of ornamental grasses and perennials (including sedums, yarrows and daisies) that are impressive in their own right and unite to create a tapestry-like meadow effect. Meandering among the beds are white walkways with wooden benches, some protected by shades, where it is possible to soak up the ambience and enjoy the views of downtown Toronto.

**Dr Sun Yat-Sen
Classical Chinese
Garden**
Vancouver, BC

● 6
578 Carrall St,
BC V6B 5K2
Open: see p.369
Admission fee

There are in fact two green spaces in Vancouver's Chinatown named after the first president of the Republic of China: the publicly accessible Park, designed in Chinese style by the landscape architects Joe Wai and Don Vaughan using North American materials, and – linked to it by an informal pool – the Classical Chinese Garden. Conceived by Wang Zu-Xin and inspired by Ming Dynasty (1368–1644) scholars' gardens, it was, when it opened in 1986, the first scholar garden outside China. With its arrangement of pavilions and covered walkways (constructed using fourteenth-century methods – no glue, screws or power tools), fantastical Taihu rocks imported from Lake Tai in eastern China, pebble-mosaic paving and calm, mirroring pond, the design adheres to the philosophical principles of Taoism and the mythology of the Islands of the Blessed. Those familiar with Suzhou's gardens will notice, too, that Vancouver's climate supports many of the same taxa, including flowering plum, lotus and winter-flowering jasmine. Guided tours are available at no additional cost.

**Vancouver Public
Library**
Vancouver, BC

📍 7
350 West Georgia St,
BC V6B 6B1
Open: see p.370
Free

It took more than two decades to come to fruition, but in 2018, as an integral element of the $15 million expansion and enhancement of Vancouver's Colosseum-esque central library, the 'garden in the sky' opened to the public. In the 1990s the architect Moshe Safdie had envisaged a public roof garden as part of his competition-winning design, but the space realized by the landscape architect Cornelia Oberlander was an inaccessible albeit successfully environment-ameliorating green roof. As part of the revamp, Oberlander has remodelled the roof garden with its wavy drifts of plants native to British Columbia (blue and green fescue grasses and the shrubby kinnikinnick, or bearberry) symbolizing the water, shore and forest of the Fraser River, which flows through the region; and planted trees, to create a 2,400-square-metre contemplative area that is in keeping with the Roman character of the building. Visible from the neighbouring building, the new design has also opened up the building's upper levels to create a two-storey glass atrium and north and south planted terraces.

Museum of Contemporary Art Denver
Denver, CO

📍1
1485 Delgany St,
CO 80202
Open: see p.370
Admission fee

On the roof of this contemporary building – designed by Sir David Adjaye in 2007 to minimize the boundaries between the exterior spaces of the city and the interior galleries of the museum – is *Sky Trapezium*, a permanent garden art installation by Karla Dakin. The geometric, silver-coloured containers on the decked roof are jauntily tilted and angled – deliberately so, in order to manifest a sculptural form that challenges expectations of what a container garden is, as well as to withstand snow loads and high winds. The planters on poles form a roof-on-a-roof, creating a sheltered spot in which to enjoy a coffee from the rooftop cafe and contemplate both the views of distant mountains and the inspiration for the garden: notably the pools at Marble Mines in Colorado and the turf (sod) roofs of pioneers' log cabins, described in novels by Willa Cather and Laura Ingalls Wilder. Introducing a thread of education, the planting uses the native Rocky Mountain flora, and the alpine feel is enhanced by gravel mulch. The use of climate-appropriate taxa has created a successful, well-established floral display.

**Cultural Gardens at
Daniel K. Inouye
International Airport**
Honolulu, HI

● 2
342 Rodgers
Boulevard, HI 96819
Open: 24/7
Free

Honolulu airport has a most unusual departure area, for here international travellers can await their flight outdoors. Designed by the
landscape architect Richard C. Tongg in 1962 are three gardens, one
for each of the islands' most populous cultures: Hawaiian, Chinese
and Japanese. The three are connected by waterways, symbolizing
the intermingling of the cultures, and by paths, bridges and stepping stones. The Hawaiian Garden is a tropical paradise of koi-
filled lagoons, bubbling springs and lava-backed waterfalls. *Hala*
(pandanus) and *kukui* (candlenut) trees shade *ti* (cabbage palm),
exotic ferns and many types of ginger. Planted with native Chinese
flowering trees, the Chinese Garden has rocky crags, a bright-red
pavilion and an arched bridge that symbolizes crossing the seas
to achieve world peace. Also naturalistic, the Japanese Garden
features a commemorative pagoda, a zigzag bridge (to confuse
evil spirits) and a shingle-roofed shelter with stone benches. For
those flying inter-island, the C.B. Lansing Garden (1995) is on the
ground level of Terminal 2, near the walkway to the Main Terminal.

**Bellagio Conservatory
and Botanical Garden**
Las Vegas, NV

● 3
Bellagio Hotel, 3600
South Las Vegas
Boulevard, NV 89109
Open: 24/7
Free

Across the lobby from the front desk as you enter this famous hotel is the elegant 1,300-square-metre Conservatory. Protected within is a floral extravaganza, a breathtaking display of flowers massed in their thousands, designed around a structure of trees, gazebos, bridges and ponds (although water features can be added or removed). The displays are changed five times a year, and every year the seasonal designs are different. The season begins with Chinese New Year and a showcase of traditional motifs. Spring brings a Japanese feel and cherry blossom, followed by a summer playground of fragrant flowers. Autumn is of course dominated by fiery reds, oranges and yellows, and after Thanksgiving the Christmas display begins, widely regarded as the most stunning of all, with extraordinary colours and complementary fragrances. When the displays rotate, 90 per cent of the plants are recycled as mulch. Do check the website for the dates of display changes: during replanting, the Conservatory doesn't look its usual amazing self for a couple of days.

Blue Ribbon Garden
Los Angeles, CA

● 4
Walt Disney Concert
Hall, 111 South Grand
Ave, CA 90012
Daily: 07.00–22.00
(closed before and
after performances,
see p.368)
Free

The Frank Gehry-designed Walt Disney Concert Hall, with its dazzling stainless-steel exterior, is instantly recognizable. Opened in 2003 and home to the Los Angeles Philharmonic Orchestra, it also hides a secret, for on the roof terrace (most easily accessed from the corner of South Grand Avenue and West 2nd Street) is the Blue Ribbon Garden, named after the centre's volunteer support group. Designed by the landscape architect Melinda Taylor and covering nearly 4,000 square metres, the informal and sublimely quiet garden is paved with pale limestone that harmonizes with the building's metal exterior. Sinuous, lushly planted island beds define winding paths. Scattered among the shrubs, perennials and ornamental grasses are seasonal vegetables and herbs grown and harvested for the complex's Patina restaurant. Walking through the garden beneath the shade-giving trees or sitting at one of the tables allows a softer, more intimate interaction with the striking building than that experienced at street level. The garden is available to hire, and can be closed in the event of a private function.

**James Irvine
Japanese Garden
(Seiryu-en, Garden
of the Clear Stream)**
Los Angeles, CA

📍5
Japanese American
Cultural & Community
Center, 244 South San
Pedro St, CA 90012
Open: see p.369
Free

Just ten minutes' walk from City Hall and entered via the Japanese American Cultural & Community Center (JACCC), this small, triangular garden mostly below street level was designed by the landscape architect Takeo Uesugi. Named after the foundation that generously made it possible, it is also called Seiryu-en (Garden of the Clear Stream) for its 52-metre-long meandering, tumbling and chattering boulder-edged watercourse. The design is a version of the Japanese strolling garden style (to be entered, not merely viewed), but Seiryu-en is much smaller and more intimate than a traditional strolling garden. It is also more densely planted, with a greater diversity of flora, but the native Japanese plants – the perennials, shrubs and trees (in spring the *sakura* blossom is followed by azaleas) perfectly complement the garden's compact form and topography. Other features include a handcrafted cedar bridge, stone lanterns and a stone *tsukubai* or ritualistic hand-washing bowl and fountain, reminiscent of a Tea Ceremony garden. Do also visit the adjacent JACCC Plaza designed by Isamu Noguchi.

Spring Street Park
Los Angeles, CA

📍6
428 South Spring St,
CA 90013
Daily: dawn–dusk
Free

Opened in 2013 on a former car park between two historic high-rise condominiums, this pocket park of 2,800 square metres between 4th and 5th streets brought much-needed green space to downtown Los Angeles. With its bright-red path taking a direct route across the L-shaped space and linking the pavement to the oval green lawn, the asymmetrical mix of geometry and sinuous forms and the strong use of colour are clearly modern Californian. It provides something for everyone: concrete benches and seating, flower beds of native species, a splendid waterfall that cascades from an angled steel wall into a pool whose edge doubles as seating, a path (looking like a running track with lanes – it is for exercise), a small, blue-surfaced children's play area and a dog run (some dog owners don't clean up after their hounds as they should, so watch your step). There is even a security guard. Overall, this is not a place of great tranquillity and repose, but in this busiest part of town it is refreshing to be able to pause, rest weary limbs and catch one's breath.

Moorten Botanical Garden and Cactarium
Palm Springs, CA

● 7
1701 South Palm Canyon Drive, CA 92264
Open: see p.370
Admission fee

This 4,000-square-metre family-owned botanical garden is on the very western fringes of the city, a seven-minute drive south of the Palm Springs Art Museum (see opposite). It is home to an impressive collection of over 3,000 taxa of cacti and other desert-adapted plants, yet is as quirky as it is prickly, with bits of kitsch ornamentation here and there. Nevertheless, the arrangement of architectural and sculptural specimens in beds defined by large boulders or simply rising up out of the dry soil, in combination with the lawns, palms, elegant house and hilly desert backdrop, is stunning. The garden is owned and run by Clark Moorten, son of Chester 'Cactus Slim' Moorten. The latter, a skilled horticulturist with a passion for cacti, also had a Hollywood career, acting alongside W.C. Fields and Buster Keaton, among others. Tuberculosis put paid to his movie stardom, and in 1933 he moved to Palm Springs and revived his passion for cacti. In 1939 he met Patricia Haliday, who became his wife, and together they plant-hunted and established and ran this unique cacti museum until his death in 1980.

Dorothy and Harold Meyerman Sculpture Garden, Palm Springs Art Museum
Palm Springs, CA

● 8
101 North Museum Drive, CA 92262
Open Fri–Tue:
10.00–17.00;
Thu: 12.00–20.00
(see also p.369)
Admission fee

On the western edge of downtown Palm Springs, this small museum punches above its weight with exhibitions of contemporary, Native American, Western and Pre-Columbian art, and two exquisite L-shaped sculpture gardens. Sunk below street level, partly shaded by the building's overhang and with slightly cooler air thanks to the fountains in the jaggedly shaped, asymmetric pools, in both gardens the artworks are complemented by sculptural, native plantings of drought-resistant plants and trees set in beds of rocks and gravel. Enjoy a refreshing drink – the chairs and tables are for cafe patrons – and plan a trip to the Palm Springs Art Museum in Palm Desert, twenty-five minutes' drive along routes 111B and 111 (72-567 Highway 111, Palm Desert, CA 92260). There, the beautifully landscaped garden of the Faye Sarkowsky Sculpture Garden (lower picture), a 1.6-hectare oasis of water features, winding paths, robust native plantings and natural rock benches, is the perfect backdrop for works by Donald Judd, Betty Gold and Yehiel Shemi, among other modern masters.

Lan Su Chinese Garden
Portland, OR

● 9
239 Northwest Everett St, OR 97209
Open: see p.369
Admission fee

Covering an area of about 4,000 square metres and occupying a city block a little north of the downtown area in Chinatown, this little bit of China in Oregon hides behind a white wall pierced with ornate 'leak windows' that frame views in and out. This beautiful space is arranged around the large, central Lake Zither, and for maximum enjoyment do keep your pace leisurely. Stroll under the covered walkways and over bridges, explore the fantastical water-sculpted rocks (imported from Lake Taihu) and sit beneath the pavilions to enjoy the picturesque vistas. More than 400 Chinese taxa make up the planting, including collections of magnolia, peony, camellia and bamboo. Built in 2000 by 65 Chinese artisans to a design by Kuang Zhen Yan, Lan Su is said to be one of the most authentic Chinese gardens outside China. It was inspired by the great classical scholar gardens of Portland's Sister City, Suzhou, and sounds from the names of both cities inspired the garden's name – which also translates as 'Gardening of Awakening Orchids'. There is an authentic tea house and free guided tours.

Keller Fountain Park
Portland, OR

● 10
SW 3rd Ave & Clay St,
OR 97201
Open: 24/7
Free

Designed by the American landscape architect Lawrence Halprin (see also p.292), this park became part of his Open Space Sequence, a vision for the transformation and re-greening of neglected city blocks. The 3,700-square-metre city-block park, which opened in 1970, was renamed in 1978 to honour Ira Keller, head of the Portland Development Commission (1958–72). It is fringed with grass and native lodgepole or shore pine (*Pinus contorta*). The fountain was designed by Halprin's colleague Angela Danadjieva and, with 49,000 litres of water a minute pouring over concrete cascades, it has a geometric, abstracted naturalism inspired by waterfalls in the Columbia River Gorge. From the pavement steps lead down to a pool into which the fountain cascades. With its large, square stepping stones the pool was designed for accessibility and interaction, and Danadjieva saw it as a refuge from the city streets. Visitors are encouraged to stroll over or sit on the stepping stones, and even to play in the water, giving varying perspectives on the dramatic fountain with its cooling cascades.

Tanner Springs Park
Portland, OR

● 11
NW 10th Ave,
OR 97204
Open: 24/7
Free

Located in the Pearl District, north of downtown, Tanner Springs Park occupies a block and stands on what was Couch Lake and a wetland fed by streams including Tanner Creek. Today the lake is beneath 6 metres of landfill. This 'urban waterscape' is a charming and thoughtfully integrated juxtaposition of naturalistic and artistic. In its calming, gently running streams and cobbled paths meandering through plantings of tall native grasses, there are echoes of the lost natural landscape. But walk the jigsaw-edged boardwalks over the water, or sit on the grassy steps and take in the view of the *Artwall* running along the eastern perimeter with its backdrop of residential blocks, and you could only be in a very contemporary urban green space. The *Artwall* installation is composed of 368 reclaimed train track rails from Portland, set on end and interspersed with 99 pieces of local blue glass, hand-painted by sculptor and landscape architect Herbert Dreiseitl with images of amphibians and insects. The 3,700-square-metre park was designed by Ramboll Studio Dreiseitl and GreenWorks PC and opened in 2003.

Church of Jesus Christ of Latter-day Saints Conference Center
Salt Lake City, UT

♦ 12
60 North Temple,
UT 84150
Daily: 09.00–21.00
Free

Built on a 4-hectare plot, this vast conference centre is symbolically deferential to the smaller Salt Lake Temple immediately to its south, so its architectural mass was reduced by submerging the building into the rising landscape. Its northern and eastern sides are clad entirely with huge stepped terrace planters filled mostly with native coniferous and deciduous trees. To the west of the main entrance, steps enlivened by tall cascading waterfalls ascend to the roof. From here, and aligned on the building's main axis, the roof garden rises in four broad flights of steps and terraces. Each terrace is flanked by large, rectangular tree-filled planters and water basins, into which fall wall fountains. At the high point stands a fountain in a square pool within a circle of tree-planted beds. To the west, the roof is covered with a 2-hectare alpine meadow designed by the landscape architects Laurie Olin and Susan K. Weiler, and showcasing twenty-one taxa of local grass. The overall effect is that the centre becomes a landscape unto itself, harmonizing with the mountainous terrain of the Wasatch Range, in full view beyond.

**New Mexico Museum
of Art**
Santa Fe, NM

● 13
107 West Palace Ave,
NM 87501
Open: see p.370
Admission fee

Just northwest of the historic Santa Fe Plaza, and offering a welcome
escape from the sun, this rustic-looking adobe building is in Pueblo
Revival style, a synthesis of Native American and Spanish Colonial
architectural forms. Designed in 1917 by Isaac Rapp, it is home to the
state's oldest art museum, with a rectangular courtyard garden at
its centre. Surrounding the garden space is a carved, red-and-blue-
painted wooden beam and adobe peristyle (covered walk), sometimes decorated with red chillies drying in the sun. The garden is laid
out geometrically, with four perpendicular concrete paths converging
on the tall, dark, sculptural stone fountain down which water gently
trickles. The four defined spaces are lawn fringed with beds in which
the mixed planting includes ornamental grasses, dahlias, hollyhocks,
hostas, dwarf pine and roses. Don't miss the museum's two sculpture
gardens, in walled courtyards to the east and west of the main building.
In the western courtyard, sit on a bench underneath the wisteria-
smothered pergola and study the bronzes and other works.

Waterfall Garden Park
Seattle, WA

● 14
219 2nd Ave South,
WA 98104
Open Mon–Fri:
    08.00–15.45
Free

At the corner of 2nd Avenue South and South Main Street, this park can be heard before it's seen. In spring and summer the surprise is heightened by the enclosing foliage, which precludes a clear view into the park. This small (446 square metres), delightful and entirely unexpected pocket park features a covered L-shaped terrace with chairs and tables surrounding a sunken courtyard, offering views of and access to the brick-paved seating area below. Enlivened with seasonally planted circular containers and evergreens in granite-edged beds, and shaded by Japanese maples, this lower area adjoins a pool on two sides. The walls are clad in large rocks and in the northwestern corner white water cascades over boulders at a rate of 50,000 litres a minute. Created in 1977 to commemorate the birthplace of the United Parcel Service (UPS) in 1907, the garden has echoes of New York City's Greenacre Park (p.332). The Japanese-influenced design by the landscape firm Sasaki, Dawson & DeMay is powerful and the space imparts a strong, lasting impression.

Freeway Park
Seattle, WA

📍15
700 Seneca St,
WA 98101
Daily: 06.00–22.00
Free

Perhaps the most unusual thing about this iconic park is its location, perched above Interstate 5. But also surprising are the Brutalist concrete landforms. They are in fact abstracted expressions of Seattle's topographic undulations. The park is composed of three irregular, intertwined plazas that bridge and reconnect Downtown and First Hill. Differentiated water features give each plaza its own identity, but the park is unified through the common use of materials: board-formed concrete containers and walls, broadleaf and evergreen trees, and furnishings. Opened in 1976 and incorporating George Tsutakawa's Naramore Fountain, the 2.2-hectare park was designed under the direction of Angela Danadjieva, then at Lawrence Halprin & Associates (see p.287). In 1990 Danadjieva's practice was commissioned to extend Freeway Park; and a renovation in 2010 revamped the mature trees, grassy areas and seasonal planting. Many landscape professionals acknowledge that this precedent-setting park 'single-handedly defined a new land-use typology for American cities'.

Cottage Row Mini Park
San Francisco, CA

📍 16
Between 1900
& 1942 Sutter St,
CA 94115
Daily: 06.00–22.00
Free

Walk east along Sutter Street from its junction with Fillmore Street and after about 80 metres, on the left-hand side, is a signpost for Cottage Row. A narrow red-brick path ascends northwards from here to exit on Bush Street, and along it stand twenty-two small, charming and well-maintained wooden houses. They were built by William Hollis during the late 1860s and 1870s, and most are on the National Register of Historic Places. The small park runs next to the houses. Greeting you at the entrance on Sutter Street are low, stone raised beds planted with pink roses and blue agapanthus, among other shrubs and perennials. Behind are two small lawns with benches on which to sit and enjoy this delightful little time capsule that offers a glimpse of pre-earthquake San Francisco. Continuing upwards, the path is edged with a mixed border, and in front of the houses, a narrow bed. Planting includes bamboo, bird of paradise and bougainvillea, softening the path's linearity and creating a welcoming green tunnel. This is a residential area: do respect sociable hours.

343 Sansome Rooftop Deck
San Francisco, CA

📍 17
343 Sansome St,
CA 94104
Open Mon–Fri:
  10.00–17.00
Free

In the busy heart of the downtown Financial District, this roof terrace is accessed via the lobby of 343 Sansome Street – take the elevator up to the 15th floor. This stylish space has a grove of olive trees planted in huge white concrete pots shading a paved area amply provided with benches, tables and chairs. Raised beds of granite filled with mixed planting add a softer dimension to the textures, forms and colours of an otherwise formal space. At the eastern end of the rectangular terrace is the multicoloured sculpture *Four Seasons Obelisk* (1987) by Joan Brown, standing in the centre of geometric flooring in grey, red, white and black. The combination of features and planting subtly makes this relatively large space feel welcoming and intimate. The roof garden is an example of POPOS, or Privately Owned Public Open Space, which since 1985 the City has required developers in downtown commercial districts to include with the intention of providing 'quality open space in sufficient quantity and variety to meet the needs of downtown workers, residents and visitors'.

Fay Park
San Francisco, CA

● 18
2366 Leavenworth St,
CA 94133
Daily: 10.00–16.00
Free

In 1957 Mary and Paul Berrigan commissioned the eminent landscape architect Thomas Church to design the 1,000-square-metre garden behind their house (built 1912). On her death in 1988, Mary bequeathed the property to the city, and after Paul's passing in 1998 the garden was opened as Fay Park. The only publicly accessible example of a Thomas Church garden, it is entered through a simple gate in the white fence that runs up steep Leavenworth Street. The formal, symmetrical garden – characteristic of Church's subtlety, elegance and grace – rises in three terraces, each with stacked stone retaining walls and ornamented on the upper terrace with a white balustrade. The flower beds, some edged with trimmed box, are filled with roses, perennials, ornamental shrubs and fruit trees. Focal points are the twin latticed gazebos that stand sentinel on the main (top) terrace, from where there is a view down over the garden and over the house to San Francisco Bay beyond. The tall light rising from the lower terrace of the stairs was once a street lamp in Copenhagen.

**Grace Marchant
Garden**
San Francisco, CA

● 19
**202 Filbert St,
CA 94133**
Open: 24/7
Free

To fully enjoy this lovely linear garden, which runs beside Filbert Steps on the eastern side of Telegraph Hill, start at the bottom. The steps begin at the end of Filbert Street, between 1299 and 1301 Sansome Street. Ascend over a climber-clad rocky outcrop and turn to admire the first view, of the Golden Gate Bridge. It is here, where the wooden steps start, that the garden proper begins. Either side of the railings is a riot of annuals, climbers, perennials and shrubs – among them angel's trumpet, busy lizzies, ceanothus, glory bush, *Hedychium* spp., palms, roses, wisteria and *Zantedeschia aethiopica*. The beauty continues to build as the garden reaches Napier Lane, where Grace Marchant lived. She began planting the steep hillside in 1949, and pursued the project until her death thirty-three years later. Today the garden is protected by the Trust for Public Land. Take the path ever upwards, looking out for the flock of parrots that lives here, across Montgomery Street and Telegraph Hill Boulevard to the top of Telegraph Hill, from where the views over the bay and city are truly superb.

Alcatraz Island
San Francisco, CA

● 20
Alcatraz Island,
CA 94122 (take the
ferry from Pier 33)
Daily: 8:45–18:30
  (dependent on ferry;
  closed Thanksgiving,
  Christmas & New
  Year's Day)
Free (fee for ferry)

A garden might not be the obvious reason to visit this infamous island, but truly the gardens are a highlight and provide fascinating insight into the lives of those who lived – and gardened – there, be they Civil War soldiers, civilian criminals or families of officers and guards. There are seven to explore, all of which have been accurately restored since 2003. On the way up from the Dock, stop to admire the Rose Terrace and Greenhouse before moving on to the neat little flower beds of the Officers' Row gardens (pictured). Each is filled with flowers that would have been cut for the house: bearded iris, marigold, red valerian and roses, among others. At the top of the main road is the Warden's House garden and the Cell House Slope, while on the western side the Prisoner Gardens cascade down in bold, colourful drifts. At their best from January to September, the gardens peak in spring. Free guided tours are offered on Friday and Sunday mornings at 09.45, starting at the Dock. Ferries to the island leave San Francisco from Pier 33, and it is advisable to book well in advance.

**The Rooftop Garden,
The Paul S. Russell, MD
Museum of Medical
History and Innovation**
Boston, MA

📍1
2 North Grove St,
MA 02114
Open: see p.370
Free

Often called the Russell Museum, this small collection is within the campus of Massachusetts General Hospital (MGH), a fifteen-minute walk northwest of the Old State House in the city's historic heart. Atop the award-winning, two-storey, copper-clad building by Leers Weinzapfel Associates is an open-air retreat designed by James A. Heroux of Brown Sardina with lovely views over the surrounding neighbourhoods. The dominant element is the giant white metal pergola that engenders a sense of comforting and peaceful enclosure. The structure of the garden is defined by the regular squared paving paths and the artfully shaped raised beds of varying heights in Cor-Ten steel, among which are scattered wooden benches. The planting makes use of more than thirty taxa and is also structural, with a focus on a mix of deciduous and evergreen shrubs and small trees, ornamental grasses, ferns and ground cover carefully selected to give an impact whatever the season. Do also visit the fascinating museum, which offers an insight into the history of MGH, healthcare in Boston and anaesthesia.

Franklin Street Park
Cambridge, MA

📍 2
494 Franklin St,
MA 02139
Open: 24/7
Free

Near Harvard University's main campus is Franklin Street, a typical Cambridge residential street. Except, that is, for number 494, which is not a clapboard house but a 'parklet'. The 409-square-metre wheelchair-accessible park has been a beloved spot in this dense neighbourhood since its inauguration in 2003. It has what one would politely call a passive character; that is to say, the onus is on the visitor. First of all to find it: the lack of a house is a useful pointer, as is the substantial granite-and-bronze arch, with its echoes of a Japanese *torii* gate, created by local sculptor Murray Dewart. And then, entering by means of the descending paved path flanked by raised beds, to use it. It is attractive and interesting, lush and serene, and perhaps the most conducive way to use the shaded space is to sit and relax, enjoy the sound of the fountain, and soak up the peace created by the informal layout and the natural materials, which include rocks and low ground-cover plantings. Kids will want to investigate the unusual metal dome that emerges from plastic grass at the back of the space.

**Kendall Square
Roof Garden**
Cambridge, MA

● 3
4 Cambridge Center,
Kendall Square,
MA 02142
Daily: 06.00–20.00
Free

From the street, branches can be seen hanging over of the top of a severe concrete structure, a tantalizing hint of what awaits. The unlikely location for this garden is six storeys up, on the roof of the Cambridge Center's parking garage. There is an entrance sign for the garden next to the Green Garage entrance on Broadway. Designed by the landscape architect Richard Kattman and opened in 2001, the garden was originally about the size of a football field (5,350 square metres), but sadly a new building linking the tower blocks on either side has since covered about half of it. It is well maintained and informally laid out, with a mix of lawns dotted with trees and beds planted with shrubs, perennials and bulbs, past which curve brick-paved paths punctuated by circular courts with benches and tables. There is also a small stone sculpture. Raised vegetable beds form part of an education programme on urban gardening run by the building's owners. This fortuitous spot, with its views of the Boston skyline and Cambridge's universities, is all the more welcome for its unexpectedness.

**Heyward-Washington
House**
Charleston, SC

⬤ 4
87 Church St,
SC 29403
Open Mon–Sat:
  10.00–17.00; Sun:
  12.00–17.00 (closed
  Easter, Thanksgiving,
  Christmas Day &
  New Year's Day)
Admission fee

A couple of blocks south of Charleston City Hall, in the midst of the old town, is a Georgian-style, brick, double-fronted house built in about 1772, and behind it, enclosed by climber-clad brick walls, is a small, rectangular garden. Created in the 1930s, it is designed in a formal, late eighteenth-century style, with a stone sundial surrounded by domed topiary. Walk the gravel paths and enjoy the geometric, stone-edged beds enclosed by neatly clipped hedges – the planting features period-correct taxa commonly used in the South Carolina Low Country, including some splendid camellias. Admire the pyramidal supports for climbers, and perhaps take a seat on the elegant white bench. In 1930 the property opened as Charleston's first historic house museum – it was once home to Thomas Heyward Jr, one of four South Carolina signatories to the Declaration of Independence. Moreover, George Washington stayed here in May 1791. The courtyard just behind the house has associated outbuildings: former slave quarters and the only 1740s kitchen building open to the public in Charleston.

Unitarian Church Cemetery
Charleston, SC

📍 5
4 Archdale St,
SC 29401
Daily: 09.00–16.00
Free

The Society of Dissenters began constructing this, the oldest Unitarian church in the South of the United States, in 1772, and it was finally consecrated in 1787. In 1852 the local architect Francis D. Lee was commissioned to enlarge and remodel the building in the English Perpendicular Gothic Revival style. Today volunteers give free tours (donation expected). In the adjacent cemetery the paths are maintained but, in accordance with Unitarian doctrine, the grave plots enclosed by low wrought-iron railings are allowed to return to nature. There is a great diversity of plants, and the wild feel and overgrown look – in particular the huge swags of Spanish moss (actually an epiphytic flowering plant, *Tillandsia usneoides*) hanging from the trees – contrast strongly with the neatly trimmed Lutheran graveyard next door. There is peace and a serene sense of nature and the cycle of life, but also sadness: a deliberately unmarked grave contains the remains of young Anna Ravenel, with whom a youthful Edgar Allan Poe fell in love. It is widely believed here that her tragic story inspired his last poem, 'Annabel Lee'.

North & South Stanley McCormick Memorial Court, The Art Institute of Chicago
Chicago, IL

📍6
111 South Michigan Ave, IL 60603
Open: 24/7
Free (fee for museum)

Either side of the pedimented entrance of the Art Institute of Chicago is a square pocket park. The north garden (pictured right) is a sculpture court designed by the landscape architect Laurie Olin in 1990. The more famous south court (1962–7) was designed by the lauded landscape architect Daniel Kiley, and it remains his best-preserved public commission. The intimately scaled design is simple in both composition and materials. A pair of long raised beds determine the southern boundary; planted with honey locust trees (*Gleditsia triacanthos*) with privet and spring-flowering bulbs beneath, they screen the garden from the busy street. A central axis runs from the entrance to the sculpture *Fountain of the Lakes* (1903) by Loredo Taft, set against the wall of the institute's Morton Wing. In front is a low rectangular pool with fountain jets, and either side, in square raised planters, a gridded bosquet of sixteen cockspur thorns (*Crataegus crus-galli* var. *inermis*), whose crowns form a dense canopy. The institute's Modern Wing also features a small garden with planting by Roy Diblik.

Nasher Sculpture Center
Dallas, TX

📍 7
2001 Flora St, TX 75201
Open: see p.370
Admission fee
  (includes museum
  & sculpture garden)

A fifteen-minute walk north of Main Street downtown, one of the world's finest collections of modern and contemporary sculpture waits to be discovered. The Nasher Sculpture Center opened in 2003 and contains more than 300 masterpieces of the Raymond and Patsy Nasher Collection. Juxtaposed with the museum building (by architect Renzo Piano) is the tranquil 8,100-square-metre garden (by Peter Walker). Stroll the manicured lawns and study works by Matisse, Moore, Picasso and others. The sculptural forms break up the garden's rectangular shape and formal layout, their verticality contrasting with the expanse of flat, green sward and harmonizing with the groves of shade-giving trees. Walk to the garden's end, where two canals run perpendicular to the museum. Separated by a decked path, one has bubbler fountains, the other is still, reflective. Here, too, stepped beds planted with trees and seasonal colour ascend to the boundary, a diametric contrast to the terracing of the open-air theatre descending towards the museum's auditorium at the other end of the garden.

**Simpson Park
Hammock**
Miami, FL

● 8
Corner of SW 15th Rd
& South Miami Ave,
FL 33129
Daily: 08.00–17.00
Free

This remnant of local regional ecology in a highly developed downtown area is technically an urban wild or passive park. Its history began in 1913, when a group of far-sighted individuals persuaded the City to purchase 2.2 hectares to preserve one of the last remaining tracts of Brickell Hammock. (A tropical hardwood hammock is a closed-canopy forest dominated by diverse evergreen and semi-deciduous trees and shrubs, mostly of West Indian origin, that grows at a very low elevation.) The resulting Jungle Park was renamed in 1927 and enlarged in 1940 to its current 3.2 hectares. Today it is home to fifteen endangered plant species, most notably the gulf licaria (*Licaria triandra*), and nine threatened plant species. The recently added pavilion provides an unobtrusive entrance and a meandering loop path of white gravel contrasts with the deep shade and greens of the canopy. Here and there are natural pools and benches, but the main purpose of visiting is to experience a rare survivor of what was once the largest hammock in south Florida. Take ID: visitors are required to sign in.

Loring Greenway
Minneapolis, MN

● 9
1234 Lasalle Ave,
MN 55403
Open: 24/7
Free

This linear park, ornamental pedestrian walkway and urban garden all rolled into one is southwest of the downtown area. Designed by M. Paul Friedberg & Partners in the 1970s, it connects the Lawrence Halprin-designed Nicollet Mall in the east with the Berger Fountain in the historic Loring Park to the west. The surrounding urban landscape is predominantly high-density, low-rise residential and the greenway is a popular commuter route, but out of rush hour it is a very pleasant place to stroll. It provides a winding, ever-changing sequence of varied and human-scale events, and a harmonious admixture of hard landscaping and planting; an entry plaza with attractive brick water feature; additional water features in the form of fountains, rills and cascades; sculptures, pavilions and seating areas; tree-shaded pathways, sloping brick planters and planted bowls; lawns, flowering shrubs and seasonal colour; a pedestrian bridge and a sunken kid's play area; and, at Loring Park, the finale of the mist fountain. Once here, do explore the expansive park and venture west to the renowned Minneapolis Sculpture Garden.

US Courthouse Plaza
Minneapolis, MN

📍 10
300 South 4th St #202,
MN 55415
Open: 24/7
Free

The landscape architect Martha Schwartz has never been one to shy away from controversy in her work, and this plaza (2002) – is it garden or sculpture installation? – continues to generate comments. The 4,645-square-metre roughly rectangular space is stone paved, the pale honey and dark-grey pinstripe laid perpendicular to 4th Street contrasting with the granite strips. Rising from it and inspired by Minnesota's glacial geomorphology is a field of twenty-one variously sized, teardrop-shaped sculptural 'drumlins' (landforms left by retreating glaciers). These are covered with Kentucky blue grass and wild flowers, and the larger ones are planted with native Jack pine (*Pinus banksiana*). To symbolize the region's cultural and natural history and man's manipulation of the landscape, the rough tree-trunk benches are pointers to the state's timber industry. (More comfortable and practical grey metallic benches were added later.) Bronze sculptures by artist Tom Otterness add a touch of playfulness, and the wood-panelled Federal Cafe nearby, offers a warm retreat in cold weather.

Beauregard-Keyes House
New Orleans, LA

📍 11
1113 Chartres St,
LA 70116
Open Mon–Sat:
 10.00–15.00
Admission fee

This historic residence (1826), in an unusual but effective mix of Creole cottage and Greek Revival styles, is now a museum focusing on past residents, notably the Confederate general P.G.T. Beauregard (1818–93) and the writer Frances Parkinson Keyes (1885–1970). The latter undertook considerable restoration, returned the garden to its 1830s appearance, and established the Keyes Foundation, which has owned and run the property since her death. A stone-flagged court behind the house contains camellias and a fountain, but the ornamental garden proper is in an adjacent courtyard. The contrast with the shady, generally informal Latrobe Park (see opposite), a mere block away, is striking. The open, rectangular, formal garden owes much to the Baroque style: its geometric form is defined by brick paths, and beds of white standard roses edged with low hedges of clipped box surround a pool and tall fountain. The museum's entrance is opposite the Old Ursuline Convent Museum (do glance in at its formal courtyard garden), but the garden may be entered via Ursulines Avenue.

Latrobe Park
New Orleans, LA

📍12
1016 Decatur St,
LA 70116
Daily: 06.00–18.00
Free

The French Market District of New Orleans covers six blocks, from grassy Jackson Square to the Farmers' and Flea markets on Barracks Street. This small park (just 1,000 square metres) is about halfway along, on the corner of Decatur Street and Ursulines Avenue. It is dedicated to Benjamin Latrobe (1764–1820), a British man who was one of the first formally trained, professional architects to work in the new United States. He was responsible for the design of the White House porticoes, and spent his last years in New Orleans, where he died from yellow fever while engaged in a waterworks project. The shady park – with its statues, raised beds of shrubs and ground cover, straight, stone-flagged paths and metal benches – stands on part of that project. The main feature, down three steps in a sunken octagonal court and surrounded by benches, is a low octagonal pool with an attractive copper fountain. This is a great place to sit, to people-watch and to listen – there is often live music playing close by. Don't miss the dynamic Gazebo Cafe behind the park.

John F. Collins Park
Philadelphia, PA

📍13
1707 Chestnut St,
PA 19103
Open Mon–Fri:
   08.30–17.00;
   Sat: 10.45–17.00;
   Sun: 12.00–17.00
Free

Formerly called Chestnut Park and tucked next to one of the busiest streets of Philadelphia's bustling business district, this tiny park is easy to miss. Behind a pair of splendid and ornate wrought-iron gates (one of which is usually closed, and so may be admired) is exactly what the weary downtowner yearns to stumble on. This green haven with its welcoming wooden benches, funky tables and chairs, trees casting sun-dappled shade, unusual paving and cheerfully planted concrete tubs and raised beds is a welcoming and hushed retreat for office workers and tourists alike. And it contains a secret, for inside the space opens up and there is an abstract sculptural water feature with jets spouting out over and water flowing between cubist concrete columns. The associated pool is sunken, with steps that can be sat on. Designed by its namesake and opened in 1979, the park was refurbished after 2010, and the new subtle lighting is a great addition. You can even rent the park for a private party or wedding, should you wish.

The Rail Park
Philadelphia, PA

● 14
340 North 12th St
#419, PA 19107
Open: see p.370
Free

A little north of the Center City district runs a 4.8-kilometre stretch of abandoned railway lines that once belonged to the Philadelphia and Reading Railroad. Inspired by New York's famous High Line, a group of enthusiasts is transforming this industrial relic into a modern park or greenway, with plans developed by Studio Bryan Hanes. The ground-breaking for Phase One took place in late 2016, and a 400-metre section from Broad Street southeast to Callowhill Street was completed in 2018. Much of the existing steel structure was restored and further augmented with four large platforms, benches and guardrails of a similar industrial character. Along this linear route a path moves among areas of diverse planting, using taxa that reflect the park's rugged character, and terminates in a series of iconic swings. Eventually the Rail Park will be twice as long and wide as the High Line, with three sections: the Viaduct, the Cut and the Tunnel. However, at the time of writing it is ongoing, and all the more exciting for that. Pay a visit to see the progress, but do check the website first for the latest updates.

**The Secret Gardens
of Independence Park**
Philadelphia, PA

⬥ 15
18th Century Garden
339 Walnut St,
PA 19106 (see p.370
for other locations)
Open: 09.00–dusk
  (closed public
  holidays)
Free

The 22-hectare Independence National Historic Park was created in 1948 in order to preserve sites associated with the American Revolution and the nation's founding history. It includes much of Philadelphia's historic district and several lovely, infrequently visited gardens within a stone's throw of Liberty Bell. The 18th Century Garden (pictured) is a formal, English-inspired period garden with a white-painted pergola fronted by sixteen small, wood-edged, seasonally planted beds. A small orchard contains period-correct heritage varieties. Further along Walnut Street, on the corner of 3rd Street, is the Benjamin Rush Garden (also called the Bishop White Garden), on the site of that Founding Father's house. The Rose Garden is hidden in a landscaped alley that joins Locust and Walnut streets between 4th and 5th streets. Dedicated in 1971 and at its best in June, it features some ninety-six antique cultivars. Almost opposite the Locust Street-end of the path is the Magnolia Garden (best in mid-March), with its pool, lawn and a different magnolia for each of the original thirteen colonies.

Spanish Governor's Palace
San Antonio, TX

● 16
105 Plaza De Armas,
TX 78205
Open Tue–Sat:
    09.00–17.00; Sun:
    10.00–17.00
Admission fee

What the National Geographic Society has called 'the most beautiful building in San Antonio' is next to City Hall in the city's downtown district. This historic white-painted adobe building is all that remains of the early eighteenth-century Presidio San Antonio de Béxar fort complex, built when the city was in the province of Spanish Texas (1690–1821). Moreover, the single-storey building of ten rooms and an 891-square-metre (supposedly haunted) courtyard is the only remaining example of an aristocratic eighteenth-century Spanish Colonial town residence in Texas. In front of the enclosed patio, and set in a square pebble-mosaic floor with a repeating S-motif, stands an octagonal raised pool of roughly hewn stone, its trickling fountain encrusted with a verdant growth of maidenhair fern (*Adiantum capillus-veneris*). The rest of the courtyard boasts beds of shady trees underplanted with tropical species including ornamental gingers, cycads and *Philodendron* spp. Here and there are planted terracotta pots and rustic wooden benches offering shady and enchanting spots to rest.

Briscoe Western Art Museum and River Walk
San Antonio, TX

● 17
210 West Market St,
TX 78205
Open: see p.368
Free (admission fee
for museum)

The Briscoe Western Art Museum celebrates the art, heritage and history of the American West, and a new addition in 2014 was the McNutt Sculpture Garden. On a large crazy-paved patio in ochre and honey tones stands a climber-clad pergola, under which is a wall-mounted bronze. To one side a straight brick path zigzags between beds planted with native taxa and seasonal colour. The sculptures set in the beds and the courtyard include works from across the country, by Sandy Scott, Herb Mignery, Denny Haskew and Doug Hyde. The museum – the brainchild of the architect Robert H.H. Hugman, and completed in March 1941 – sits on an island formed by a loop of the River San Antonio, and is connected at the rear to the San Antonio River Walk. The paved, swamp cypress-shaded path winds gently for 5 kilometres along both banks through the city centre, dotted here and there with lush green spaces. But the walk is also a lively place, with restaurants and bars and an open-air theatre where the sights, sounds and flavours of Native America, Old Mexico and the Wild West blend effortlessly.

Owens-Thomas House
Savannah, GA

● 18
124 Abercorn St,
GA 31401
Open Tue–Sat: 10.00–
17.00; Sun & Mon:
12.00–17.00 (closed
public holidays)
Admission fee

This small, charming courtyard garden is to be found behind an elegant double-fronted house with a Classical portico, perhaps the finest example of English Regency architecture in America. It was built in 1816–19 for the cotton merchant and banker Richard Richardson by an Englishman, William Jay (one of the first professionally trained architects practising in the fledgling United States). The Revolutionary War hero Marquis de Lafayette, staying there in March 1825, addressed an enthusiastic crowd from the veranda at the back. And from here a twin flight of steps flanking a stone urn on a plinth descend into the garden, which is laid out in a hybrid of English knot and Colonial formal styles. Low brick walls contain raised perimeter beds with mixed plantings, while next door's pair of stately *Magnolia grandiflora* add to the composition. Sit on one of the benches and enjoy the formal central area, with its four box-edged beds filled with seasonal colour. Beyond is the Carriage House, which contains one of the earliest intact urban slave quarters in the American South.

Lightner Museum
St Augustine, FL

● 19
75 King St, FL 32084
Daily: 09.00–17.00
(closed Christmas
Day)
Admission fee

In the heart of America's oldest city and opposite Flagler College (the splendid courtyard garden of which is visitable on a guided tour) stands the former Alcazar Hotel, built in 1888. In front is a public garden in Islamo-Hispanic style, with four lawns and a central pool. However, within the Mudéjar-style building is a hidden square courtyard garden, made at the same time as the hotel. The central feature is a geometric pool running the length of the courtyard, home to clumps of papyrus, colourful koi and burbling fountains that create a soothing ambience. An addition to the original design is the perpendicular path and palm-fringed bridge – a popular spot for weddings. The four quarters of the garden are of lawn edged with hedging, ornamented with statuary and stone benches. A victim of the Depression, the hotel closed in 1932, but thankfully the building was saved by the publisher Otto C. Lightner, who opened it as a museum in 1948 to show his vast collections of arts and antiques. Today it is home to one of the American nation's finest collections of nineteenth-century fine and decorative arts.

FOOD ROOF Farm
St Louis, MO

● 20
1335 Convention Plaza,
MO 63101
Open Mon-Fri:
 06.00–18.00
Free

Downtown St Louis has become increasingly populous in recent years, and hidden away atop a two-storey building on the northeast corner of Convention Plaza, close to the popular City Museum, is the FOOD ROOF Farm. Opened in 2015, this community garden with its backdrop of the cityscape has a central paved area with wooden benches and tables, used as both an outdoor classroom and a gathering space for community events. It is a great perch from which to admire this admirable project. Paved and gravel paths provide access among mounded beds of vegetables that thrive on the 790-square-metre roof space. Poles support beans, tomatoes and squash, and there are raised beds of flowers and herbs, a greenhouse, beehives, a chicken coop and innovative approaches to urban agriculture, including hydroponics and vertical farming. FOOD ROOF Farm is the brainchild of Urban Harvest STL, a thoughtful non-profit that establishes urban farms and food projects to grow food 'for people who need it most in our communities', those 'living in nearby food deserts'.

**Hirshhorn Museum
and Sculpture Garden**
Washington, DC

● 21
Independence Ave SW
& 7th St SW, DC 20560
Daily: 10.00–17.30
Free

To the north of the museum by Modernist architect Gordon Bunshaft lies the 0.6-hectare sunken, rectangular sculpture garden displaying over sixty works. Terraced, with a pebbled floor echoing the museum's concrete aggregate and a central reflecting pool, Bunshaft's austere design was remodelled In 1977 by the landscape architect Lester Collins, who also increased the planting. The garden today retains much of the original geometric framework but softened by mature plantings. Indeed, Collins's design better displays the sculptures, allowing them to appear and disappear as one moves about the space. In deliberate contrast to the buildings surrounding it, the museum is part of the Smithsonian Institution but named for Joseph Hirshhorn (1899–1981) who endowed it with his modern art collection. It is in the form of an open cylinder elevated on four massive legs, with a large illuminated fountain in the central, paved courtyard. While here do also visit the picturesque and intimate Mary Livingston Ripley Garden located a short walk northwest of the museum.

**TechWorld Plaza,
Washington DC**

● 22
Techworld Plaza,
DC 20001
Open: 24/7
Free

TechWorld is a pair of very distinctive buildings overlooking Mount Vernon Square in Chinatown, and at first glance the stone, steel and glass edifices connected by a skybridge would not appear to have anything to do with public green space. However, hidden within each building is a courtyard garden. Those with an inquisitive nature will stroll the pedestrianized TechWorld Plaza that separates the buildings at street level and connects I Street NW to K Street NW, and seek out the hidden, shaded passages that pierce the buildings and lead to their courtyards. Bathed in an effective mix of direct and reflected light, each space boasts a small and appropriately Chinese-influenced garden. As delightful as they are unexpected, the garden installations are simple yet effective. The main features are the sculptural arrangements of water-washed rocks resembling Taihu from Lake Tai. The rocks define raised beds surfaced in places with larger cobbles and planted with tall, umbrella-like Japanese maples and lower shrubs, including *Aucuba japonica* and heavenly bamboo (*Nandina domestica*).

Tudor Place
Washington DC

⬥ 23
1644 31st St NW,
DC 20007
Open Tue–Sat: 10.00–
16.00; Sun: 12–16.00
Admission fee

Hidden in Georgetown, four minutes south from Dumbarton Oaks and its famous formal garden by Beatrix Ferrand, this Federal-style house was designed by Dr William Thornton (architect of the US Capitol building) and completed in 1816. Built for Thomas and Martha Custis Peter (step-granddaughter of George Washington), it remained a family home for their descendants until 1983. With its open, sweeping lawns, quaint garden buildings, hidden nooks, natural woodland and collection of mature trees as well as fountains and formal garden rooms (the Knot Garden was added in 2012), the 2.2-hectare garden is varied, beautiful and picturesque. And although successive generations have added their touches, it retains many original design and planting elements. A highlight, therefore, is the collection of unusual heritage varieties still grown here, including yesterday, today and tomorrow forget-me-nots, Florentine tulips and the grape cultivars that smother the North Garden Arbor. This rare surviving example of an intact urban estate from the Federal Period may be explored as you will.

● N

0 450 900 1350 yd.

The Lotus Garden
New York City, NY

● 24
250 West 97th St,
NY 10025
Open: see p.369
Free

New York City has several pocket parks on plots cleared by demolition. The Lotus Garden on the Upper West Side is different, for it was specifically engineered to be a green roof on a low-rise parking garage belonging to a condominium tower. Pass through a wrought-iron gate just to the east of the garage, on the south side of West 97th Street between Broadway and West End Avenue, climb the concrete stair to 7 metres above street level, and be amazed at what it is possible to squeeze into just 650 square metres. The original design, by the horticulturist Carrie Maher and architect Mark Greenwald, is informal and eclectic: woodchip paths snake among amorphous island beds filled with fragrant flowers and foliage, while climbers scrambling over supports and mature trees add a vertical element. The centrally positioned dwarf peach unaccountably grew 4 metres tall, and the three *Amelanchier arborea* trees were donated by the horticulturalist at the Rockefeller Center. Ornaments include statuary and two ponds with goldfish and lotus, which gave the garden its name.

West Side Community Garden
New York City, NY

● 25
123 West 89th St,
NY 10024
Daily 07.30–22.30
Free

Pass through the iron gates with their brick-and-stone pillars on West 89th Street between Amsterdam and Columbus avenues and be greeted by the floral amphitheatre. Descending gently to a sunken oval lawn – used to stage performances and screen films – are steps and twenty-six tiered, wood-retained beds that provide somewhere to sit and are also beautifully planted (the spring tulips are impressive). The Flower Park of which the amphitheatre is the dominant element covers about two-thirds of the garden's 1,500 square metres; other features include a shade garden, ornamental shrubs and a large rockery. The rest of the space is occupied by (fenced-off) members' vegetable beds, with a communal herb bed and espaliered fruit trees. The initiative began life in the 1970s as a guerrilla garden on a vacant, rubbish-strewn plot, and after negotiations with the City Planning Commission, it finally gained permanent status. The concept was developed by members of the community, the award-winning design was executed by Terry Schnadelbach and the garden opened in 1988.

The Frick Collection
New York City, NY

● 26
1 East 70th St,
NY 10021
Open: see p.369
Admission fee

The Gilded Age mansion designed by Thomas Hastings and built in 1914 for Henry Clay Frick (1849–1919), an industrialist and art collector, boasts three gardens. On the lawn of the Fifth Avenue Garden are three magnolias – two saucer magnolias (*Magnolia x soulangeana*) and a star magnolia (*M. stellata*) – planted in 1939 and some of the city's largest. Inside, the classical rectangular and glass-roofed peristyle Garden Court (1935), with its formal pool, ornate fountain and small beds filled with tropical taxa, was designed by John Russell Pope for the museum's opening. The real gem, however, is the formal 70th Street Garden by Russell Page (1977). This is a viewing garden with a rectangular lily pool flanked by tree-planted lawns and gravel paths: a combination designed to create the illusion of space and distance. At the perimeter are low hedges of box and low, colourful plantings in narrow beds. Page said: 'What I was aiming for in this small garden [was] tranquillity, because that is what I feel inside the Frick Collection, and that is the quality shown by the greatest gardens I have known.'

Abby Aldrich Rockefeller Sculpture Garden, MoMA
New York City, NY

● 27
11 West 53rd St, NY 10019 (enter via West 54th Street)
Daily: 10.30–17.30
Admission fee (museum and garden; see p.368)

To visit this hidden, rectangular 2,000-square-metre sculpture garden free of charge, enter via the west gate on West 54th Street between 5th and 6th Avenues, any day between 09.30 and 10.15. But to get the best view, visit the museum's Terrace 5 cafe. Paved with pale-grey Georgia marble, the courtyard is elevated on the three sides abutting the museum, while the central sunken space features two staggered, parallel rectangular canals with fountains and marble bridges, mini-groves of silver birch and beds of ivy, moveable seating, and of course the sculptures. Works include Pablo Picasso's playful *She-Goat* (1950), Tony Smith's *Free Ride* (1962), Ellsworth Kelly's *Green Blue* (1968) and Anthony Caro's *Midday* (1960). Named after one of the museum's founders, this gem was created in 1953 by the architect Philip Johnson and the landscape architect James Fanning. It was enlarged in 1964 by Johnson and the landscape architect Zion & Breen, and restored by Zion Breen & Richardson Associates in 2000–4, who introduced lighter coloured paving and a screen.

Paley Park
New York City, NY

● 28
3 East 53rd St,
NY 10022
Open: 24/7
Free

Walking between the towering blocks of downtown Manhattan you sometimes feel small and insignificant. It is a relief, then, to reconnect with human scale in the compelling, graceful and eye-catching Paley Park. The 390-square-metre rectangular pocket park was designed by the landscape architect Robert Zion as a gift to the city from William Paley, who named it in memory of his father, Samuel, founder of the CBS network. Opened in 1967 and rebuilt to exactly the same design in 1999, it has a Zen-like, sparse beauty. The park entrance is surfaced with red-brown paving, and beyond with granite cobblestones (on which stand sixty Harry Bertoia-designed chairs and twenty marble-topped tables) and it is edged with raised planters of pink granite. Its dominant feature is the 6-metre-high illuminated glass waterfall at the back; the gentle roar of the 6,800 litres of water a minute drowns out the sounds of the city. The planting is as minimalist as the hardscaping, with ivy on the walls, seasonal colour in the planters and a bosquet of honey locust trees (*Gleditsia triacanthos*) in a quincunx pattern.

Greenacre Park
New York City, NY

📍 29
217 East 51st St,
NY 10022 (between
2nd Ave & 3rd Ave)
Open: see p.369
Free

Up a short flight of steps under a pergola and hidden between skyscrapers is a different world. Commissioned in 1971 by the Greenacre Foundation to provide New Yorkers with 'moments of serenity in this busy world', this delightful Midtown haven continues to do exactly that. The rectangular Greenacre Park is a mere 505 square metres, but clever design with lush evergreens, varying textures, sculpted stone walls and a dramatic water feature skilfully creates the illusion of a far larger space. The entrance court, with its grey brick floor, boasts a formal grove of honey locust trees (*Gleditsia triacanthos*), in the shade of which are colourful chairs and tables. Here, a small outpost of Birdbath Neighborhood Green Bakery serves treats. A bed of rhododendrons forms the inner terminus of the courtyard and partially hides a second, sunken seating area in front of the park's dominant feature, the 7.6-metre-high sculptural stone cascade. The soothing noise from the water-fall blocks out the city din. The brick walls are clad thickly with ivy, and to the left is a raised, covered seating area.

**Ford Foundation
Atrium Garden**
New York City, NY

● 30
320 East 43rd St,
NY 10017 (between 1st
Ave & 2nd Ave)
Open Mon–Fri: 09.00–
17.00 (closed public
holidays)
Free

New York City is justly proud of its many small, hidden, ground-level green spaces. It is rare, though, to find a secret conservatory garden, but there is one – on Broadway, in Midtown, not far west of Tudor City (see p.334). And what a splendid discovery it is: a veritable jungle of subtropical taxa, towering trees and cascading vines, foliage and ferns. This tiered garden of three terraces steps down to the focal point, a square, still pool. The terracing is a neat solution to the 4-metre height difference between the entrances on 42nd and 43rd streets. From the atrium's lowest point the bold, exotic and unexpected plantings appear to reach the roof of the 49-metre-high glass-enclosed atrium, but in fact the effect is achieved through planters installed along the edges of the second, third, fourth and tenth floors. The building, completed in 1967 and named a New York City Landmark in 1997, was a collaboration between the landscape architect Dan Kiley and the architects Kevin Roche and John Dinkeloo. Kiley's planting was referenced and refreshed as part of a major refurbishment in 2017–18.

Tudor City Greens
New York City, NY

● 31
24–38 Tudor City Place,
NY 10017
Daily: 07.00–22.00
Free

These two small, tree-shaded parks, one either side of East 42nd Street, are formally laid out, with straight, cobble-edged paths delineating seating or gathering areas and geometric beds. The latter are planted with trees and flowering shrubs, including Judas tree, hydrangeas, holly, magnolia, Japanese maples, Japanese pagoda tree and rhododendrons, complemented by an attractive and varied mix of perennials. These are supplemented in spring by thousands of tulips and in summer by bedding plants. When illuminated, the gardens take on a whole new persona, as they do when covered with a fall of snow. Enjoy the great view of the United Nations building, too. Built in 1927 on a Prospect Hill cliff as a middle-class residential suburb, Tudor City was the world's first residential skyscraper complex. Its far-sighted developer, Fred F. French, set the twelve apartment buildings among parks and open spaces. After a chequered history – in 1972 they were dramatically saved from being built on, by residents obstructing a bulldozer – the gardens were revamped in the late 1980s.

Jefferson Market Garden
New York City, NY

● 32
70 A Greenwich Ave,
NY 10011
Open: see p.369
Free

Beside the imposing High Victorian Gothic of the landmark Jefferson Market Library in historic Greenwich Village, this delightful garden transports you out of the city of cities. Pass through the splendid entrance gates on Greenwich Avenue (between 6th Avenue and West 10th Street), perambulate around the manicured lawn and take in the borders filled with a riot of herbs, annuals and perennials. Soak up the atmosphere on one of the wooden benches along the path before venturing on to explore some of the features, which include a greenhouse and a koi pond with waterfall. The garden is a veritable haven throughout the year, but seasonal highlights include magnolia, ornamental cherries and tulips in spring, and the heady perfume and bright blooms of the box-edged rose garden in summer. Created in 1975 to designs by the landscape architect Pamela Berdan on the site of the Women's House of Detention (noted inmates included Ethel Rosenberg, Valerie Solanas and Angela Davis), the garden was a community project; and it continues to be maintained by volunteers.

St Luke in the Fields
New York City, NY

● 33
487 Hudson St,
NY 10014
Open Mon–Sat:
  08.00–dusk; Sun:
  08.00–17.00 (closed
  public holidays)
Free

With ten terraced houses of similar age, this church (1821) occupies a 0.8-hectare city block forming what the New York City Landmarks Register hails as the 'most significant architectural ensemble in the West Village'. Today five linked gardens cover most of the block, but the first evidence of gardening here was the planting in 1842 of a cutting of the famous Glastonbury thorn (*Crataegus monogyna* 'Biflora'). Its scion still lives in the North Garden, which is dominated by two century-old silver maples (*Acer saccharinum*). In the 1950s Barbara Leighton created the tranquil, saltire-patterned Barrow Street Garden in the southeastern corner, with four richly planted triangular beds and benches encouraging quiet reflection (the use of mobile phones is prohibited throughout). To the northwest is the Gene Morin Contemplation Corner (pictured), its bluestone paving harmonizing with the soft pink, lavender and white planting. The South Lawn, with its butterfly- and bird-friendly trees and shrubs is another quiet place simply to sit and unwind on the sward. Lastly, just south of the church is the Rectory Garden with its delightful roses.

Creative Little Garden
New York City, NY

● 34
530 East 6th St,
between A Ave
& B Ave, NY 10009
Open: see p.369
Free

A block south of Tompkins Square Park, on the site of a tenement that burned down in 1970, this East Village oasis opened in 1978 as a result of the hard work and foresight of a local resident, Françoise Cachelin. At only 7.3 metres wide and 30.5 metres deep, it is more community backyard than garden, but no space is wasted. A winding birch-chip path with ample bench seating leads to a slate patio in the shade of a large willow tree. Stone-edged borders either side of the path are filled with azaleas, tulips, hydrangeas, ferns, roses and perennials, and eight sculptures and a waterfall add more interest. Leave this minuscule oasis, turn right to the junction of Avenue B, and right again to the entrance of the 6 & B Community Garden, which opened in 1983. With its mix of edibles and ornamentals in 125 raised beds and community spaces, this lush 1,650-square-metre plot offers beauty, peace, education and entertainment for residents and visitors alike. The 6BC Botanical Garden on East 6th Street is also worth a visit and only two minutes' walk away (see opposite).

6BC Botanical Garden
New York City, NY

◆ 35
622 East 6th St,
NY 10009 (between
B Ave & C Ave)
Open: see p.368
Free

A little east of two other small gardens on East 6th Street (see opposite) is an ivy-clad black iron fence, marking this beguiling botanic garden. Created in 1981 on a plot formerly occupied by a tenement, it was founded as a community garden – with members contributing to shared spaces. In 1995 a change of direction was made and 6BC became an official botanical garden, the first and only one in Manhattan devoted to biodiversity, horticultural education, neighbourhood beautification and community programming. Pass through the double gate and a weathered red-brick path extends under a climber-smothered wooden pergola. At the end of this tunnel-like approach, the garden opens up, and the path meanders around an assemblage of informal yet well-maintained island beds. An artful melange of bulbs, perennials, shrubs, trees and climbers produces a harmonious and diverse display throughout the seasons. Combined with rock sculptures and rockery beds, ponds, ornamental climbing supports and intimate seating areas, this creates a sumptuous haven that feels much larger than it is.

**Elizabeth Street
Garden**
New York City, NY

● 36
Elizabeth St, NY 10012
Open: see p.369
Free

Little Italy and SoHo have 0.23 square metres of green space per resident, despite the city's goal of at least 10.12 square metres. That makes this calm refuge all the more important. The story of this creative little L-shaped space began in 1989, when gallery owner Allan Reiver decided to clean up a vacant, rubbish-strewn 2,000-square-metre plot and added statues and monuments. The resulting garden was not open to the public at first, but that changed in 2012 with the establishment of the Friends of Elizabeth Street Garden. Today the Friends are fighting city planners to preserve this popular garden as permanent parkland. A wide gravel path punctuated by park benches divides this block-wide park into two almost mirrored halves. Nearest the entrance is mostly lawn, ornamented with an eclectic mix of stone sculpture. Further in, recycled stone balustrading encloses flower beds planted with a mix of perennials and shrubs that delineate nooks where it is possible to hide away and sit in peace. This is not only a lovely space to visit, but also a much-needed sanctuary for local residents.

Teardrop Park
New York City, NY

● 37
Warren St, NY 10005
Open: 24/7
Free

Enclosed by four residential towers at the northern end of Battery Park City, this 0.8-hectare park was designed by the landscape architect Michael Van Valkenburgh and opened in 2004 at a cost of $17 million. It is of mixed use but with an emphasis as a landscape for children, and its aim is to be a natural habitat – a bit of the Hudson Valley in the city – in order to stimulate young minds and provide a safe space for inventive nature play. Yet there is much for older users: the topography, interactive fountains, rocky outcrops, lawns, meandering paths and intimate plantings (almost all the 16,000-odd plants are natives of New York state) combine to create a stimulating environment complemented by precisely choreographed views. A highlight is *Ice Wall*, a magnificent artwork by Ann Hamilton and Michael Mercil. Local sedimentary rocks are stacked to resemble natural strata, and in winter water flows over it, forming icicles. The contiguous Rockefeller Park and North Meadow on the Hudson River is a couple of minutes' walk west, and Washington Market Park a couple of blocks east.

The Elevated Acre
New York City, NY

📍 38
55 Water St, NY 10004
Open: 24/7
Free

Its gridiron street plan and towering architecture mean that most of Manhattan's hidden gardens are shady and enjoy limited views. The Elevated Acre is an exception. On the east side of the busy Financial District, this 0.4-hectare roof garden is accessed via an anonymous-looking recessed flight of steps and escalator between 55 and 60 Water Street. Designed by Rogers Partners atop a four-storey parking garage and tying into Lower Manhattan's 'green necklace' of parks, this secretive space has a large lawn enclosed to the south by an L-shape of stepped seating that creates an amphitheatre setting. Ascend the stone bleachers and the hardwood viewing terrace offers a magnificent panorama over the harbour and the East River to Brooklyn. The decking also fronts the adjacent meadow area. With ample fixed benches and moveable furniture, the paved surface is set with island beds, their asymmetric linear geometry softened by the forms and textures of a glorious mix of ornamental grasses, perennials, shrubs and trees, whose height opens and closes shifting views.

**The Old Stone House
and Washington Park**
New York City, NY

📍 39
336 3rd St, NY 11215
Open: see p.370
Free (admission fee
for house)

Both a Historic House Trust of New York City site and listed on the National Register of Historic Places, the Old Stone House in Brooklyn is at the centre of the 1.2-hectare Washington Park and J.J. Byrne Playground, between 4th and 5th avenues and 3rd and 4th streets. Its small garden has been developed sustainably since 2004 in order to encourage wildlife, and references the site's history. The layout is uncomplicated, with beds under the windows and set in lawn, and enclosed by a wooden post-and-rail fence. The planting is a vibrant riot of period-correct taxa, most of which are useful as food, medicine or dye, and many of which are native. The garden is also an educational resource, and is used by the community. The first farmhouse built on the site, by a Dutch settler, Claes Arentsen Vechte, and his son Hendrick in 1699, was razed in 1897, and the house seen today is a reconstruction from 1933, using stones retrieved from the ruins. Interestingly, the house was situated at the centre of the Battle of Brooklyn (also known as the Battle of Long Island), fought on 27 August 1776.

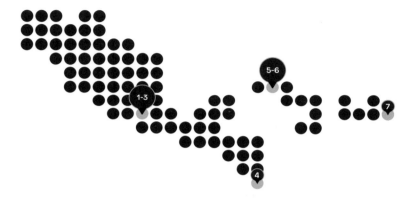

**Museo Casa de la Bola
(Museum of the House
of the Ball)**
Mexico City

◆ 1
Parque Lira 136, Miguel
Hidalgo, Tacubaya
Open Sun: 11.00–17.00
(or by appointment)
Admission fee

Casa de la Bola was first occupied in 1616 by Francisco Bazán y Albornoz, who served as Inquisitor of the Holy Office. The villa (now a museum) retains many of its colonial architectural features, including the cobbled, colonnaded central courtyard that offers a tempting glimpse of the garden beyond. The present garden dates to the 1940s, covers 0.79 hectares and was created by its last private owner, Don Antonio Haghenbeck. He built the beautiful terrace and raised conservatory, and developed a European-style garden with red-tiled walks, ornate fountains and classically inspired sculptures. The ornamental features now peep out from among luxuriant tropical taxa, many of them Mexican natives. Above is a thick, shady canopy of mature trees – although sadly all the original olive trees and magueys (an agave that yields the alcoholic drink *pulque*) have long since vanished. Vestiges of the colonial garden have survived, however, namely the three ponds and the mud channels now colonized by lush vegetation.

**Museo Franz Mayer
(Franz Mayer Museum)
Mexico City**

● 2
Avenida Hidalgo 45,
Centro Histórico,
Guerrero
Open Tue-Fri: 10.00–
17.00; Sat & Sun:
10.00–19.00
Admission fee

In the historic centre of Mexico City, across the wide avenue from the expansive Alameda Central park and next to the small, elegant Plaza de la Santa Veracruz, is the former monastery and hospital of San Juan de Dios (Holy St John). The complex dates from 1582, and the eighteenth-century building that is now on the site has been renovated to house what is often called Latin America's largest collection of decorative arts. Shaded by orchid-encrusted trees and with a gently splashing fountain, the verdant ambience of the stone-flagged former cloister offers a cool, calm contrast to the galleries. The colonnaded courtyard garden with its central stone-edged pool has a distinctively Islamic-cum-Spanish-cum-Colonial feel. However, the pattern of the beds is saltire rather than cruciform. The four beds surrounding the elegant pool are enclosed by low, clipped hedges, and the trees are underplanted with ground cover from which rise azaleas. Flower-ing shrubs in terracotta pots add additional colour. There is also a very good cafe.

**Biblioteca
Vasconcelos
(Vasconcelos Library)
Greenhouse**
Mexico City

● 3
Eje 1 Norte Mosqueta
S/N, Buenavista,
Cuauhtémoc
Daily: 08.30–19.30
Free

A little northwest of the old city stands the remarkable 'hanging library of Mexico City' (2007) by the architect Alberto Kalach. To the north, detached from and almost perpendicular to it, is a remarkable part of the library's garden: an elegant greenhouse, an invigorating architectural union of new glazing and the infrastructure of an abandoned factory building. The artistic combination of new and old extends to the contrasting unity of the planting and Zen-like cobbled dry 'stream' landscaping with the rusty industrial artefacts. Parts of the conservatory stand in a naturalistic pool, which both creates a dramatic setting and helps to unite the structure with the 2.6-hectare botanic garden that surrounds the library. Isolated from the roar of the urban landscape, the garden is a sublime escape. Containing a collection of native and endemic Mexican flora, it is divided into different sections, as Kalach explains: 'You can enter the garden of aromas, and from there you walk on through a forest on the plateau of the city, and then to the side there is the orchard [with] a section devoted to herbs.'

Garden of the Museo Nacional de Costa Rica (National Museum of Costa Rica)
San Jose

📍 4
Calle 17 (between Avenida Central & Avenida 2)
Open: see p.370
Admission fee

To the east of the Plaza of Democracy and the Abolition of the Army (it covers the site of a former barracks) is the martial-looking, mustard-yellow building of the National Museum of Costa Rica. In fact it has two gardens to enjoy. The first, at the entrance, is a lovely 500-metre-square glass atrium butterfly garden. The raised path passes through a riot of tropical plants which are home to twenty-five butterfly species native to the Central Valley. The second garden, a central rectangular courtyard, is open-air and offers views out over the city. Surfaced with an eye-catching asymmetric pattern of concrete and grass and enclosed on three sides, trees soften the architectural geometry of the space and shade corners where it is possible to sit in quietude. The cannons scattered here and there are a reminder that the museum is inside the Bellavista Fortress. Formerly the army headquarters, it experienced fierce fighting during the 1948 civil war. The courtyard was a parade ground, but instead of cannonballs, stone spheres – hand-carved by indigenous civilizations – now ornament a peaceful garden.

**Museo Napoleónico
(Napoleon Museum)**
Havana

● 5
San Miguel & Ronda
Open Tue–Sat:
   09.30–17.00; Sun:
   09.30–12.30
Admission fee

Displaying more than 7,000 objects associated with the life of Napoleon Bonaparte, the first emperor of France, this museum has a deserved reputation as one of Cuba's finest. On San Miguel in the west of the city, near the junction with Ronda, it is housed in the Villa Fiorentina, a vast Renaissance-style palazzo built in the 1920s as the residence of the former politician Orestes Ferrara (the pieces on show are his and those of the sugar baron Julio Lobo). As well as beautiful architecture, the museum boasts an eclectic garden. The view down into the courtyard from the elegant mansion reveals a formal structure of two terraces, fountain, rill, pool and flower beds all set within the grid-like pattern of red tiles and white lines of crazy paving. Once in the garden, sit on a bench and enjoy the planting. While you are in the area, do also walk the short way southwest to the Museo de Historia Natural Felipe Poey. Pass beneath the impressive classical facade and be astonished by the unusual courtyard, shaded by lofty trees and palms that cast a verdant glow.

**Jardín Diana de Gales
(The Diana of Wales
Garden)**
Havana

📍 6
Desamparados
Malecón
Daily: 09.00–18.00
Free

Old Havana is a delight to explore, but if you need a moment or two
of cool quietude, head for this small garden dedicated to the late
Diana, Princess of Wales. It is next to the harbour and bordered by
three roads: Obrapía, Baratillo and the Malecón. Pass through the
iron gate (the crown on top does seem a touch incongruous in this
most communist of countries) under the ironwork pergola and walk
the neat stone and gravel paths. Sit in the shade cast by the kapok
trees, palms and wayfarer's palm, and admire the tropical foliage
underplanting, including *Caladium* spp., *Codiaeum* and ferns. From
the middle of the circular, tiled pool with its fountain jets, which
generate a calming burble, rises a 3-metre-tall Cubist column by the
Cuban artist Alfredo Sosabravo. There is also an engraved Welsh
slate-and-stone plaque from Althorp, Diana's childhood home.
Five minutes' walk west is another small, shady retreat: Parque
Rumiñahui on the corner of Mercaderes and Lamparilla, a tribute
to the twentieth-century Ecuadorian artist Oswaldo Guayasamín,
whose sculpture-fountain, a gift to Fidel Castro, is the focal point.

**La Fortaleza
(The Fortress)
San Juan**

● 7
63 Calle Fortaleza
Open Mon–Fri:
   09.00–16.00
Free

Built in 1533–40 to defend the harbour of San Juan, this UNESCO-listed fortress is also known as Palacio de Santa Catalina (St Catalina's Palace). To the north is a small, formal, sunken garden accessed via white balustraded steps descending from a narrow terrace ornamented by clipped weeping fig in terracotta pots. The main feature of this Spanish Colonial-inspired garden is the oval lawn defined and quartered by a path of brick and stone flags, with a central stone pool ornamented with Islamic-inspired geometric patterns and a fountain. The planting is mostly of foliage plants, including *Dracaena* spp., *Philodendron* and *Schefflera*, and large mango trees cast welcome shade. A second, smaller lawn is home to a modern sculpture – pause here and enjoy the views from the tile-covered brick seats. Since its construction, the fortress has been the official residence of the Governor of Puerto Rico, making it the oldest executive mansion in continuous use in the Americas. A major reconstruction in 1846 gave it its pale blue-and-white facade, which evokes the grace of colonial Spanish architecture.

South America

Brazil, Peru, Chile & Argentina

1 Praça cívica do Quartel
  General do Exército,
  Praça dos Cristais
  (Civic Square, General
  Army HQ, Crystal
  Square) Brasília, p.355
2 Palácio Itamaraty
  (Itamaraty Palace)
  Brasília, p.356
3 Parque Lage (Lage Park)
  Rio de Janeiro, p.358
4 Luciana Brito Galeria
  (Luciana Brito Gallery)
  São Paulo, p.359
5 Casa de Aliaga (Aliaga
  House) Lima, p.360

6 Convento de Santo
  Domingo (Convent of
  St Dominic) Lima, p.361
7 Casa Museo La Sebastiana
  (La Sebastiana Museum
  House) Valparaíso, p.362
8 Museo de Arte Español
  Enrique Larreta
  (Enrique Larreta Museum
  of Spanish Art) Buenos
  Aires, p.363

Praça cívica do Quartel General do Exército, Praça dos Cristais (Civic Square, General Army HQ, Crystal Square)
Brasília

● 1
Praça Duque de Caxias, SMU – Federal District
Open: 24/7
Free

Literally meaning 'Crystal Square' and inaugurated in 1970, this garden (actually an equilateral triangle) is in the Urban Military Sector of Brazil's capital city. Off the beaten track, it is a rarely visited gem by Brazil's most famous and influential modern garden designer, Roberto Burle Marx, and his assistant Haruyoshi Ono. Its dynamic, geometric layout, with no clear start or end, is characteristic of Burle Marx's style; and his coloured plan of the garden could pass as an avant-garde painting. Roughly central to the garden is an asymmetric pool in which stand Ono's four sets of large concrete sculptures; they echo the rock crystals that inspired the garden. The pool reflects the sculptures and sky, and contains islands of planting. The paving is a mix of granite slabs and Portuguese stone laid in various geometric patterns that introduce another element of dynamism to the garden and into which are set geometric flower beds. These are planted with Brazilian natives in masses of the same taxa, creating bold blocks of colour. Notable, too, are the large specimens of *buriti*, a local palm (*Mauritia flexuosa*).

**Palácio Itamaraty
(Itamaraty Palace)**
Brasília

● 2
Esplanada dos
Ministérios,
Bloco H, Palácio
do Itamaraty, Zona
Cívico-Administrativa
Open: see p.370
Free

The impressive Itamaraty Palace (1970) was designed by the architect Oscar Niemeyer, to house the Ministry of Foreign Affairs. It is surrounded by a reflecting lake containing ten abstractly shaped islands planted by the garden designer Roberto Burle Marx using tropical Amazonian taxa. This masterclass in planting design is reason enough to visit, but inside the 'Palace of the Arches' (also home to one of the largest public art collections in Brazil) is another garden, also by Marx, hidden on the top floor. It is not an open rooftop garden per se, but something more subtle and delightful. The dim light of the large, roofed reception areas accentuates the splendid views out over the Esplanade and the National Congress, and contrasts with the central rectangular garden. Intended as a viewing garden, it is illuminated by bars of sunlight cast by the slatted roof. Walking around it, the mix of surfacing materials harmonizes with the raised beds of native vegetation, which are artistic forms in their own right; specimen plants act as focal points, as does the sculpture.

**Parque Lage
(Lage Park)
Rio de Janeiro**

📍 3
Rua Jardim Botânico
330, Jardim Botânico
Daily: 08.00–19.00
Free

Just 1.5 kilometres northeast of the entrance to Rio's must-see botanic garden, and on the same street, is an imperial palm-lined winding driveway leading to an imposingly grand mansion. The garden of the Roman palazzo is geometric and European-inspired, with terraces, trim lawns, a circular fountain and, beyond, ponds and islands. Here, too, built of mortar imitating logs and rocks, are a tower and caves, one of which has twelve aquaria set into its walls. The mansion, once owned by the industrialist Enrique Lage, is now home to the Visual Arts School of Parque Lage, and the highlight is the picturesque swimming-pool courtyard. The excellent cafe serves a superior weekend breakfast. Behind and in striking juxta-position are the steep sides of the 710-metre-tall granite peak of Corcovado, cloaked in 52 hectares of Atlantic rainforest. Pierced by winding pathways and flights of steps, the quiet forest with its streams, pools and many endemic species is a peaceful contrast to the craziness of Copacabana. For the very fit and determined, there is a path to the top and the statue of Christ the Redeemer.

**Luciana Brito Galeria
(Luciana Brito Gallery)**
São Paulo

📍 4

Avenida Nove de Julho
5162, Jardim Europa
Open Tue–Fri:
   10.00–19.00;
   Sat: 11.00–18.00
Admission fee

To the southwest of downtown, on a busy yet tree-shaded street, the Luciana Brito Galeria is housed in a striking white structure: the epitome of postmodern elegance. Approaching the entrance, you pass by beds set into the concrete paving, from which rise cycads, dragon trees and traveller's palm underplanted with tropical ground cover. The gallery's light and airy architecture makes much use of glass, and the interior landscaping displays enforce the sensation that there is little boundary between inside and out. Though the conservatory doors may be slid back to allow access, these are primarily viewing gardens and have something of an art installation feel. Architects and landscape designers worked collaboratively here, using tropical ground cover and sculptural specimen plants (including *Monstera deliciosa Dracaena* spp. and *Philodendron*), combined with large rust-red cobbles set like stepping stones. Established in 1997, the gallery plays a significant role in both disseminating the works of Brazilian artists to a global audience and locally promoting the work of non-native artists.

**Casa de Aliaga
(Aliaga House)
Lima**

📍 **5**
Jirón de la Unión 224,
Cercado de Lima
By reservation only
(see p.370)
Admission fee

Sometimes you are lucky enough to come across a hidden gem that is beautiful, fascinating and unique all at once. This enchanting colonial house near Lima's Plaza Mayor is just such a treasure, and at its heart is a delightful little square courtyard. Surrounded by yellow-painted walls and a wooden-balustraded, tiled walkway on two storeys, the courtyard is accessed from the lower level via a flight of stone steps leading to a pebble floor on which stands a circular stone pool with an ornamental metal fountain. Around the rim of the pool and along the walls are pots of anthurium, delicate maidenhair ferns, cut-leaved Swiss cheese plant and palms, while the branches of a broad-trunked fig form an umbrella above the patio. The house dates from the founding of Lima, in 1535, when the Spanish conqueror Francisco Pizarro granted his ally Jerónimo de Aliaga y Ramírez land next to his residence (today the Government Palace). Aliaga built his home there, and seventeen generations later his descendants still live in it, making it the oldest dwelling in the Americas to be inhabited continuously by the same family.

Convento de Santo Domingo (Convent of St Dominic) Lima

📍 6
Jirón Camaná 170, Cercado de Lima
Daily: 09.30–18.30
Admission fee

A few blocks from Plaza Mayor in the historic centre of Lima, the late sixteenth-century church and convent of Santo Domingo form the oldest and best-preserved religious complex in the city. There are five cloisters, two of which contain gardens that may be visited. The architecture of both is Mudéjar and clearly shows the Islamic influence. The large main cloister is surrounded by a two-storey arched colonnade, the lower level of which is painted red and white. The pillars and walls are decorated with Seville tiles and paintings depicting the life of St Dominic, the Castilian priest who founded the Dominican Order. The turfed garden is enclosed by a low stone wall and divided into four by perpendicular tiled paths that converge on a raised octagonal pool, in which stands a tall bronze fountain. The beds defined by the paths are planted mostly with roses. The smaller cloister is simpler in layout, with a white central fountain, but both encourage one to revel in the silence, and are the perfect place to revivify during a day's sightseeing or after exploring the convent's catacombs and bell tower.

**Casa Museo
La Sebastiana
(La Sebastiana
Museum House)
Valparaíso**

●7
Ricardo de Ferrari 692,
Región de Valparaíso
Open: see p.370
Admission fee

About twenty minutes' uphill walk south from the esplanade brings you to the Bellavista neighbourhood and this eclectic house with its shady garden. Built by Sebastián Collado but left incomplete at his death in 1949, the building was abandoned until 1959, when the poet and later Nobel laureate Pablo Neruda, wishing to leave Santiago, sent his friends Sara Vial and the sculptor Marie Martner an impossible-to-fulfil list of requirements for a house that he hoped to find in Valparaíso. Although too big, La Sebastiana was almost perfect, and Neruda and his wife shared it with Martner and her husband. The view from the concrete terrace north over the city to the Pacific Ocean is spectacular, and the mature terraced gardens beside and below the house with lawns, tall trees (including fig, jacaranda and palms) and beds of flowers and foliage are intimate. Here and there a sculpture by Martner introduces a focal point, and look out for the Cor-Ten steel bench with its back in the silhouetted form of the poet. Entry to the house and garden is limited and on a 'first come, first served' basis, so it is advisable to arrive early.

Museo de Arte Español Enrique Larreta (Enrique Larreta Museum of Spanish Art)
Buenos Aires

● 8
Juramento 2291,
Belgrano
Open: see p.370
Admission fee

In the Belgrano district, and across the road from the impressive Plaza Manuel Belgrano, is a neo-colonial villa dating from 1886. Now a museum holding Argentina's premier collection of Spanish art, it was previously the home of the writer Enrique Larreta (1875–1961). As well as collecting art, Larreta also transformed the orchard surrounding the house into an elegant Islamic-Spanish-inspired garden. A veranda, its walls adorned with tiles from Granada, connects the house to the geometrically structured garden. At the foot of six steps is an almost labyrinthine oasis in which the various beds enclosed by low clipped hedges and filled with exotic species are shaded by tall palms, ginkgo, cypress and bitter orange trees. Paths of brick or gravel lead you between the beds to the various features, which include tiled pools and fountains, large pots and stone busts, and the monumental granite sculpture *Sideways* by Pablo Larreta. This garden is truly a delight for the senses, with sweet scents, burbling fountains and verdant vistas – the perfect antidote to the modern city.

Visitor Information

Addresses and opening times are noted on the individual garden entries where possible. Additional visitor information is listed here, including tour details, websites and opening times where these vary depending on the season. Please note that while every care has been taken to ensure accuracy throughout the book and in the information below, details are subject to change and it is advisable to check times and access information prior to visiting or arranging travel. Gardens listed below are organized alphabetically by name for ease of reference.

A number of cities organize seasonal opening events during which it is possible to visit gardens that are otherwise inaccessible. Some events are organized by local groups, for example in Amsterdam, London and Prague. Others by national organizations such as the National Gardens Scheme (UK), the Garden Conservancy (USA) and My Open Garden (Australia).

Oceania

Docklands Community Garden
Melbourne
Located between Bourke & Collins Sts. Volunteers run regular planting days and social events. *docklandsgarden.org*

Eden Garden
Auckland
edengarden.co.nz

Highwic
Auckland
Entrance off Mortimer Pass. Special events often run. *highwic.co.nz*

Himeji Garden
Adelaide
Located in Wita Wirra park, in the Adelaide Park Lands. Open daily, April–Sept, 08.30–17.30 (weekends and public holidays closes 16.30) and Oct–Mar from 08.30 (see website for closing). *adelaideparklands.com.au*

Katherine Mansfield Birthplace
Wellington
Open Tue–Sun, 10.00–16.00. Closed Christmas Day, Good Friday and for private functions. *katherinemansfield.com*

Lex and Ruby Graham Gardens
Sydney
Part of Cremorne Point Reserve, situated at the end of Milson Rd (access via Murdoch St, off Military Rd). *northsydney.nsw.gov.au*

Old Parliament House
Rose Gardens
Canberra
Summer opening hours are from the first Sun in Oct until the first Sun in April. *fophrg.org.au*

Olveston Historic Home
Dunedin
Entry to the house is by guided tour only (admission fee). *olveston.co.nz*

Riccarton House and Bush
Christchurch
House open daily for guided tours (admission fee). Closed Christmas Day. *riccartonhouse.co.nz*

The System Garden
Melbourne
Entrance off Royal Parade, via a path between the Percy Grainger Museum and Veterinary Sciences building. Another entrance is off Professors Walk. Tours available by appt. *sustainablecampus.unimelb.edu.au*

Te Wepu Native Garden
Christchurch
Open daily, 10.00–17.00, by appt only. Contact Jo Kerr by phone: +64274123422 or email: joker_938@hotmail.com

Vaucluse House
Sydney
Take the 325 bus from Watson's Bay ferry terminal, or walk along the shoreline via Parsley Bay. House open Wed–Sun, 10.00–16.00. Closed on public holidays, Good Friday and Christmas Day. Tearoom open Wed–Fri, 10.00–16.30, and Sat and Sun, 08.00–16.30 (open every day except Christmas Day during school holidays). *sydneylivingmuseums.com.au*

Wendy's Secret Garden
Sydney
A short walk from North Sydney or Milsons Point railway stations. There are no signposts – take the descending steps from the junction of Walker St and Lavender St, or ascend from Lavender Bay ferry wharf. Look for the large fig tree outside Wendy's house, with a distinctive white tower. *wendyssecretgarden.org.au*

Asia

Ann Siang Hill Park
Singapore
Entrance via Ann Siang Rd, Ann Siang Hill and Amoy St. National Parks run free events – check website for listings. *nparks.gov.sg*

Asakura-choso-kan
Tokyo
Located west of Yanaka Cemetery and a five-minute walk from Nippori Station. Open daily, 09.30–16.30. Closed Mon and Thu, and 29 Dec–3 Jan. When a holiday falls on a Mon or Thu, the museum will be open but is closed the next day. *taitocity.net*

Darat al Funun
Khalid Shoman Foundation
Amman
Open Sat–Thu, 10.00–19.00 (15.00 during Ramadan). Closed in Aug and on public holidays. *daratalfunun.org*

Denpo-in Teien
Tokyo
Part of Senso-ji Temple Complex. Open during spring only (usually Mar–May), 10.00–16.00. Contact garden for details. *senso-ji.jp/*

Gong Wang Fu
Beijing
Open daily, 15 Mar–31 Oct, ticket office: 8.00–17.00 (closing time 18.30). Closed on Mon from 1 Nov–14 Mar, ticket office: 9.00–16.00 (closing time 18.30). *pgm.org.cn/*

Happo-en
Tokyo
Open Mon–Fri, 10.00–20.30, and Sat–Sun, 09.00–20.30 (closed New Year's Day). There is an open-air cafe and restaurant. *happo-en.com*

Huwon Garden
Changdeokgung Palace
Seoul
Visitors must pre-book a guided tour (available in English) to view the garden. Check website for opening hours, tour times and to book tours. *eng.cdg.go.kr*

Lavigerie Garden
Church of St Anne
Jerusalem
Open Apr–Sept, 08.00–12.00 and 14.00–18.00 (Sun until 17.00). Oct–Mar, 08.00–12.00 and 14.00–17.00.

Lin Ben Yuan Yuandi
New Taipei City
Open daily, 09.00–17.00 (19.00 on Fri). Closed on first Mon of the month, Chinese New Year's Eve and Day. Ticket includes an introductory video. Guided tours are available – tours in English should be booked one week in advance.
en.linfamily.ntpc.gov.tw

Marble Palace
Kolkata
Open daily, 10.30–16.00 (closed Mon and Thu). A permit must be obtained to visit. Contact the West Bengal Tourism bureau. *wbtdcl.com*

Mughal Gardens
Rashtrapati Bhavan
Delhi
Gardens open Aug–Mar on Fri, Sat and Sun, 09.00–16.00. Museum open year-round, Tue–Sun. Closed on government gazetted holidays. Pre-booking is essential.
presidentofindia.nic.in

Namba Parks
Osaka
Guided tours available weekdays, from 14.00. *nambaparks.com*

Namikawa-ke
Kyoto
Open daily, 10.00–16.30 (closed Mon and Thu). When a holiday falls on a Mon or Thu, the museum will be open but is closed the next day.

Nezu Bijutsukan
Tokyo
Tue–Sun, 10.00–17.00. Closed during exhibition installations and over New Year. When a public holiday falls on a Mon, the museum will be open but is closed the next day. Cafe on site. *nezu-muse.or.jp/en*

Osaka Station City Roof Gardens
Osaka
Yawaragi-no-niwa is on the 10th floor, Kaze-no-hiroba on the 11th floor and Tenku-no-noen on the 14th floor. Regular garden events take place throughout the year.
osakastation.com

Rashtrapati Niwas
Shimla
Open Tue–Fri. 1 May–30 June, 09.00–19.00; 1 July–30 April, 09.00–17.00. Closed on public holidays. *iias.ac.in/*

Shigemori Mirei Kyutaku
Kyoto
By reservation only (usually Tue–Sun, 11.00–14.00). Contact via the website. *est.hi-ho.ne.jp/shigemori/association.html*

Swapna Bagalcha
Kathmandu
gardenofdreams.org.np

Europe

Abbey Gardens
Westminster Abbey
London
The College Garden and two further gardens are located south of the church. The Garth is located within the abbey's cloisters. Donations are welcome.
westminster-abbey.org

Addison's Walk
Magdalen College
Oxford
Access is via Magdalen College. Open daily, Oct–late June, 13.00–18.00 (or dusk, whichever is earlier), and June–end of Sept, 12.00–19.00. Check website in case the college is closed. *magd.ox.ac.uk*

Alter Botanischer Garten
Zurich
bg.uzh.ch/de/altergarten.html

Aptekarsky Ogorod
Moscow
Open daily. Nov–Apr, 10.00–19.00; May–Aug, 10.00–22.00; Sept–Oct, 10.00–21.00. Closed in Mar and Apr during the thaw, for part of Sept for planting, during severe weather and for special events. Check website for details. Weekend and evening tours availble. *hortus.ru/en*

Arktisk Alpin Botanisk Hage
Tromsø
A cafe is open in the morning during summer.
en.uit.no/tmu/botanisk

Arundells
Salisbury
Open mid-Mar–1 Nov. General admission Sat–Tue, 11.00–17.00, Wed, guided tours only (book in advance via the website). *arundells.org*

Assistens Kirkegård
Copenhagen
Open 1 Apr–30 Sept, 07.00–22.00, and 1 Oct–31 Mar, 07.00–19.00. Cultural centre and garden tours available. There is a cafe on site.
assistens.dk

Barbican Centre
London
Beech Gardens: open 24/7. Conservatory: open Sun and bank holidays, 12.00–17.00. Lake Terrace: open Mon–Sat, 09.00–23.00; Sun, 11.00–23.00; bank holidays, 12.00–23.00 (closed 24–26 Dec).
barbican.org.uk

Basiliek van Sint Servaas
Maastricht
From Sept–June: Mon–Sat, 10.00–17.00, and Sun, 13.00–17.00. From July–Aug: Mon–Sat, 10.00–18.00, and Sun, 13.00–17.00.
sintservaas.nl

Biblioteka Uniwersytecka
Warszawie Roof Garden
Warsaw
buw.uw.edu.pl

Bishop's Palace
Wells
Open daily, 27 Mar–29 Oct: 10.00–18.00, and 30 Oct–26 Mar: 10.00–16.00. Closed 23 Dec–6 Jan. Check website for other closures. Twice-daily guided tours at 12.00 and 15.00 are included in the admission fee. *bishopspalace.org.uk*

Bonnington Square Garden
London
bonningtonsquaregarden.org.uk

Botanisk Have
Copenhagen
Entrance on corner of Gothers-gade and Øster Voldgade. Open daily: 1 Apr–30 Sept, 08.30–18.00, and 1 Oct–31 Mar, 08.30–16.00. See website for greenhouse opening times. *botanik.snm.ku.dk*

Camley Street Natural Park
London
Open Mon–Sat: 10.00–17.00 (summer); 10.00–16.00 (winter). Self-guided activities available and there is an outdoor eating area.
wildlondon.org.uk

Ca' Morosini del Giardino
Venice
Visits by appt only. Contact Mariagrazia Dammicco, email: giardini.storici.venezia@gmail.com. Donations appreciated.

Carmen de los Mártires
Granada
Open daily. 1 Apr–14 Oct: Mon–Fri, 10.00–14.00 and 17.00–19.00, and Sat, Sun and public holidays, 10.00–19.00. 15 Oct–31 Mar: Mon–

Fri, 10.00–14.00 and 16.00–18.00, and Sat, Sun and public holidays, 10.00–18.00. *lovegranada.com/ places/carmen-martires*

Chelsea Physic Garden
London
Main season (2 Apr–30 Oct): open Mon, 11.00–17.00 (via 66 Royal Hospital Rd), and Tue–Sun, 11.00–18.00 (via Swan Walk gate). The cafe is open Tue–Fri, 11.00–17.00. Hours vary during the off-season– check website.
chelseaphysicgarden.co.uk

Chester Cathedral Cloisters
The Refectory Cafe, in the monks' dining hall, is open Mon–Sat, 09.30–16.30, and Sun, 12.00–16.00. Donations appreciated.
chestercathedral.com

Chiesa del Santissimo Redentore
Venice
Open Mon, 10.30–16.00, and Tue–Sat, 10.30–16.30. Closed New Year's Day, Easter, 15 Aug and Christmas Day.
chorusvenezia.org

Church of Our Lady and St Nicholas
Liverpool
livpc.co.uk

Le Cloître Lucien Wercollier Neumünster Abbey
Luxembourg
Check for private event closures.
neimenster.lu

Clos des Blancs Manteaux
Paris
A red watering-can sign is placed by the garden entrance during opening times. Open weekends: from 13.30 on Sat and 10.30–12.30 on Sun, then opening again at 13.30. Closing times vary (both days): 18.30 (July–Sept), 17.30 (Oct), 17.00 (Nov–Dec). Closed bank holidays. *en.parisinfo.com*

College Gardens
University of Oxford
Worcester College: open daily, 14.00–17.00. Closed some bank holidays, over Christmas and occasionally at other times. New College: open daily, mid-Oct–mid-Mar, 14.00–16.00, and mid-Mar–mid-Oct, 11.00–17.00.
It is advised to phone ahead.
worc.ox.ac.uk | new.ox.ac.uk

College Gardens
University of Cambridge
Christ's College grounds and garden: open daily, 09.00–16.00 (Fellows' Garden closed on weekends). Clare College Fellows' Garden: open daily, 10.00–17.00. Call before visiting as the gardens can be closed for events.

Comenius-Garten
Berlin
Opening times vary, please call +49 030 6866106 or email: comenius-garten@t-online.de *comenius-garten.de*

Cromhouthuis
Amsterdam
cromhouthuis.nl

DakAkker
Rotterdam
The garden runs regular events such as harvest parties, dinners and workshops. See website. You can view the garden from the terrace of the cafe Op Het Dak, open Wed–Sun, 09.00–17.00. To visit the DakAkker itself, email Wouter Bauman: wouter.bauman@dakakker. nl.*luchtsingel.org*

Dubh Linn Garden
Dublin
dublincastle.ie/the-castle-gardens

Estufa Fria
Lisbon
Free Sun and bank holidays until 14.00. *estufafria.cm-lisboa.pt*

Františkánská Zahrada
Prague
Accessible from Jungmannovo Square or via passages from Vodickova St or Wenceslas Square. *prague.eu*

Fundación Rodríguez-Acosta
Granada
fundacionrodriguezacosta.com

An Gairdín Cuimhneacháin
Dublin
opwdublincommemorative.ie

Galerija Meštrović
Split
mestrovic.hr

Geffrye Museum Garden
London
Front Gardens: open daily, 08.00–17.00. Herb and Period Gardens: open Apr–Oct on Tue–Sun and bank holidays, 10.00–17.00. *geffrye-museum.org.uk*

Giardini Vaticani
Rome
Access is only by tour (pre-book via the website). Day tickets include entry to the Vatican Museums and Sistine Chapel. *museivaticani.va*

Giardino dell'Iris
Florence
Open 25 Apr–20 May, Mon–Fri, 10.00–13.00 and 15.00–19.30, and Sat and Sun, 10.00–19.00. Visits at other times of the year are by appt. Donations are appreciated. *societaitalianairis.com*

Herschel Museum of Astronomy Garden
Bath
Open Mon–Fri, 13.00–17.00, Sat–Sun and bank holidays, 11.00–17.00. Check website for Dec closures. *herschelmuseum.org.uk*

The Hidden Gardens
Glasgow
Open Tue–Sun. Apr–Sept: Tue–Thu, 10.00–17.00 (closes at 19.00 from 14 June–12 Aug); Fri and Sat, 10.00–19.00; Sun, 12.00–18.00. Oct–Mar: Tue–Fri, 10.00–15.30; Sat and Sun, 12.00–15.30. *thehiddengardens.org.uk*

Hof Meermansburg
Leiden
meermansburg.nl

Hôtel Le Vergeur Museum
Reims
Located opposite the northern corner of the place du Forum. *museelevergeur.com*

Huerto de las Monjas
Madrid
Entrance is via a gateway at 7 Calle del Sacramento, southwest of the Plaza de la Villa. *esmadrid.com*

Inns of Court
London
Inner Temple: open Mon–Fri, 12.30–15.00. Middle Temple: open Mon–Fri, 12.30–15.00, May–July and Sept only. Lincoln's Inn: open Mon–Fri, 07.00–19.00 (North Lawn 12.00–14.30). Gray's Inn: open Mon–Fri, 12.00–14.30. *innertemple.org.uk | middletemple.org.uk | lincolnsinn. org.uk | graysinn.org.uk*

Japanese Roof Garden SOAS
London
Accessed via 1st floor of the Brunel Gallery. Open Tue–Sat, 10.30–17.00. Closed on bank holidays, for private

functions and when exhibitions are changing. Call for details: +4420 7898 4046. *soas.ac.uk*

Jardin Anne-Frank
Paris
Open daily from 10.00. Closing at: 19.00 (1 Oct–end of daylight saving), 17.30 (end of daylight saving to end Feb), 18.30 (1 Mar–start of daylight saving), 20.00 (start of daylight saving–30 Apr), 21.00 (1 May–31 Aug), 20.00 (1 Sept–30 Sept).

Jardin du Palais Saint-Pierre
Lyon
mba-lyon.fr

Jardin Rosa Mir
Lyon
rosa.mir.free.fr

Jardins del Palau Robert
Barcelona
Located on the corner of Passeig de Gràcia and Avinguda Diagonal. *lameva.barcelona.cat/en*

Jardins Renoir
Musée de Montmartre
Paris
Le Café Renoir is open 12.15–17.00 (18.00 during the high season). *museedemontmartre.fr*

Kabinettsgarten
Munich
residenz-muenchen.de

King Henry's Walk Garden
London
khwgarden.org.uk

Leeds University Sustainable and Edible Garden
Located between Roger Stevens Building and Chancellor's Court. To get involved with planting or research (no experience needed), contact: sustainability@leeds.ac.uk or bardongrangeproject@luu.leeds.ac.uk | *sustainability.leeds.ac.uk/biodiversity/sustainable-garden/*

Liebieghaus
Frankfurt
liebieghaus.de

Listasafn Einars Jónssonar
Reykjavik
Museum open Tue–Sun, 10.00–17.00. *lej.is/en*

Museo Sorolla
Madrid
mecd.gob.es/msorolla

Museum Willet-Holthuysen
Amsterdam
Open Mon–Fri, 10.00–17.00, and Sat, Sun and public holidays, 11.00–17.00. On 5, 24 and 31 December, closing time is 16.00. Closed on King's Day (27 April), Christmas Day and New Year's Day. *willetholthuysen.nl/en*

Natuurtuin Slatuinen
Amsterdam
Guided tours available – call Marijke Kooijman: +31204124361.

Ny Carlsberg Glyptotek Museum
Copenhagen
Museum address: Dantes Plads, 71556. Museum open Tue–Sun, 11.00–18.00 (22.00 on Thu). See website for holiday closures. Entrance to the museum must be purchased to visit the cafe. *glyptoteket.com*

Onze-Lieve–Vrouw Sint-Pieterskerk
Ghent
Open Tue–Fri, 10.00–17.15. Sun (Apr–Oct) 10.00–12.30 and 15.30–20.00. Sun (Nov–Mar), 10.00–12.30 and 18.00–20.00.

Orto Botanico di Pisa
Pisa
ortobotanicoitalia.it

Orto Botanico di Padova
Padua
Open daily. Apr–Sept: 09.00–19.00; Oct: 09.00–18.00; Nov–Mar, 09.00–17.00. Closed working Mons, except Apr–May. *ortobotanicopd.it/en*

Palacio de Viana
Cordoba
Check the website for public holiday opening times. *palaciodeviana.com/en*

Palazzo Corsini al Prato
Florence
To arrange a visit, call +39 3402514033 for details.

Palazzo del Quirinale
Rome
Admission by guided tour only (book in advance). Access via the Porta Giardini on Via del Quirinale and bring ID. *palazzo.quirinale.it*

Palazzo Podestà
Genoa
Admission fee includes a guided tour. Reservation recommended. *palazzolomellino.org/en*

Patsy R. and Raymond D. Nasher Sculpture Garden
Peggy Guggenheim Collection
Venice
guggenheim-venice.it

Petersfriedhof
Salzburg
stift-stpeter.at

Phoenix Garden
London
Located behind the Phoenix Theatre, north of Shaftesbury Ave and east of Charing Cross Rd. Donations via website are welcome. *thephoenixgarden.org*

Plantation Garden
Norwich
plantationgarden.co.uk

Queen Elizabeth Hall Roof Garden
London
southbankcentre.co.uk

Rockoxhuis
Antwerp
Open Tue–Sun, 10.00–17.00. Closed on New Year's Day and 2 Jan, Ascension Day, Christmas Day and Boxing Day. *rockoxhuis.be*

The Roof Gardens
London
Opening times vary – call +4420 7937 7994 to check. If the garden is closed for an event, part of it can be viewed from the Babylon restaurant and bar. *virginlimitededition.com/en/the-roof-gardens*

Rubenshuis
Antwerp
Open Tue–Sun, 10.00–17.00. Closed on New Year's Day, 1 May, Ascension Day, 1 Nov and Christmas Day. Free entry on the last Wed of the month. *rubenshuis.be*

The Sackler Garden
at the Garden Museum
London
Garden open Mon–Thu, 08.00–17.00; Fri, 08.00–21.00; Sat, 09.00–16.00; Sun, 09.00–17.00. Closed on first Mon of the month, Christmas Day and Boxing Day. *gardenmuseum.org.uk*

St Nicholas Garden
Provand's Lordship
Glasgow
Open daily. Tue–Thu and Sat, 10.00–17.00; Fri and Sun, 11.00–17.00. Closed Mon and bank holidays.

The Secret Garden and Discovery Terrace
Library of Birmingham
The Secret Garden is located on the 7th floor of the library and the Discovery Terrace on the 3rd floor. Open Mon–Tue, 11.00–19.00, and Wed–Sat, 11.00–17.00. Closed bank holidays. *libraryofbirmingham.com*

Skip Garden
London
Located at the northern end of Lewis Cubitt Park, just off Handyside St. The Skip Garden Kitchen is open Tue–Sat, 10.00–16.00 (lunch 12.00–14.00). *globalgeneration.org.uk*

Slottsträdgården
Malmö
slottstradgarden.se

Sofia University Botanic Garden
ubg-bg.com

Square Saint-Gilles-Grand-Veneur
Paris
Accessible via rue de Hesse from rue Villehardouin or via rue du Grand Veneur from rue des Arquebusiers. Open daily: Mon–Fri from 08.00 and Sat, Sun and public holidays from 09.00. Closing times vary: 18.30 (1 Oct–end of daylight saving), 17.00 (end of daylight saving–end Feb), 18.00 (1 Mar–start of daylight saving), 19.30 (start of daylight saving–30 Apr), 20.30 (1 May–31 Aug), 19.30 (1 Sept–30 Sept).

Square Vinet
Bordeaux
Located between rue du Cancera and rue Maucoudinat. Open daily, 1 Apr–31 May, 08.00–19.30; 1 June–31 Aug, 08.00–20.00; 1 Sept–31 Oct, 08.00–18.30; 1 Nov–14 Feb, 08.00–17.30; 15 Feb–31 Mar, 08.00–18.30. *bordeaux.fr/l907*

Tarragona Cathedral Cloister
Tarragona
Generally open Mon–Sat, 10.00–17.00 (1 Nov–17 Mar), 10.00–19.00 (18 Mar–10 June and 11 Sept–31 Oct), 10.00–20.00 (2 June–9 Sept). Open on Sun in July, Aug and the first two weeks of Sept, 15.00–20.00. Check the website in case of reduced opening hours. *catedraldetarragona.com*

Treasurer's House
York
Check website for off-season opening hours. *nationaltrust.org.uk*

UNESCO Garden of Peace (Japanese Garden)
Paris
Visits to UNESCO are by appt only, in groups. However, regular public events are held. Visit the website or call ahead. *unesco.org*

La Vigna di Leonardo
Milan
Tours start every 15 minutes. Check the website for closures due to private events. *vignadileonardo.com*

Vrtbovská Zahrada
Prague
vrtbovska.cz

Wildlife Garden at the Natural History Museum
London
During winter, garden visits are welcome by appt. Ask at an information desk inside the museum or email: wildlifegarden@nhm.ac.uk | *nhm.ac.uk*

The Writers' House of Georgia
Tbilisi
writershouse.ge/eng/index

Africa

Le Jardin Secret
Marrakech
Open daily. Feb, Mar and Oct, 09.30–18.30; April–Sept, 09.30–19.30; Nov–Jan, 09.30–17.30. The cafe and shop follow the same times. *lejardinsecretmarrakech.com*

Oranjezicht City Farm
Cape Town
Located next to the corner of Sidmouth Ave and Upper Orange St, adjacent to Homestead Park (entrance at 87 Upper Orange St). The farm operates a weekly market at Granger Bay on the V&A Waterfront. *ozcf.co.za*

Tangier American Legation Institute for Moroccan Studies
Tangier
Guided tours of the museum are available. *legation.org*

North & Central America

6BC Botanical Garden
New York City
Open Apr–Oct. Sat–Sun, 12.00–18.00, and Mon–Fri, 18.00–dusk. The garden is open at other times when a member is present. *6bcgarden.org*

Abby Aldrich Rockefeller Sculpture Garden, MoMA
New York City
To visit the garden for free, enter via the west gate on West 54th St between 5th and 6th Aves, between 09.30 and 10.15 on any day. Museum admission applies at other times. *moma.org*

Alcatraz Island
San Francisco
Ferries operate to and from the island roughly every 45 minutes, from Pier 33. Check website for full schedules and ticket prices. Free guided tours of the gardens are offered on Fri and Sun mornings at 09.45, starting at the Dock. *alcatrazgardens.org* *alcatrazcruises.com*

Beauregard-Keyes House
New Orleans
Museum entrance opposite the Old Ursuline Convent Museum. Garden may be entered via Ursulines Ave. Tours begin on the hour and last 45 minutes – first tour 10.00 and last 15.00. *bkhouse.org*

Bellagio Conservatory and Botanical Garden
Las Vegas
Located across the lobby from the front desk of the Bellagio Hotel. Broad display dates are as follows, but check the website as the gardens close during changeovers. Chinese New Year: Jan–Mar; Spring: Mar–May; Summer: June–Sept; Autumn: Sept–Nov; Winter/Christmas: Dec–Jan. *bellagio.com*

Blue Ribbon Garden
Los Angeles
Accessed from the corner of S. Grand Ave and W. 2nd St. The garden closes 90 mins prior to a performance and re-opens 30–60 mins after a morning/matinee performance, but remains shut after evening performances. *laphil.com*

Briscoe Western Art Museum and Riverwalk
San Antonio
Museum open Tue, 10.00–21.00, and Wed–Sun 10.00–17.00. Museum free on Tue, 16.00–21.00. Closed on Battle of Flowers Fiesta Parade, Thanksgiving, Christmas Day and New Year's Day. *briscoemuseum. org | thesanantonioriverwalk.com*

Château Ramezay
Montreal
Museum open daily all year. From Canadian Thanksgiving–31 Oct, 10.00–17.30; from 1 Nov–31 May, 10.00–16.20; from 1 June–Canadian Thanksgiving, 09.30–18.00. While the garden is officially open from 1 June–Canadian Thanksgiving, it can be viewed year-round (call ahead). *chateauramezay.qc.ca*

Church of Jesus Christ of Lat-ter-day Saints Conference Center
Salt Lake City
Tours available from Apr–Oct Call +18012400075 to confirm times. *templesquare.com*

Creative Little Garden
New York City
Open daily, 1 Apr–1 Nov, 11.00–18.00 (weather permitting). The nearby 6 & B Garden is located at 6th St and Ave B, and is open Apr–Oct, on Sat and Sun only, 13.00–18.00. *creativelittlegarden.org newsite.6bgarden.org*

Devonian Gardens
Calgary
Located on the 4th floor of the CORE Shopping Centre. Open daily: Mon–Wed and Sat, 10.00–18.00; Thu and Fri, 10.00–20.00; Sun and public holidays, 12.00–17.00. Closed Easter Sunday, Christmas Day and New Year's Day. Note: at the time of going to press, parts of the Devonian Gardens were closed. Please check website for latest information. *coreshopping.ca*

Dr Sun Yat-Sen Classical Chinese Garden
Vancouver
Open daily. 1 May–14 June and Sept, 10.00–18.00; 15 June–31 Aug, 09.30–19.00; 1 Oct–30 Apr, 10.00–16.30 (closed on Mon, 1 Nov–30 April). A guided tour is included in the ticket price. *vancouverchinesegarden.com/*

Dorothy and Harold Meyerman Sculpture Garden
Palm Springs Art Museum
Free admission on the second Sun of every month. *psmuseum.org* The Faye Sarkowsky Sculpture Garden at Palm Springs Art Museum in Palm Desert is about 25 minutes' drive along routes 111B and 111 (72–567 Highway 111, Palm Desert, CA 92260). Located at Entrada del Paseo at the westernmost intersection of Highway 111 and El Paseo. The garden is open during museum hours. *psmuseum.org/palm-desert*

Elizabeth Street Garden
New York City
Usually open Mon–Fri, 11.00–16.00; Sat–Sun, 10.00–16.00. Seasonal times vary – see website. *elizabethstreetgarden.org*

Fay Park
San Francisco
sfrecpark.org

FOOD ROOF Farm
St Louis
Accessible to the public during events, tours and community days only. See website for details. Drop-in community days every Sat, 1 Apr–31 Oct, 09.00–12.00. *urbanharveststl.org*

Ford Foundation Atrium Garden
New York City
Note: at the time of going to press, the garden was closed for renovation and due to reopen autumn 2018. Check website for update. *fordfoundation.org*

La Fortaleza
San Juan
Guided tours of the palace are available, except for public holidays. Donations are encouraged.

Freeway Park
Seattle
Check website for details of the park's regular events programme. *freewayparkassociation.org*

The Frick Collection
New York City
Museum and garden open Tue–Sat, 10.00–18.00, and Sun, 11.00–17.00. Open until 21.00 on first Fri of every month (not Sept and Jan). Closed public holidays. Admission free 18.00–21.00 on first Fri of every month (not Sept and Jan). *frick.org*

Grace Marchant Garden
San Francisco
Steps to the garden begin at the end of Filbert St, between 1299 and 1301 Sansome St. *gracemarchantgarden.com*

Greenacre Park
New York City
Open 10 Apr–1 May, 08.00–18.00; 1 June–9 Oct, 08.00–20.00; 10 Oct–20 Dec, 08.00–18.00. Closed 21 Dec–31 Mar. Check website for other closures. *greenacrepark.org*

Heyward-Washington House
Charleston
charlestonmuseum.org

Hirshhorn Museum and Sculpture Garden
Washington DC
Tours are available daily, Mon–Thur at 12.30, and on Fri, Sat and Sun at 12.30 and 15.30. *hirshhorn.si.edu*

James Irvine Japanese Garden
Los Angeles
Enter via the Japanese American Cultural & Community Center, a ten-minute walk from City Hall. Open Tue–Fri, 10.00–17.00; Sat and Sun, 10.00–16.00 (closed for private events or in bad weather, call +12136282725 to check). *jaccc.org*

Jefferson Market Garden
New York City
Entrance on Greenwich Ave (between 6th Ave & West 10th St). Open 1 Apr–31 Oct. Tue–Fri, 09.00–1800, Sat and Sun, 10.00–18.00. *jeffersonmarketgarden.org*

John F. Collins Park
Philadelphia
Located between Chestnut and Ranstead Sts. Check website for details of events. *centercityphila.org/parks/john-f-collins-park*

Kendall Square Roof Garden
Cambridge
Located on top of the Green Garage, accessible from both Broadway and Main St. *kendallcenter.com*

Lan Su Chinese Garden
Portland
Open daily. 15 Mar–31 Oct, 10.00–19.00; 1 Nov–14 Mar, 10.00–16.30. Closed Thanksgiving, Christmas Day and New Year's Day. Free tours available. *lansugarden.org*

Lightner Museum
St Augustine
Guided and self-guided tours available daily. *lightnermuseum.org*

Loring Greenway
Minneapolis
loringgreenway.org

The Lotus Garden
New York City
Open from second week in Apr–first week in Nov, Sun only, 13.00–16.00. *thelotusgarden.org*

Moorten Botanical Garden and Cactarium
Palm Springs
Open Thu–Tue, 09.00–13.00, (21 Jun–21 Sept); Thu–Tue, 10.00–16.00 (22 Sept–20 Jun). Closed public holidays. Tours included in admission fee – check website.
moortenbotanicalgarden.com

Museum of Contemporary Art Denver
Open Tue–Thu, 12.00–19.00; Fri, 12.00–22.00; Sat and Sun, 10.00–17.00. The on-site cafe and bar (next to garden) is open at the same times. *mcadenver.org*

Museo Franz Mayer
Mexico City
Admission free on Tue.
ingles.franzmayer.org.mx

Museo Nacional de Costa Rica
San Jose
Garden and museum open Tue–Sat, 08.30-16.30; Sun, 09.00-16.30. Closed Mon and on public holidays. *museocostarica.go.cr*

Museo Napoleónico
Havana
napoleon.org

Nasher Sculpture Center
Dallas
Open Tue–Sun, 11.00–17.00. Closed on Independence Day, Thanksgiving, Christmas Day and New Year's Day. Cafe open from 11.00–16.00. *nashersculpturecenter.org*

New Mexico Museum of Art
Santa Fe
Opening times vary, check the website for specific hours.
nmartmuseum.org

North & South Stanley McCormick Memorial Court
The Art Institute of Chicago
Museum open daily from 10.30–17.00 (20.00 on Thu). Closed on Thanksgiving, Christmas Day and New Year's Day. *artic.edu*

The Old Stone House and Washington Park
New York City
Open daily, dawn–dusk. The house is open on Fri, 15.00–18.00, and Sat and Sun, 11.00–16.00.
theoldstonehouse.org

Owens-Thomas House
Savannah
Daily tours are given every 20 minutes. Last tour at 16.20. *telfair.org*

The Rail Park
Philadelphia
Note: at the time of going to press, Phase 1 of the Rail Park's development was underway and due to open in 2018. Check website for updates and details of walking tours. *therailpark.org*

The Rooftop Garden, Paul S. Russell, MD Museum of Medical History and Innovation
Boston
Open Mon–Fri, 09.00–17.00; Sat, 11.00–17.00 (Apr–Oct). Closed public holidays. *massgeneral.org/museum*

St Luke in the Fields
New York City
stlukeinthefields.org

The Secret Gardens of Independence Park
Philadelphia
18th Century Garden, 339 Walnut St; Benjamin Rush Garden, corner of Walnut St and S 3rd St; Magnolia Garden, 433 Locust St; Rose Garden, 422 Walnut St, PA 19106. *nps.gov/inde*

Spanish Governor's Palace
San Antonio
spanishgovernorspalace.org

Teardrop Park
New York City
Located between Warren St and Murray St, east of River Terrace and west of North End Ave. Check website for details of games and projects for children (May–Oct). *bpcparks.org*

Tudor City Greens
New York City
Located on Tudor City Place on either side of East 42nd St, east of Second Ave. Donations welcome. *tudorcitygreens.org*

Tudor Place
Washington DC
Self-guided garden tours include a map. House tours run on the hour from 10.00. *tudorplace.org*

Unitarian Church Cemetery
Charleston
The cemetery can also be accessed via a gate next to 161 King St. To access outside the usual opening hours, call +18437234617. Tours of the church are available on Fri and Sat, 10.00–13.00, and Sun, 12.30–15.00 (Sept–mid-June).

Vancouver Public Library
Open daily (excluding public holidays). Check the website for opening times. Note: At the time of going to print, the library's expansion programme was in progress. The garden is due to reopen in Spring 2018 – check website. *vpl.ca*

West Side Community Garden
New York City
Entrance is on West 89th St between Amsterdam Ave and Columbus Ave.
westsidecommunitygarden.org

South America

Casa de Aliaga
Lima
Open Mon–Sun, 09.30–17.00, by reservation only. *casadealiaga.com/en*

Casa Museo La Sebastiana
Valparaíso
Mar–Dec, open Tue–Sun, 10.00–18.00. Jan and Feb, Tue–Sun, 10.00–19.00. Fee includes an audio guide. *fundacionneruda.org/en*

Convento de Santo Domingo
Lima
conventosantodomingo.pe

Palácio Itamaraty
Brasília
Free tours run on the hour from 09.00–17.00 (Mon–Fri). On weekends, tours at 09.00, 11.00, 14.00, 15.00 and 17.00. Visitors will not be allowed in if wearing shorts, miniskirts, minidresses, sleeveless tops or flip-flops on weekdays. Email: visita@itamaraty.gov.br or call +6120308051 to book. *itamaraty.gov. br/en/visit-the-itamaraty-palace*

Luciana Brito Galeria
São Paulo
lucianabritogaleria.com.br

Museo de Arte Español Enrique Larreta
Buenos Aires
Open Tue–Fri and weekday holidays, 12.00–19.00. Weekends and weekend holidays, 10.00–20.00. Guided tours run at 12.30, 14.00 and 17.00 during the week, and at 16.00 and 18.00 on weekends. *buenosaires.gob.ar*

Index

Page numbers in *italics* refer to illustrations

Phaidon Press Limited
Regent's Wharf
All Saints Street
London N1 9PA

Phaidon Press Inc.
65 Bleecker Street
New York, NY 10012

phaidon.com

First published 2018
© 2018 Phaidon Press Limited

ISBN 978 0 7148 7612 2

A CIP catalogue record for
this book is available from the
British Library and the Library
of Congress.

Designed by João Mota

Printed in China

Author's Acknowledgements

Til Vibeke.
Tak fordi du altid er der for mig.

This book is the result of a team
effort and I have been fortunate
to work with an exceptional group
of people throughout the whole
process. I should therefore like
to express my heartfelt thanks to
the following, and should there
be anyone forgotten, it is my
fault alone and please accept
my apologies.

First and foremost to Victoria
Clarke, commissioning editor at
Phaidon and all round good egg.
Thank you for placing your trust
in me and making this project
happen. Thank you too for all your
unfaltering wise council, resolute
hard work, ceaseless patience and
much appreciated good humour –
especially on Friday afternoons! It
has been a pleasure and an honour
to work with you.

To all those knowledgeable souls
at Phaidon and further afield who,
when asked, were kind enough to
offer suggestions for gardens to
be included – many of which have
been: Dominic Aveiro, Sara Bader,
Siobhan Bent, Caroline Bourrus,
Katja Bremer, Tania Compton,
Capucine Coninx, Chris Conti,
Rasmus Frisk, Thomas Gooch, Kate
Greenberg, Nadja Hempel, Amy
Hordes, Ian Kennaway, Micaela
Lade, Pedro Martin, Hélène
Gallois-Montbrun, Rebecca Morrill,
RoseMary Musgrave, Bill Noble,
Meg Parsont, Belle Place, Gisela
Rosell and Emily Takoudes.

A special mention of thanks
to Jeremy Case, the editor of
the *Wallpaper* City Guides* at
Phaidon, who advised on gardens
in Havana, Cuba and also reached
out to his local contacts in various
cities for their input. And of course
a big thanks to them too for their
helpful suggestions: Catherine
Balston, Matt Chesterton, Nicholas
Gill, Sandra Lane, Marie Elena
Martinez, Shonquis Moreno, Sorrel
Moseley-Williams, Sean O'Toole,
Adrian Sandiford, Paul Sullivan and
Laurice Taitz.

At Phaidon, the in-house and
freelance team who worked
so creatively, diligently and
professionally to create such a
beautiful book. A special thank
you goes to the talented João
Mota for the book's design, but
thanks are also due to: Jane
Birch (proofreader), Vanessa Bird
(indexer), Adela Cory (production
controller), Rosie Fairhead
(copyeditor), Christopher Lacy
(artworker), Jen Veall (picture
researcher), Tom Wainwright (fact
checker), and the editorial team
of Lucy Kingett, Sophie Kullmann,
Catalina Imizcoz, Eddie Royle,
Federica Sala and Sarah Scott.

A huge debt of gratitude is
owed to to my ever-patient,
ever-tolerant, ever-cheerful and
ever-lovely wife, Vibeke. Thank you
for your support and strength.

And last but in no means least,
thank you to our splendid hound
Mirkko, faithful writing companion
and champion foot warmer.